P9-DXZ-550

The Family
Handyman
BEST
PROJECTS
TIPS & TOOLS

The Family
Handyman
BEST
PROJECTS
TIPS & TOOLS

by The Editors of *The Family Handyman* magazine

Reader's
Digest

THE READER'S DIGEST ASSOCIATION, INC.
PLEASANTVILLE, NEW YORK / MONTREAL

FOR THE FAMILY HANDYMAN
Executive Editor: Spike Carlsen
Managing Editor: Mary Flanagan
Archives: Shannon Hooge
Contributing Designer: Teresa Marrone
Contributing Copy Editor: Amy Orchard

Editor in Chief: Ken Collier

READER'S DIGEST PROJECT STAFF
Senior Editor: Don Earnest
Senior Design Director: Elizabeth L. Tunnicliffe
Production Technology Manager: Douglas A. Croll

Editorial Director: Christopher Cavanaugh
Marketing Director: Dawn Nelson

READER'S DIGEST HOME AND HEALTH BOOKS
Editor in Chief: Neil Wertheimer
Vice President and General Manager: Keira Krausz

THE READER'S DIGEST ASSOCIATION, INC.
Editor in Chief: Eric W. Schrier
President, North America Books and Home Entertainment: Thomas D. Gardner

Warning: *All do-it-yourself activities involve a degree of risk. Skills, materials, tools, and site conditions vary widely. Although the editors have made every effort to ensure accuracy, the reader remains responsible for the selection and use of tools, materials, and methods. Always obey local codes and laws, follow manufacturer's operating instructions, and observe safety precautions.*

Copyright © 2003 by The Reader's Digest Association, Inc.
Copyright © 2003 by The Reader's Digest Association (Canada) Ltd.
Copyright © 2003 by The Reader's Digest Association Far East Ltd.
Philippine Copyright © 2003 by The Reader's Digest Association Far East Ltd.
All rights reserved. Unauthorized reproduction, in any manner, is prohibited.

Reader's Digest is a registered trademark of The Reader's Digest Association, Inc. The Family Handyman and Handy Hints are registered trademarks of RD Publications, Inc. Ask Handyman, Using Tools, Wordless Workshop, Workshop Tips, You Can Fix It, and ⌂ are trademarks of RD Publications, Inc.

Library of Congress Cataloging-in-Publication Data:
The Family handyman best projects, tips & tools/by the editors of the Family handyman magazine.
     p. cm.
    Includes index.
    ISBN 0-7621-0443-7 (hardcover)
    ISBN 0-7621-0455-4 (paperback)
    1. Dwellings–Maintenance and repair–Amateurs' manuals. I. Title: Best projects. II.
Family handyman.

TH4817.3.F3397 2003
643'.7–dc21   2002031919

Address any comments about *The Family Handyman Best Projects, Tips, and Tools* to:
Editor in Chief
Reader's Digest Home and Health Books
Reader's Digest Road
Pleasantville, NY 10570-7000

To order additional copies of *The Family Handyman Best Projects, Tips, and Tools,* call 1-800-846-2100.

rd.com For more Reader's Digest products and information, visit our Web site.

Printed in the United States of America

1 3 5 7 9 10 8 6 4 2 (hardcover)
1 3 5 7 9 10 8 6 4 2 (paperback)
US 4266A/L—US

ABOUT THIS BOOK
and the magazine it comes from

Selecting the best material from the hundreds of articles and tips published in *The Family Handyman* magazine in 2001 and 2002 for this "Best of —" collection was tough. Tough, because we think every article we produce is the best. What makes us think that?

Well, for starters, we're the best do-it-yourself magazine in the world. Over four million people read *The Family Handyman* each month. We've been helping homeowners and do-it-yourselfers for 51 years.

We have the best readers. Heck, they submit the material for four of our most popular departments—Handy Hints, Workshop Tips, Wordless Workshop and Great Goofs.

We have the best editors with the best experience; every one of us earned our bread and butter as a carpenter, builder or contractor for 10 years or more. We live and breathe what we write about.

We use the best consultants and experts. Take our electrical consultant, Al Hildenbrand. Not only is he a licensed master electrician (with a degree in electrical engineering to boot), he's also out there every day, running wire, tracking down electrical gremlins and solving real-life problems.

And we use the best architects, designers, illustrators, photographers and experts to deliver safe, solid information.

Of course, what's best to one reader isn't necessarily best to the next. Some think nitty-gritty articles about sweating pipe and hanging drywall are the best, others love big outdoor landscaping projects. Even for one individual, what's best one month, might not be best the next. When you're standing knee-deep in water and your spouse brings down that recent issue on emergency plumbing repairs—well, that's got best written all over it!

But we gave it our best shot. We pulled together and organized dozens of projects and hundreds of useful tips and techniques. You'll even find information you won't find in *The Family Handyman* magazine; information about product recalls, the best and cheapest places to buy tools and hard-to-find items and more.

Best of luck in all your projects.

Spike Carlsen and *The Family Handyman*

Contents

1 INDOOR PROJECTS, IMPROVEMENTS & REPAIRS

2 OUTDOOR PROJECTS & IMPROVEMENTS

3 IN THE WORKSHOP

4 HOUSE SYSTEMS

5 YARD & GARDEN PROJECTS & IMPROVEMENTS

6 ENERGY SAVINGS & HOME SAFETY

RESOURCES

TOPICS AND TRENDS SHAPING THE
DO-IT-YOURSELF WORLD

NEW CODES AND PRODUCTS AFFECT YOUR PROJECTS

Safer electrical systems. As of January 2002, the National Electrical Code requires arc-fault circuit-interrupters in 15- and 20-amp bedroom branch circuits. These breakers trip when they detect low-level arcing (electrical shorts) that won't trip a standard breaker. Not all communities require them so ask your inspector.

Another recent regulation requires grounding all light switches, dimmers and similar controls. Up until recently, most ground wires were simply tucked into the back of the box.

Changing building codes. Though building codes vary from state to state and region to region, you may find your home improvement projects affected in a few areas.

- Deck railings. New codes prohibit building decks with all horizontal rails. Why? Kids use them as ladders to climb up and risk falling over the top.
- Smoke detectors. If you spend $1,000 or more on improving your home, many communities are requiring the installation of battery-operated smoke detectors in every bedroom and on each level of the house.
- Basement windows. In many areas if you build a new house or addition, the basement must include an egress window (one with a clear opening at least 20 in. wide, 24 in. high and 5.7 sq. ft. total area) for fire safety.

New kinds of treated wood. Lumber treated with chromated copper arsenate (CCA) is not considered a health hazard by the EPA. But because of continuing health concerns about arsenic in the preservative, the treated wood industry is voluntarily switching over to non-arsenic wood preservatives for the residential market. The changeover will be complete by the end of 2003.

Non-arsenic lumber is sold under brand names such as ACQ Preserve, NatureWood and Wolmanized Natural Select. Nearly one billion board feet of ACQ treated lumber alone will be sold in the U.S. in 2002.

Residential fire sprinkler systems. They're a reality—especially if you're building a new home. Installation typically costs 1% to 1-1/2% of the cost of a new home. In conjunction with fire alarms they reduce the risk of home fire deaths by 82%, they're inconspicuous, they can even help cut your insurance premiums. One fire chief said installing a residential sprinkler system has become so painless, he'd never consider building a home or addition without one.

For more information visit www.homefiresprinkler.org or call (888) 635-7222

FEMALE DO-IT-YOURSELFERS HAMMER THE HOME IMPROVEMENT MARKET

True or false? 1) Nearly half of all home-center purchases are by women. 2) More women would rather spend their leisure time on a home-improvement project than shopping at a mall. 3) Nearly 65% of women plan on doing a home-improvement project within two or three years.

If you answered "true" to all the above, you're tuned in to one of the biggest trends in home improvement. Women are involved in 90% of all home-improvement decisions, and tackling projects in record numbers. A current survey showed 54% of women are in the process of planning a home improvement project. The most popular? Painting (32%), landscaping (32%), wallpapering (21%), tiling (15%) and installing light fixtures (13%). And everyone from tool companies to work glove manufacturers are creating products directed toward women.

One company, Tomboy Tools, specializes in finding, developing and selling tools that are lighter, fit smaller hands and geared to female DIYers. The company even offers in-home workshops. Its motto is "No Pink Tools." Find more information at www.tomboytools.com.

DIY VOLUNTEER GROUPS MAKE A DIFFERENCE

What started as a trickle, has become a flood. Habitat for Humanity, one of the first and best known "hammer swinging" volunteer organizations, has built more than 125,000 houses in 83 countries around the world. But Habitat volunteers aren't the only ones pitching in to help others. The volunteer organization Rebuilding Together (formerly Christmas in April), has helped renovate 63,000 homes. In 2002 more than 250,000 volunteers pitched in over 2-1/2 million hours of working time.

Gardeners are getting into the act, too. The "Plant a Row for the Hungry" program sponsored by the Garden Writers Association of America, contributed over one million pounds of fruits and vegetables to food shelves over the past year. The Scotts Company "Give Back to Grow" program salutes volunteers who use their green thumbs to help others. The company offers $5,000 prizes in the categories of Good Neighbor Gardener of the Year, Classroom Gardener of the Year, Outstanding Young Gardener of the Year, and Urban Greenup Gardener of the Year.

The Minwax Community Craftsman Award honors individuals and groups that have improved their communities by working with wood.

For information about getting involved, contact the organizations below:

Habitat for Humanity
121 Habitat St.
Americus, GA 31709
(800) 422-4828
www.habitat.org

Minwax Community Craftsman Award
c/o Brushfire, Inc.
110 South Jefferson Rd.
Whippany, NJ 07981
www.minwax.com

Plant a Row for the Hungry
10210 Leatherleaf Ct.
Manassas, VA 20111
(877) 492-2727
www.gwaa.org//par

Rebuilding Together
1536 Sixteenth St., N.W.
Washington, DC 20036
(800) 473-4229
www.rebuildingtogether.com

Scotts Give Back to Grow
c/o Weber Shandwick Worldwide
100 South Fourth St., Ste. 1200
St. Louis, MO 63102
(800) 551-5971
www.scottscompany.com

PRICES KEEP COMING DOWN

The negotiating power of "big box" stores, a global economy, the Internet and more efficient manufacturing processes have driven down the prices of many products. What's cheaper? High-end kitchen appliances, granite countertops, cordless tools and composite decking have all become more affordable. What's more expensive? Cedar lumber and concrete (because many sand and gravel quarries are becoming depleted near urban areas).

HOW WE LIVE

- Americans spent 163 billion dollars on remodeling and repairs in 2002.
- Sixty-seven percent of Americans own their own homes; an all-time high.
- Two-thirds of all major home improvement projects (building decks, room additions, etc.) are done by do-it-yourselfers.
- Based on a survey, the average cost of a kitchen makeover by National Kitchen and Bath Association members is $36,200 about 40% of their jobs cost $25,000 or less.
- Americans spend an average of 35 minutes per day in the bathroom; 42% read in the bathroom; 16% have telephone conversations and 17% sing in the shower. Fifty percent take showers every day and more than 6% take more than one shower a day.
- The EPA estimates that air in most new homes is likely to be two to five times more polluted than outside air; Americans spend about 90% of their time indoors.

10 PROBLEM-SOLVING
NEW PRODUCTS

INDESTRUCTIBLE WORK LIGHT

Anyone who's worked in a poorly lit garage, basement or remodeling space knows the benefit of halogen work lights: They cast a blast of light that makes it seem like you're working in broad daylight. But there are disadvantages: They're awkward to move, focus light on a limited area, are scorching hot to the touch—and if one tips over, run for your life.

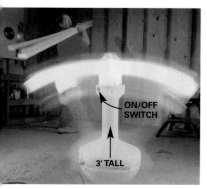

ON/OFF SWITCH

3' TALL

The Wobble Light addresses all these problems:

■ Its unibody construction and weighted base make it easy to move around and set up.

■ The brilliant 500-watt halogen bulb casts light in 360 degrees (and has an estimated lifespan of 2,000 hours).

■ An internal blower and vented dome help keep the bulb dome in the safe temperature range.

■ Its "Bozo the clown" construction means that when you knock it over, it swings right back up. Shock-absorbing springs cushion the bulb from breakage.

SHOCK-ABSORBING SPRINGS

While testing the 3-ft. tall light, we punched, knocked, banged and dropped it. The "bulletproof" dome lived up to its name and it returned to its upright position flawlessly. It has a handy on-off button plus a built-in receptacle for plugging in an additional extension cord.

Compared with other work lights, it's a bit expensive, but in terms of safety (and as a conversation piece) it's got 'em all beat. People even use them to light up their basketball courts and barbecue pits. Cost is $99 plus shipping from the manufacturer. Wobble Light, 4518 North Kedzie Ave., Chicago, IL 60625; (773) 463-5900. www.wobblelight.com.

HOOK YOURSELF SOME LUMBER

No more excuses that you can't put up new gutters because you can't haul them home. Siderax turns your van, car or SUV into a gutter-toting, lumber-hauling, ladder-carrying machine.

The concept is simple. You open your passenger-side windows, set the hooks in the openings, lock 'em in place with bungee cords, tie

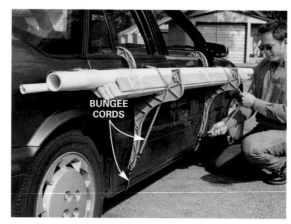

BUNGEE CORDS

your load down, then drive away. Great for long skinny stuff up to 40 lbs.—carpet, millwork, pipe, you name it. The padded hooks help protect the finish on your vehicle, and you can store 'em in your trunk when you're not using them. You can even hang 'em over the bed of your pickup truck if you don't have a rack for hauling. They cost about $25 plus shipping. Siderax, 23 Lower Truro Rd., Truro, NS B2N 5E8, Canada. (877) 620-4994. www.siderax.com

A HANDY INFLATER

If you're tired of the huff-and-puff method of blowing up air mattresses, water toys and other inflatables, you need the Air Daddy. The Air Daddy is a simple gadget with a standard car tire–like valve on one end and a tapered nozzle on the other. You can hook it up to a compressor, bike pump or gas station air

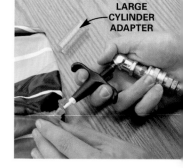

LARGE CYLINDER ADAPTER

hose and blow away. The $5 price (with shipping) includes a large cylinder adapter for really big valves. You can also use it to blow off your tools and workbench, clear water lines or to "blow clean" the inside of your car. MT Synergy, 1020 Swan River Rd., Bigfork, MT 59911; (406) 837-0706. Fax: (406) 837-0806. www.mtsynergy.com

"FLAT-FREE" WHEELBARROW TIRE

Here's a wheelbarrow tire that keeps rolling through rain, snow, nails and glass. The Carefree Tire isn't filled with air but with a special polyurethane foam-like material that contains hundreds of thousands of microscopic air cells. The tires simply don't go flat. It's the same technology used in the tires of golf carts, wheelchairs and heavy-duty construction equipment.

The Carefree Tire provides a smoother ride, and according to the manufacturer, requires up to 40% less effort to move heavy loads. (How do they figure that stuff out?) Lifetime guarantee, too.

The tires are available in two rim diameters, three tread patterns and two hub lengths. Best of all, they're available in red, green, yellow and blue. About $45 at home centers, hardware stores and garden centers. Carefree Tire, 5141 Firestone Place, South Gate, CA 90280; (877) 352-8776. www.carefreetire.com

LOG SPLITTER FOR SUBURBAN LUMBERJACKS

The maul and wedge routine for splitting wood is draining, and renting a gas-powered hydraulic splitter is expensive. The splitter is also tough to haul around and sounds like a Mack truck. The solution? The new electric Fisch Log Splitter. It will split more than 100 logs in less than an hour, safely and (almost) effortlessly. The requirement of two hands to operate the splitter—one on a safety button, the other on the hydraulic lever—eliminates hand injuries common with splitters. It's surprisingly quiet and the splitting carriage at shin level makes it easy to load and unload logs. It will handle logs up to 20 in. long and 12 in. in diameter and automatically retracts when you remove your hand from the lever.

The lightweight (under 100 lbs.) and affordable (about $450) splitter is equipped with wheels and is the size of a vacuum cleaner. The 2-hp electric motor requires a 20-amp circuit and hefty extension cord. This splitter is a dream for the suburban lumberjack on a budget. Fisch Precision Tools, (724) 663-9072. www.fisch-woodworking.com

PUT A PHONE ANYWHERE

If you wish you had a phone in your shop, basement, laundry room or spare room—but there's not a phone jack in sight—check out this wireless system from RCA. It's a two-unit system

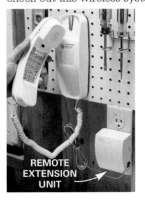

REMOTE EXTENSION UNIT

that turns your electrical system into a telephone transmission line.

You position the base unit (not shown) where a phone jack and electrical outlet are close together. Use a standard phone cord to connect the base unit to the wall phone jack, and another phone cord to plug the existing phone into the base unit. Then plug the base unit into the outlet. Trust me—it's simple. Finally, plug the remote extension unit (shown) into any outlet and a phone into the extension unit. Presto, you're connected. You can add as many extension units as you want once the base system is in place.

RCA has also developed a wireless computer modem jack (No. RC930, about $100) that allows you to connect a computer to the Internet using the same technology. The wireless phone system (No. RC926) costs about $50. Additional extension units (No. RC920) cost about $30. Available at Radio Shack, home centers and discount stores. Find a dealer at www.rca.com or by calling (800) 409-5111. Thomson Consumer Electronics, 11721 Alameda Ave., Socorro, TX 79927; (800) 338-0376.

FLEXIBLE BRUSH

Here's a wire brush with a new twist —it bends! The Armadillo brush's curved ends and nine segments allow the brush to accommodate irregular shapes and curves. Great for removing rust and paint from pipes, machinery, grills and outdoor furniture.

It's made from sturdy polyethylene, fits well in the hand and contains 163 wire tufts (no, I didn't count them). It's No. 1838 and costs about $8.95. Wooster Brush, 604 Madison Ave., Wooster, OH 44691; (800) 392-7246. www.woosterbrush.com

SUPER RIPPING GUIDE

We've experimented with circular saw edge guides in the past—and found most to be inaccurate, too limited or too hard to set up. But the Craftsman Accu-Rip is so well designed and simple to use that we got one for the workshop. You secure the front edge of your circular saw base to the guide with a set of pins. You then adjust the small sliding cutting guide to the width of cut you want and run it along the edge of the board or sheet good you're cutting.

It will make accurate rip cuts up to 24-in. wide. And we were pleasantly surprised to discover we could shave off strips as thin as 1/8 in. You need to "freehand" the last 2 in. of any cut, but the blade tends to track in the existing kerf

CUTTING GUIDE

and guide itself for that short distance.

Another nice feature: When you need to use your saw for crosscuts, you can leave the guide in place. It sure beats wrestling a 4 x 8 sheet of plywood through your table saw. Accu-Rip (No. 25980) is available in Sears stores for $39.99. Check the Sears Web site: www.sears.com

WARMER, DRIER CONCRETE FLOORS

Anyone who's hassled with installing sleepers and plywood over concrete to create a drier, "friendlier" surface for floor coverings will love this product. The Subflor system consists of 2 x 2-ft. tongue-and-groove OSB panels with dimpled plastic laminated to the bottom. The OSB is impregnated with water-resistant waxes and resins, and the plastic dimples raise the OSB off the floor 5/16 in. to protect it from moisture and to create a thermal break. Subflor provides a ready surface for installing carpet, floating wood, laminate flooring and sheet goods.

DIMPLES

OSB PANEL

To install the panels, you simply tap them together using a hammer and block of wood. The panels interlock so tightly that there's no need to glue them to one another or to the concrete floor. The panels are only 7/8 in. thick, making the floor about half as thick as a conventional sleeper-and-plywood floor. And they're a heck of a lot easier to handle and haul home than 4 x 8-ft. sheets of plywood and 12-ft. long furring strips. OSB will irreversibly swell if subjected to water repeatedly or for long periods of time, so keep it out of areas that could be flooded, particularly bathrooms and laundry rooms.

Each panel costs about $7, making the price of finishing a 10 x 10-ft. room about $175. See the Web site below or call for a dealer near you. Lamwood Products Ltd., 44 Woodbine Downs Blvd., Rexdale ON M9W 5R2, Canada; (866) 782-3567. www.subflor.com

GARDENING TOOLS THAT GROW ON YOU

These tools may look like something out of a science fiction novel, but Earth Bud-Eze tools are the real thing. Ergonomically designed and constructed of heavy-duty steel, these are the most comfortable, easy to use gardening tools around. The rubber hand grip and arm cuff combine to take strain and pressure off your wrist and hand and transfer it up to your arm and shoulder.

They take a few minutes to get used to—you pull instead of push for most tasks—but once you get the hang of them, they're almost effortless to use. Good for any gardening enthusiast—and great for folks with arthritis or repetitive stress

injuries. Available in three styles: the cultivator shown in use, the trowel shown at left and a smaller, similarly shaped V-hoe. The price is $12.95 per tool or $38.85 for the trio (plus shipping). Available at United Hardware, Trustworthy Hardware and Hardware Hank stores or from the Web site listed below. Earth Bud-Eze, 880 S.W. 15th St., Suite 2, Forest Lake, MN 55025-1306; (877) 504-9800. www.earthbudeze.com

PRODUCT RECALLS
AND SAFETY ALERTS

Tackling home improvement projects is challenging enough without having to worry about the safety of the tools and products are you're using. If you own any of the recalled items listed below, contact the manufacturer for more information on what to do. You can stay on top of the latest recalls by checking www. safetyalerts.com.

Horizontal Window Blinds
Problem: Pull cords and inner cords can form a loop and cause strangulation.
Models affected: Any of the approximately 85 million window blinds sold each year if they have cords that can form a loop.
What to do: Contact the Window Covering Safety Council at (800) 506-4636 or visit www.windowcovering.org for a free repair kit.

Kohler Shower Doors
(about 41,000 units recalled)
Problem: Hinges can fail, causing shower door to fall and injure those nearby.
Models affected: Kohler Helios and Sterling Freestyle models made from January 1997 through September 2001.
What to do: Contact Kohler at (866) 782-6329 or visit www.kohler.com to receive a replacement door.

Lakewood Electric Heaters
(about 107,000 units recalled)
Problem: The electrical connections inside the heater can become loose, causing the heater's metal frame to become energized. This poses a serious electric-shock hazard.
Models affected: Model numbers 797 or 797 DFT, which is stamped on the back of the unit. These units were sold between October 2000 and February 2002.
What to do: Contact Lakewood at (888) 858-3506 to receive a free repair or replacement.

Roto Zip Handheld Saws
(about 1.9 million units recalled)
Problem: The handles can separate from the body, causing the operator to be cut.
Models affected: Roto Zip Revolution (serial numbers 01 through 1,145,000), Rebel (serial numbers 01 through 415,000) and Solaris (serial numbers 01 through 270,000) Spiral Saw power tools. These units were sold from December 1999 through January 2002.
What to do: Contact Roto Zip at (800) 920-1467 or visit www.rotozip.com to receive a free replacement handle.

DeWalt Circular Saws
(about 55,000 units recalled)
Problem: The spindle may slip, causing the blade to contact the lower guard, posing a hazard to the operator from an exposed blade.
Models affected: 7-1/4-in. circular saws with the model numbers DW368, DW368K and DW369CSK. The saws have date codes 200128-F through 200152-F stamped on the bottom of the motor case. These units were sold from July 2001 through December 2001.
What to do: Return the saw to the nearest DeWalt service center for a free repair. For more information, contact DeWalt at (888) 839-3559.

Ames Wheelbarrows
(about 647,000 units recalled)
Problem: The plastic wheel assemblies (manufactured by a predecessor company) can break when being inflated with high-pressure hoses. This can result in plastic pieces exploding from the rims of the wheels.
Models affected: Ames "Mustang-" or "Douglas-" brand wheelbarrows with wheel assemblies with a black plastic rim and an approximately 14-in. diameter wheel. They have red, green or orange tubs or trays made of steel or plastic. These units were sold from January 1993 through December 2000. Wheelbarrows with metal wheel assemblies are not part of this recall.
What to do: Contact Ames True Temper at (866) 239-2281 to receive a free replacement steel wheel assembly.

Anderson Window Latches
(about 400,000 units recalled)
Problem: The latches on the lower sash can unexpectedly open, posing a potential hazard to consumers who can be struck by the window or by shattered glass.
Models affected: Only the tilt latches on the lower sash of the Andersen 200 Series Tilt-Wash Double-Hung Windows sold from May 2000 through August 2001. This recall does not apply to Andersen Builder's Select or any other Andersen products.
What to do: Call Andersen WindowCare Solution Center at (888) 888-7020 or visit www.andersenwindows.com to schedule a free in-home repair.

Ryobi Circular Saws
(about 125,000 units recalled)
Problem: The lower blade guards can stick in the open position, posing a serious risk.
Models affected: 7-1/4-in. Ryobi circular saws with a blue plastic body, a metal blade guard and the model numbers CSB120, CSB130, CSB1308, CSB130K and CSB130JS sold from October 1998 through July 2001.
What to do: Contact Ryobi's Consumer Response Team at (800) 867-9624 for a free repair kit.

Whirlpool Microwave-Hood Combinations
(about 1.8 million units recalled)
Problem: These units can overheat and catch fire.
Models affected: Microwave and exhaust fan/hood combination units installed above ranges. Sold under the Whirlpool, KitchenAid and Kenmore brand names. Their serial numbers begins with XC. Units were sold from January 1998 through September 2001.
What to do: Contact Whirlpool at (800) 785-8897 or visit www.whirlpool.com for a free repair kit.

Craftsman Radial-Arm Saws
(about 3.7 million units recalled)
Problem: These saws were sold without a guard that covers the entire blade.
Models affected: Craftsman 8-, 8-1/4-, 9- and 10-in. radial-arm saws with a model number beginning with 113. The 8-, 9-, and 10-in. saws were sold from 1958 through 1992. The 8-1/4-in. saws were sold from 1990 through 1995.
What to do: Contact Emerson Tool Co. at (800) 511-2628 or visit www.radialarmsawrecall.com for information about a free repair kit that provides a complete blade guard. For older model saws and others that cannot accept the new guard, Emerson will provide $100 for the return of the saw carriage. Saws should not be returned to Sears.

BRK First Alert Fire Extinguishers
(about 600,000 units recalled)
Problem: The extinguishers can fail to discharge when the trigger is activated.
Models affected: First Alert model FE1A10G with serial numbers beginning with RH, RK, RL, RP, RT, RU or RW are included in this recall. Units were sold from September 1999 through September 2000.
What to do: Contact First Alert at (866) 669-2736 or visit www.firstalert.com to receive a coupon for a new extinguisher.

Halogen Torchiere Floor Lamps
(more than 40 million units recalled)
Problem: These lamps have no wire or glass guard to protect combustibles, such as drapes, from coming in contact with the bulb, posing a fire risk.
Models affected: Numerous floor lamps that were manufactured before 1997.
What to do: Get a wire guard by sending a postcard to Catalina Lighting Consumer Services, 18191 NW 68th Ave., Miami, FL 33015.

DeWalt Battery Chargers
(about 1.7 million units recalled)
Problem: The battery charger can fail to automatically shut off after the battery is fully charged, which can cause the battery to burst, and poses fire, burn and electrical-shock hazards.
Models affected: Recalled DeWalt battery chargers have model numbers DW9107 and DW9108 with date codes 9616 through 9752. Recalled Black & Decker Industry and Construction battery chargers have model numbers 97015 and 97016 with date codes 9616 through 9752. These units were sold from May 1996 through August 2000.
What to do: Take the charger to a DeWalt or Black & Decker service center for a free replacement, contact DeWalt at (866) 543-3401 or visit www.dewalt.com.

Wood Industries Extension Cords and Cord Reels
(about 500,000 outdoor extension cords and 19,000 cord reels recalled)
Problem: The extension cords and cord reels are equipped with a locking plug, which is designed to keep tools plugged in. The plastic housing of the locking plug can separate or break, exposing live wires and posing shock and electrocution hazards.
Models affected: The extension cords were sold under the "Woods LockJaw" and "Yellow Jacket LockJaw" brand names in various wire gauges, lengths and colors. The cord reels are 30-ft. long, were sold under the "Woods' ACDelco" and "LumaPro" brand names and in various wire gauges and colors. These cords and reels were sold from January 1996 through July 2000. Units with a gray locking button on the side of the LockJaw plug are not recalled.
What to do: Contact Woods Industries at (888) 755-6535 to receive a replacement.

Black & Decker Cordless Drills
(about 950,000 units recalled)
Problem: These drills can overheat, posing a burn hazard.
Models affected: The drills are either orange with "Firestorm" on the label or green with "Quantum Pro" and model numbers CD632, HP532, FS1442, Q145, FS1560, FS1802, HP932 and Q185. These units were sold between March 1999 and December 2001.
What to do: Contact Black & Decker at (866) 821-5444 to arrange to have the drill repaired for free.

WORK SAFELY

As you go about your home improvement projects and repairs, stay alert for these hazards:

Aluminum wiring

Aluminum wiring, installed in about 7 million homes between 1965 and 1973, requires special techniques and materials to make safe connections. This wiring is dull gray, not the dull orange characteristic of copper. Hire a licensed electrician certified to work with it. For more information visit the Web site www.inspect-ny.com/aluminum.htm

Asbestos

Texture sprayed on ceilings before 1978, adhesives and tiles for vinyl and asphalt floors before 1980 and vermiculite insulation (with gray granules) all may contain asbestos. Other building materials, made between 1940 and 1980, could also contain asbestos. If you suspect materials you're removing or working around contain asbestos, contact your health department or visit www.epa.gov/asbestos for information.

Backdrafting

As you make your home more energy-efficient and airtight, ducts and chimneys can't vent combustion gases, including potentially deadly carbon monoxide (CO). Install an inexpensive CO detector as a safety measure.

Buried utilities

Call your utility companies to have them mark underground gas, electrical, water and telephone lines before digging. In many areas it takes just one call.

Five-gallon buckets

Since 1984 over 200 children have drowned in 5-gallon buckets. Store empty buckets upside down and store those containing liquids with the cover securely snapped.

Lead paint

If your home was built before 1979 it may contain lead paint; a serious health hazard, especially for children six and under. Take precautions when you scrape or remove it. Contact your public health department for detailed safety information or call (800) 424-LEAD to receive an information pamphlet.

Spontaneous combustion

Rags saturated with oil finishes like Danish oil and linseed oil, and oil-based paints and stains can spontaneously combust if left bunched up. Dry them outdoors, spread out loosely. When the oil has thoroughly dried, it's safe to throw them in the trash.

1

Got cold floors? A room that needs paint or wallpaper? A little mold lingering in the corner? Here's how to deal with these and more!

Indoor Projects
IMPROVEMENTS & REPAIRS

You can **fix** it™

FIX A LOOSE HINGE

Over time, many doors get heavy use, causing the hinge screws to strip out and the hinges to loosen. Once this happens, the door ceases to swing smoothly and may require lifting and pushing to get it closed because of the binding hinge. If you get teed off at a door hinge that frequently comes loose because the screws don't hold anymore, grab a hammer, knife, wood glue and your golf bag for a quick fix.

Completely remove the loose hinge from the door and frame. Remove only one hinge at a time so you don't have to take the door down. (If you have several hinges with stripped screws, however, you may want to remove the entire door.) Locate the stripped screw holes and repair with golf tees as shown in **Photos 1 and 2**. Once the hole is plugged, reattach the hinge and screws. Screwing through the golf tee will cause it to expand and tighten the hinge even more, restoring your doors to proper working condition.

GOLF TEE

TIGER WOODS

1 UNSCREW the loose hinge. Squirt wood glue on a golf tee and tap it into the stripped hole until tight. Let the glue dry for an hour.

2 CUT the golf tee flush with the door frame using a sharp utility knife, then screw the hinge back in place.

REVIVE AN AROMATIC CEDAR CLOSET

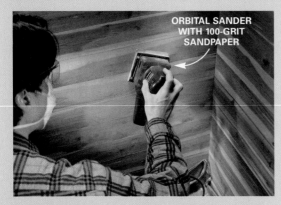

ORBITAL SANDER WITH 100-GRIT SANDPAPER

SAND the emptied closet using an orbital sander with 100-grit sandpaper. Achieve an even finish by moving the sander slowly back and forth under medium pressure and changing the sandpaper when it's clogged with dust. To avoid "chatter marks" on inside corners and door trim, grip the sander firmly and move it up and down without touching adjacent walls or trim.

Everyone likes the woodsy smell of a new aromatic cedar closet. But the fragrance diminishes once the cedar oils evaporate and dust clogs the wood pores. You can revive much of the aroma by sanding and cleaning the paneling.

Start by emptying the closet, laying down floor protection and draping the area with plastic sheeting to control the sanding dust.

For the best results, move the sander in overlapping side-to-side strokes. Clean the paneling by vacuuming and then wiping it with tack cloths (about $1 each). Avoid using a damp cloth or sponge to remove the cedar dust. Wet-cleaning may raise the wood grain and leave a rough surface and water stains.

VACUUM all the wall surfaces. Then wipe the walls with fresh tack cloths.

REPAIR VINYL FLOORING

The easy maintenance of vinyl and linoleum flooring makes it ideal for bathrooms, kitchens and other busy areas. However, heavy, hot or sharp objects can damage this tough material, and nothing looks worse in the middle of the floor than a conspicuous blemish. The Vinyl Floor Repair Kit ($20) by Homax Products allows you to repair those unsightly burns, cuts and gouges in your vinyl or linoleum flooring. It'll disguise imperfections up to the size of a quarter. The kit is available at Ace Hardware stores or directly from the manufacturer (800-729-9029).

Prepare the surface for patching as shown in **Photo 1**. Keep the tape 1/2 in. back so the repair adhesives don't glue it to the floor.

Mixing the special paint to match your flooring color is the trickiest part of the fix (**Photo 2**). The included color-matching guide will help you determine basic colors, but a closer match will require a little trial and error. An exact color match is difficult to achieve, but if it's close, it'll be virtually indistinguishable at normal viewing distances.

Check the color mix by dabbing test samples on a piece of clear packing tape laid on the floor. Add small amounts of color to the mix until you find a close match. Dark colors will lighten slightly and light colors will darken slightly after the hole is filled.

The filler and floor bond level the hole flush with the rest of the floor (**Photo 3**). If the surface appears rough after the bond dries, lightly sand it smooth with the enclosed sandpaper (be careful not to scratch the surrounding floor surface). Protect the repair with clear acrylic finish (**Photo 4**).

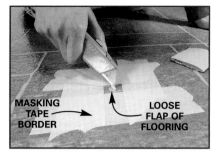

1 APPLY tape around the damaged area. Cut out any loose fragments with a utility knife. Clean dust or dirt from inside the damaged area with a damp rag, and smooth rough edges with the enclosed sandpaper.

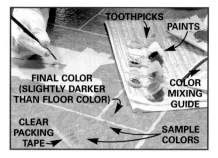

2 MIX the paint to match the floor color, and paint the inside surface and edges of the damaged area. Clean off any paint that gets on the surrounding vinyl surface. Let the paint dry for 15 minutes, or speed up the drying time with a hair dryer on low heat.

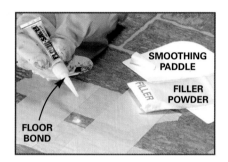

3 POUR filler powder into the hole and level it off with the enclosed smoothing paddle. Hold the floor bond right over the filler powder. Slowly drip the bond onto the filler powder until the powder is saturated (three or four drops cover a dime-size area). Let the compound harden for 15 minutes.

4 BRUSH the clear acrylic finish over the repair with a small brush, and allow two hours' drying time before walking on the area or moving appliances across it.

TIGHTEN A RATTLING DOOR

A loose, rattling door can be nerve-racking, especially at night, and if it's an exterior door, it's wasting energy, too. Most strike plates have an adjustment tab to solve that problem (**see photo**). If the door continues to rattle, you might have to remove the plate and bend the tab several times to get it just right. If the door latch doesn't catch when you close the door, bend it back until the door latches tightly. Now you can sleep in peace.

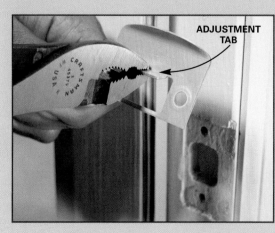

UNSCREW the strike plate from the door. Bend the small tab toward the latch bolt opening.

WARM
BATHROOM FLOORS

Under-tile heat is easy to install, cheap to operate, and takes up little or no space. Best of all, your feet will love it!

by **Spike Carlsen**

You finished that long, hot shower. You're squeaky clean and cozy warm—until you step onto the tile floor. Then you get another sensation—ice-cold feet. The solution isn't to banish tile from bathrooms—it's too durable, water resistant and easy to clean to do that. The answer is to warm up that tile from below with electric resistance heat.

Lots of pros, few cons

This in-the-floor heating system consists of one thin continuous cable heating element woven into a mat that you install under the tile. This makes it a project best done when over-

hauling or changing the floor covering of an existing room or when adding a new room. It can be installed as supplemental heat to take the chill out of the floor or as space heat to warm the entire bathroom. It's also a great project for warming entryway and kitchen floors.

The benefits

- It's easy to install. You embed a cable-laced mat in the mortar when you lay the tile. If you're not comfortable with the wiring portion, hire an electrician.
- It's safe. Once the heating system is installed, it's nearly impossible to damage. The GFCI-protected thermostat instantly cuts power in the event of a short or other problem.
- It's inexpensive to operate. At 12 watts per square foot, our 30-sq.-ft. mat drew 360 watts of power—about the equivalent of an electric blanket or large TV. If you operate it only during the high-traffic morning and evening hours, this translates into 25¢ to $1 per day, depending on your location, electrical costs and the season.
- It takes up zero space. Got a big, clunky radiator? Remove it and gain valuable square footage by installing this stuff.
- It's versatile. If your existing furnace or boiler doesn't have enough oomph to heat a newly remodeled or added space, floor heat can do the job.
- It's really, really comfortable. When your feet are warm, your entire body feels warm. You'll find yourself reading and playing games with your kids on the bathroom floor.

The downside? It can't be retrofitted under existing tile floors, the total initial cost of materials is about $15 to $20 per square foot, and you'll most likely need to run new wiring from the main circuit panel to the bathroom.

HEATING MAT

Project Facts:
- **Cost:** The floor heating mat costs **$12 to $14 per square foot; the thermostat costs $130 to $190. Add the price of tile materials, cement board and electrical work.**
- **Time:** Mat installation added 6 hours to the floor tiling project; the electrical box, conduit and thermostat installation added 3 hours.
- **Skill Level: Intermediate wiring and tile-laying skills.**
- **Most Common Mistake: Slamming the trowel down to knock off mortar, and in the process, nicking the cable.**

Where to find electrical power

For a heated floor area less than 20 sq. ft., you could (in most cases) draw power from an adjacent GFCI-protected outlet without overloading the circuit. (If the thermostat you purchase is already GFCI protected like ours, you can use any outlet. In any case, the mat must be GFCI protected.) But a larger mat on an existing circuit—a circuit that might also accommodate a 2,000-watt hair dryer—can cause overloads and nuisance circuit breaker trips. For our larger mat, we elected to install a dedicated circuit with its own wiring and circuit breaker. Both 120-volt and 240-volt mats are available.

A programmable thermostat that turns the mat on during times of normal usage, then off when you're sleeping or away, costs more initially but will save energy and money in the long run.

Special-order your custom-size mat

A number of companies offer electric resistance floor warming systems. We ordered our electric mat, thermostat and installation materials from Watts Radiant (see Buyer's Guide, p. 22). We sent them the required detailed drawing of the bathroom floor plan and location of fixtures. In two days, they faxed back a proposed mat layout and bid. The mats come in 12-, 24- and 30-in. widths and increments of 5 ft. in length (10 sq. ft. minimum). When in doubt, the company will specify a mat smaller than you need since the mat cable can't be cut. A good instructional video comes with the materials. A few common mat sizes are beginning to be available at some home centers.

When you receive the mat, use a volt-ohm meter (**Photo 1**) to obtain a resistance reading to make sure it wasn't damaged during manufacturing or shipping.

Prep your floor as you would for any tiling job. Install 1/2-in. cement backer board, securing it to the existing subfloor with mortar and cement board screws (**Photo 2**). Tape and mortar the seams to create a solid, continuous surface. Snap tile layout lines on the floor once the mortar has dried.

Test-fit the mat to avoid glitches

Before proceeding with the actual installation, do a test layout (**Photo 3**). Follow these basic guidelines:

- Install the mat up to the area where the vanity cabinet or pedestal sink will sit, but not under it; that can cause excessive heat buildup.
- Keep the mat 4 in. away from walls, showers and tubs.
- Keep the mat at least 4 in. away from the toilet wax ring.
- Keep the blue heating cable at least 2 in. away from itself (**Photo 5**). Never overlap the cable.
- Don't leave large gaps between the mats. Your feet will be able to tell!
- If your mat is undersized, give priority to the areas where you'll be standing barefoot most often!

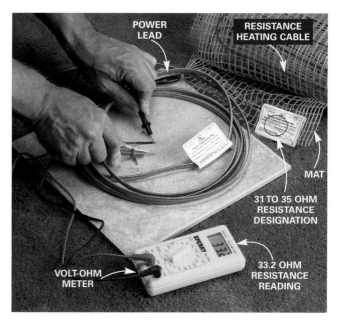

1 TEST the heating cable for manufacturing or shipping damage with a volt-ohm meter. The resistance reading on the mat label (in our case, 31-35) and the resistance registered by the meter (in our case, 33.2) should be within 10 percent of each other. If not, see the manufacturer's instructions. Digital volt-ohm meters like the one shown cost less than $30 and are easy to operate.

2 INSTALL cement board over the existing subfloor. Trowel on a layer of thin-set mortar, then secure the cement board with cement board screws. Cover the seams with mesh fiberglass tape and thin-set to create a "unibody" floor. Snap chalk lines on the floor to mark the tile layout.

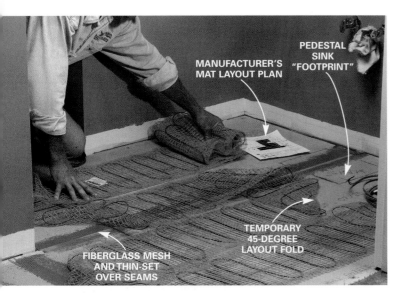

MANUFACTURER'S MAT LAYOUT PLAN

PEDESTAL SINK "FOOTPRINT"

TEMPORARY 45-DEGREE LAYOUT FOLD

FIBERGLASS MESH AND THIN-SET OVER SEAMS

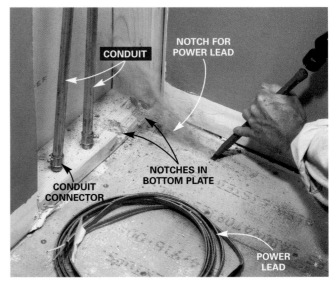

CONDUIT

NOTCH FOR POWER LEAD

NOTCHES IN BOTTOM PLATE

CONDUIT CONNECTOR

POWER LEAD

3 TEST-FIT the mat, keeping the cable 4 in. from fixtures and walls and 2 in. from one another. Give priority to those areas where you'll stand barefooted the most. You MUST NOT cut or cross the cable, so make sure the mat fits.

4 CHISEL a groove in the cement board for the enlarged portion of the power lead to nestle into. Notch the bottom plate of the wall to provide a pathway for the power lead, thermostat wires and conduit.

Following your preliminary layout, mark the path of the thick "power lead" between the mat and wall cavity (**Photo 4**) and chisel a shallow trench into the cement board. Notch the bottom plate to accommodate the two conduits that will contain the power lead and the wires for the thermostat-sensing bulb.

Glue and tape the mat in place

Install the mat, securing it lightly to the cement board with double-face tape (**Photo 5**). To make turns, cut the mat between two loops in the cable, then flip the mat and run it the opposite direction. *Never, ever cut, nick or stress the cable itself.* Where the full-width mat won't fit, or where you encounter angles or jogs, carefully cut the mat from around the cable, and hot-melt glue the cable to the floor (**Photo 6**). Continue using the full mat again when you can.

Tip Make sure no screw- or nail-heads protrude above the cement board. A sharp edge can damage the cable.

Install the entire mat complete with cuts, flips and turns to make sure it fits the space right, make any final adjustments, then press the mat firmly into the tape. Use hot-melt glue to additionally secure the mat. Don't leave any humps or loose edges; you'll snag them with your notched trowel when you're applying the thin-set mortar.

If you're not going to tile right away, lay thick corrugated cardboard over the mat to protect the cable. You'll be glad you did when your kid walks in wearing baseball cleats.

Wiring setup

Install conduit connectors to both ends of two pieces of 58-in. long 1/2-in. electrical metal tubing (EMT). Fish the power lead cable through one length of conduit. Hot-melt glue the power lead into the groove. Fish the thermostat wires through a second piece of conduit, then weave it 12 in. into the mat, keeping it equidistant from the cable on each side (**Photo 7**).

Secure the two lengths of conduit to a 4 x 4-in. metal electrical box. Secure this box to the studs so the lower ends of the conduits nestle into the notches you made in the bottom plate (**Photo 7**). Secure metal protective plates over the notches in the bottom plate to protect the wires and cable where they pass through.

Install the wiring from the area of the main circuit breaker panel (or nearby outlet) to the area of the wall cavity where the thermostat will be located. Don't do any actual wiring in the main panel yet.

Install the tile

Select tile that's at least 6 in. square so each tile will span two or more sections of cable. Smaller tiles are more likely to conform to the minor hills and valleys of the cable when you tamp them in place, creating a wavy surface.

Spread the mortar over a 5- to 10-sq.-ft. area of floor. Use the flat side of the trowel to press the mortar firmly through the mat and into contact with the cement board. You can establish a flat, uniform layer by lightly floating the trowel across the tops of the cable. Then use the notched side to comb the mortar to create ridges (**Photo 8**); a 3/8 x 1/4-in. trowel works well for most tiles. Again, lightly skim your trowel over the cable. The sheathing on the cable is tough, but you still

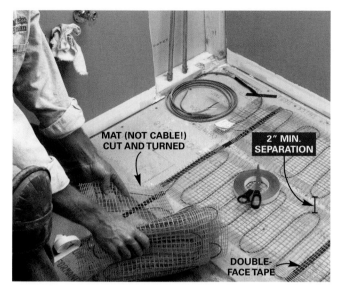

5 INSTALL the mat, securing it lightly to the floor with double-face tape. Cut the mat (NEVER THE CABLE), then reverse direction at walls.

MAT (NOT CABLE!) CUT AND TURNED

2" MIN. SEPARATION

DOUBLE-FACE TAPE

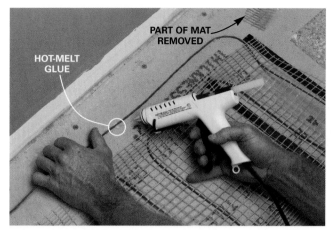

PART OF MAT REMOVED

HOT-MELT GLUE

6 SECURE individual cables to the floor using small blobs of hot-melt glue. Carefully cut and remove the orange mesh to free the cable. Do this to work around angles, obstacles and sections where full-width mats won't fit. Do not overlap the cable. When the entire mat is fitted and installed, press it firmly into the tape and hot-melt glue loose ends or humps in the mat. Perform a resistance test (shown in Photo 1) to check for damage.

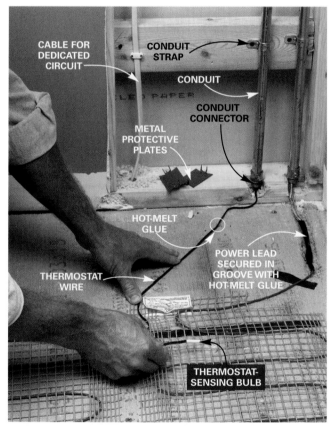

CABLE FOR DEDICATED CIRCUIT

CONDUIT STRAP

CONDUIT

CONDUIT CONNECTOR

METAL PROTECTIVE PLATES

HOT-MELT GLUE

POWER LEAD SECURED IN GROOVE WITH HOT-MELT GLUE

THERMOSTAT WIRE

THERMOSTAT-SENSING BULB

7 FISH the power lead and thermostat wires through two 58-in. lengths of conduit and connect the tops of the conduit to a 4 x 4-in. electrical box. Position the lower end of the conduits in the notches and secure the electrical box to the studs. Weave the thermostat wire through the mesh so the sensing bulb is an equal distance between wires and 12 in. into the warming area. Use hot-melt glue to secure the thermostat wires to the floor and the power lead in the groove. Cover the notches in the bottom plate with protective metal plates. Do another resistance test.

COMBED THIN-SET

FLAT-TROWELED THIN-SET

8 APPLY the mortar, first pressing it firmly into the mesh and floor with the flat side of the trowel, then combing it with the notched side. Try to "float" the trowel just above the cable. Use care not to snag the mesh or nick the cable.

 Tip The No. 1 goof that people make is slamming the edge of their trowel on the floor to knock excess thin-set loose—then nicking the cable.

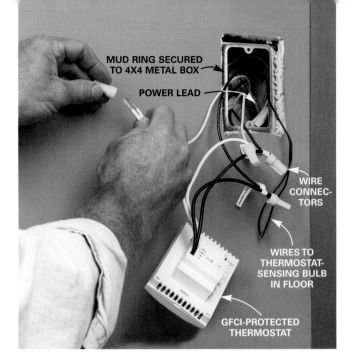

MUD RING SECURED
TO 4X4 METAL BOX

POWER LEAD

WIRE CONNEC-TORS

WIRES TO THERMOSTAT-SENSING BULB IN FLOOR

GFCI-PROTECTED THERMOSTAT

9 LAY the tile using the chalked lines as your guide. Wiggle and tap the tiles firmly into place to create a level surface. Readjust previously laid tiles so they remain in line and properly spaced; the thick mortar bed used to cover the cable and mesh allows for more movement than a standard tile installation so check and re-check the tile alignment. Grout the tile once the thin-set has properly set.

10 WIRE the thermostat according to the manufacturer's instructions. Our thermostat had individual pigtails for securing the wires from the power lead and the cable running from the main panel. Have your electrician make the final connections in the main circuit panel. Power up the system for 10 or 15 minutes to ensure that the floor heat functions, then turn it off and keep it off for two to four weeks while the mastic and grout cure and harden.

need to avoid any "sawing" type action or jabs with the trowel. It takes a little trial and error to get a flat layer.

Place the tile (**Photo 9**), then tap it firmly into place with a rubber mallet. Do two resistance tests (**Photo 1**) while installing the tile to ensure you haven't damaged the cable. (If the resistance test fails, see the manufacturer's instructions to find the problem.) Once the mortar has dried, grout the joints.

Final steps

The instructions that came with the mat and thermostat were so darn good we felt comfortable completing the wiring of the thermostat and mat (**Photo 10**). We left installing the new circuit breaker and final connections in the main circuit panel to a local electrician. We suggest you do the same. Once the wiring is complete, energize the system for a few minutes to make certain the controls work and resistance cable heats. Don't put the system into full operation until the thin-set and grout have had time to properly cure and harden—usually two to four weeks.

Then call the family together and play a game of Scrabble on your cozy, warm bathroom floor. ⌂

Another kind of in-the-floor heat

A hydronic system uses a dedicated water heater or a boiler (or even your existing water heater) as a heat source. A circulating pump moves the hot water through the PEX tubing and back to the heater. Because there can be no joints in the PEX tubing in the floor, uncut lengths of tubing snake through the floor, starting and ending at a manifold. The manifold balances the water in individual loops (lengths of tubing) and vents the system. The water returns to the bottom of the water heater near the drain about 10 degrees cooler than when it left.

During installation (inset photo), the PEX tubing is laid down in long loops spaced about 9 in. apart and carefully stapled to the floor. The mortar or concrete will then be installed on top of the tubing.

To find a hydronics specialist, look in the Yellow Pages under "Heating Contractors," or call either the Hydronics Institute at (908) 464-8200 or WIRSBO at (800) 321-4PEX.

Buyer's Guide

SunTouch floor-warming mat and thermostat by Watts Radiant, 3131 W. Chestnut Expressway, Springfield, MO 65802; (888) 432-8932. www.suntouch.net

Handy hints® from our readers...

BRUSH WRAP

After thoroughly cleaning your paint brushes, fold a paper towel around the bristles to keep them straight. Then let the brush dry while it's wrapped and store it that way. The next time you use the brush, the bristles will be as straight as the first time you took the brush out of the package.

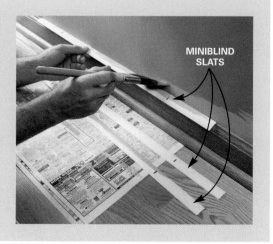

PAPER TOWEL

IN-THE-BAG PAINT STIRRING

Here's a neater way to stir a new can of paint. Place the unopened can in a grocery bag, pry off the lid and mix with gusto. All drips, dabs and dollops stay in the bag.

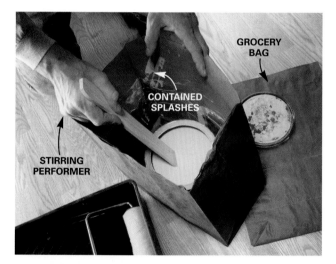

GROCERY BAG

CONTAINED SPLASHES

STIRRING PERFORMER

DISPOSABLE TOUCH-UP CONTAINER

Need a handy container for small touch-up jobs? Use the plastic measuring cup that comes with powdered laundry detergent. The handle makes for easy holding while you dip and swipe your brush, and the cup is disposable to boot.

VENETIAN BLIND PAINTING SHIELD

Slats from an old Venetian blind work great for shielding trim when you're repainting walls. Cut the strings to free the slats, then tape the string holes in the slats so paint can't leak through. To use, press the slat firmly along the junction of the wall and molding or trim. Bring several slats to the job and use a fresh one as they load up with paint.

MINIBLIND SLATS

HANGING MINIBLINDS

Marking the pilot holes for miniblind or other brackets is painstaking. Transfer the pilot holes to a piece of tape, and stick the tape where the bracket is to be fastened. Drill the holes and mount your brackets.

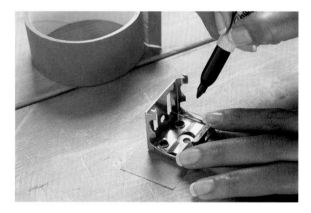

STAY-PUT DOOR HOLDER

Do you have problems keeping your door from blowing shut in the summer? Put a piece of adhesive-backed Velcro fastener on the doorstop and another piece on the wall or baseboard. The door will stay open until you pull it free.

QUICK CLEANUP CAT LITTER

Cut your litter cleanup time in half with this nifty trick! Line your litter pan with a plastic kitchen garbage bag before adding the litter. When it's time to change the litter, simply lift out the bag, tie it off and throw it all away.

INVISIBLE WALL PATCHING

After you patch small holes in a wall that you're planning to repaint, the patched area often turns out smoother than the area around it. Mimic the texture of the wall on the patched area by spraying it lightly with water, then scrub the area in a circular motion with a small scrub brush. After painting, your patch won't show.

INSULATION TRIMMER

Here's a faster, cleaner way to cut fiberglass insulation. Use a hedge shears to slice through the insulation. Unlike a utility knife, the shears won't spread loose tufts of insulation all over, and the best part is, you stay itch free.

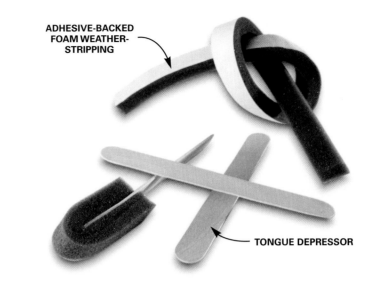

ADHESIVE-BACKED FOAM WEATHER-STRIPPING

TONGUE DEPRESSOR

5¢ SPONGE BRUSHES

Need a quick touch-up brush? If you have any leftover self-adhering foam weatherstripping, you can save yourself a trip to the store. A short piece—1/2 in. thick x 3/4 in. wide—wrapped around the end of a thin strip of wood or a tongue depressor will work as well as store-bought foam brushes for small jobs. Foam weatherstripping is made from extra-porous foam, which holds a lot of paint and smoothly applies it to flat surfaces. It also smooshes down nicely when you're coating molding contours or painting in tight corners.

LICK PICTURE-HANGING PROBLEMS

Here's how to hang pictures quickly and easily. Lick your middle knuckle and grab the hanger on the back of the picture with the wet finger. Press your knuckle against the wall when the picture is exactly where you want it. The saliva will leave a light mark for placing a nail.

TILE REPAIR

I had a small chip in a bathroom tile but didn't want to replace the tile. At the drugstore I found nail polish to match and quickly filled in the chip. Nail polish comes in a lot of glossy colors and is easy to apply with the built-in applicator.

THE RIGHT WAY TO ROLL PAINT

Forget everything you've ever heard or learned about rolling paint. Here's how to do the job quicker, smoother and neater.

by **Jeff Gorton**

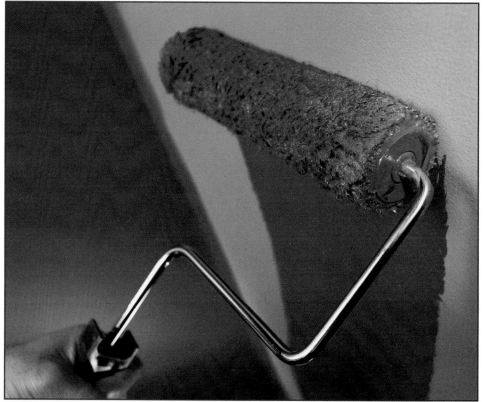

Most of you have probably used paint rollers before, with varying degrees of success. Maybe you just plunged right in and started rolling, developing your own technique as you went. Or maybe you read the instructions telling you to apply the paint in some pattern, usually a "W," before rolling it out. We're going to show you a slightly different approach. In this article, we'll teach you a simple method to quickly spread a smooth, even coat of latex paint on the wall. It's not fancy, but it gets the job done in record time and eliminates common problems like light areas, roller marks and built-up ridges that sometimes plague first-time painters.

However, even the best technique won't work with poor-quality equipment. Don't waste your money on those all-in-one throwaway roller setups when you can buy a pro setup that will last a lifetime for under $20. Start with a good roller frame. The one I like (the Wooster Sherlock, $10 at paint stores) is sturdy and

designed to keep the roller cover from slipping off while you paint (see **photo** at the top of p. 27). To extend your reach and give you better control, screw a 48-in. wood handle ($3) onto the end of the roller. You could also use a threaded broom handle.

You'll need a container for the paint. While most homeowners use paint trays, you'll rarely see a pro using one. That's because a 5-gallon bucket with a special bucket screen hung over the edge works a lot better (**photo at left**).

Here are a few of the advantages of a bucket and screen over a roller pan:

- It's easy to move the bucket without spilling.
- The bucket holds more paint. You won't have to frequently refill a pan.
- You're less likely to trip over or step in a bucket of paint.
- It's quicker and easier to load the roller cover with paint from a bucket.
- It's easy to cover a bucket with a damp cloth to prevent the paint from drying out while you're taking a lunch break.

5-GALLON BUCKET

BUCKET SCREEN

POLY/WOOL BLEND ROLLER COVER

LOAD the roller cover with paint by dipping into the paint about 1/2 in. and then rolling it against the screen. Filling a dry roller cover with paint will require five or six repetitions. After that, two or three dips are all you need. Leave the roller almost dripping with paint.

Use an old drywall compound bucket or buy a clean new bucket for about $3. Add a $2 bucket screen and you're ready to go.

Take a wool-blend roller cover for a spin

The most important part of your paint rolling setup is the roller cover, also known as a sleeve. It's tempting to buy the cheapest cover available and throw it away when you're done. But you won't mind the few extra minutes of cleanup time once you experience the difference a good roller cover makes. Cheap roller covers don't hold enough paint to do a good job. It'll take you four times as long to paint a room. And you'll likely end up with an inconsistent layer of paint, lap marks and built-up ridges of paint.

Instead, buy a 1/2-in. nap wool-blend roller cover and give it a try. (One good one is the Sherwin-Williams Poly/Wool cover, about $6, which is a combination of polyester for ease of use and wool for maximum paint capacity.) With proper care, this may be the last roller cover you'll ever buy.

Wool covers do have a few drawbacks, though. They tend to shed fibers when they're first used. To minimize shedding, wrap the new roller cover with masking tape and peel it off to remove loose fibers. Repeat this a few times. Wool covers also tend to become matted down if you apply too much pressure while painting. Rolling demands a light touch. No matter what roller cover you're using, always let the paint do the work. Keep the roller cover loaded with paint and use only enough pressure to release and spread the paint. Pushing on the roller to squeeze out the last drop of paint will only cause problems; you'll apply a thin coat and your wall will look splotchy.

STIFF METAL ARM

GRIPPING TEETH

The best coat of paint can't hide bumpy walls

Fill holes with lightweight spackling compound and sand them smooth when it dries. Then go over the entire wall with 100-grit sandpaper mounted in a drywall sanding handle. The ultimate setup for this job is a pole-mounted drywall sander with a 100-grit mesh drywall sanding screen, but any method of sanding off old paint lumps and bumps will do. Next mask off the baseboard and window and door trim. Slide the blade of a flexible putty knife along the edge of the masking tape to seal it. Otherwise paint will bleed underneath.

Tips for a perfect paint job

■ **Avoid lap marks.** Keeping a wet edge is crucial to all top-quality paint jobs, whether you're enameling a door, varnishing furniture or rolling paint on a wall. The idea is to plan the sequence of work and work fast enough so that you're always lapping newly applied paint onto paint that's still wet. If you stop for a break in the middle of a wall, for example, and then start painting after this section has dried, you'll likely see a lap mark where the two areas join. The rolling

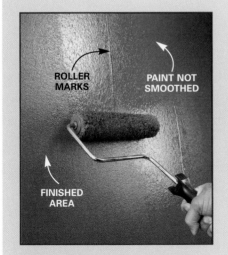

ROLLER MARKS

PAINT NOT SMOOTHED

FINISHED AREA

Smooth walls by rolling back over the wet paint without reloading the roller. Roll lightly without pressing.

Eliminate fat edges and roller marks

Ridges of paint left by the edge of the roller, or "fat edges," are a common problem. And if left to dry, they can be difficult to get rid of without heavy sanding or patching. Here are a few ways to avoid the problem:
■ Don't submerge the roller in the paint to load it. Paint can seep inside the roller cover and leak out while you're rolling. Try to dip only the nap. Then spin it against the screen and dip again until it's loaded with paint.
■ Don't press too hard when you're smoothing out the paint.
■ Never start against an edge, like a corner or molding, with a full roller of paint. You'll leave a heavy buildup of paint that can't be spread out. Starting about 6 in. from the edge, unload the paint from the roller. Then work back toward the edge.
■ Unload excess paint from the open end of the roller before you roll back over the wall to smooth it out. Do this by tilting the roller and applying a little extra pressure to the open side of the roller while rolling it up and down in the area you've just painted.

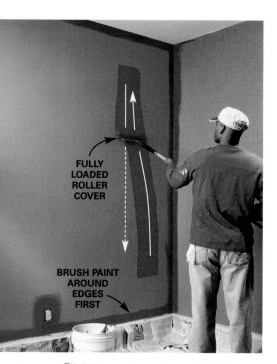

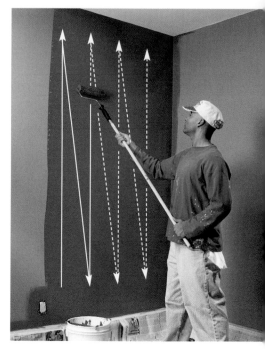

FULLY LOADED ROLLER COVER

BRUSH PAINT AROUND EDGES FIRST

1 LAY the paint on the wall with a sweeping stroke. Start about a foot from the bottom and 6 in. from the corner and roll upward at a slight angle using light pressure. Stop a few inches from the ceiling. Now roll up and down back toward the corner to quickly spread the paint. You can leave paint buildup and roller marks at this step. Don't worry about a perfect job yet.

2 RELOAD the roller and repeat the process in the adjacent space, working back toward the painted area. Use the same up and down motion and keep your roller cover loaded with plenty of paint.

3 ROLL back over the entire area you've covered to smooth and blend the paint. Don't reload the roller with paint for this step. Use very light pressure. Roll up and down, from floor to ceiling and move over about three-quarters of a roller width each time so you're always slightly overlapping the previous stroke. When you reach the corner, roll as close as you can to the adjacent wall without touching it.

Repeat Steps 1 through 3 until the entire wall is painted, then finish with steps 4 and 5:

4 SMOOTH the paint along the ceiling using a long horizontal stroke without reloading the roller with paint. If you are skilled enough to roll within an inch of the ceiling while rolling vertically, you can skip this step.

5 LAY paint on wall areas above and below windows and doors with a long horizontal stroke. Then smooth it off with short vertical strokes so the texture will match the rest of the wall.

A better way to paint: Vertical paint tray and tote

The Mobile Paint tray is Yankee ingenuity (and versatility) at its best. You can hang the tray from a ladder, haul it around by hand or set it down horizontally, vertically—even on sloped roofs—as you work. The bucket-like bottom prevents spills and holds darn near a gallon of paint. It's a step saver and mess preventer. You can use it for dipping rollers, brushes or both. Heck, you could clean it out and use it for hauling around light tools and fasteners too. Available for $8.95 plus $4.95 shipping from Wolf Mountain Products, 269 Butts Road, Morton, WA 98356; (360) 496-0037. www.mobiletray.com

technique we show avoids this problem by allowing you to quickly cover a large area with paint and then return to smooth it out—which brings us to the second important painting technique.

■ **Lay it on, smooth it off.** The biggest mistake most beginning painters make, whether they're brushing or rolling, is taking too long to apply the paint. **Photo 1** shows how to lay on the paint. Then quickly spread it out and repeat the laying-on process again (**Photo 2**). This will only work with a good-quality roller cover that holds a lot of paint. Until you're comfortable with the technique and get a feel for how quickly the paint is drying, cover only about 3 or 4 ft. of wall before smoothing the whole area off (**Photo 3**). If you find the paint is drying slowly, you can cover an entire wall before smoothing it off.

■ **Get as close as you can.** Since rollers can't get tight to edges, the first painting step is to brush along the ceiling, inside corners and moldings. This "cutting in" process leaves brush marks that won't match the roller texture on the rest of the wall. For the best-looking job, you'll want to cover as many brush marks as possible with the roller. Do this by carefully rolling up close to inside corners, moldings and the ceiling. Face the open end of the roller toward the edge and remember not to use a roller that's fully loaded with paint. With practice, you'll be able to get within an inch of the ceiling rolling vertically, and can avoid crawling up on a ladder to paint horizontally like we show in **Photo 4**.

■ **Pick out the lumps before they dry.** It's inevitable that you'll end up with an occasional lump in your paint. Keep the roller cover away from the floor where it might pick up bits of debris that are later spread against the wall. Drying bits of paint from the edge of the bucket or bucket screen can also cause this problem. Cover the bucket with a damp cloth when you're not using it. If partially dried paint is sloughing off the screen, take it out and clean it. Keep a wet rag in your pocket and pick lumps off the wall as you go. Strain used paint through a mesh paint strainer to remove lumps. Five-gallon size strainers are available at paint stores for about $1.

■ **Scrape excess paint from the roller before you wash it.** Use your putty knife, or better yet, a special roller scraping tool with a semi-circular cutout in the blade. Then rinse the roller cover until the water runs clear. A roller and paint brush spinning tool, available at hardware and paint stores for about $8, simplifies the cleaning task. Just slip the roller cover onto the spinner and repeatedly wet and spin out the roller until it's clean. 🏠

HUB

PRESSURE ROLLER

Masking made easy

When I paint, I can spend just as much time putting up masking tape as wielding a brush. That's why it was love at first sight when I met the Smart Masker. You simply load a roll of 1- to 2-in. masking tape on the large hub, weave the end of the tape over a smaller pressure roller and go to work. The Smart Masker distributes the tape straight, tight to the edge, flat and, best of all, fast. Serrated teeth help cut the tape when you move on.

With a little practice, you can use it to mask the top of baseboards (even skinny ones), the edges of window trim and inside corners. Suggested retail price is $19.95. Geo Mask, 33678 336th St., LeSueur, MN 56058; (800) 965-3580. www.geomask.com

ARE GAPS IN WOOD PLANK FLOORS INEVITABLE?

My red oak hardwood floor (3-in. plank) was installed three years ago, and some areas are showing shrinkage gaps. This is a random problem, and I wonder if there is a filler I could use in these seams.

Sorry to say, Bruce, but there's not much you can do at this point. Plank flooring expands and contracts with humidity changes and may show some gaps. In fact, on old plank floors, gaps are considered part of the "look." To minimize them, try keeping your home's relative humidity close to 50 percent. During dry seasons or heating periods, the humidity often drops and you'll need to use humidifiers. During periods of high humidity, you may have to dehumidify (although air conditioning often takes care of it).

I don't recommend that you use a filler; it may look worse than the shrinkage gaps. A non-hardening color putty will fill the cracks, but it will dry and pop out within a year and need redoing. A putty that sets hard can create larger gaps or even buckle the floorboards by not leaving any expansion space. Conversely, it will crack if the floor shrinks.

The real cure for cracks in a wood plank floor is to minimize them in the first place. There are the two main ways excessive cracks develop.

Excessive moisture

The wood flooring has too much moisture content when installed and then shrinks as it "dries out." The solution is to buy dry wood and to acclimate the flooring to the room you want to lay it in. All work that introduces moisture (concrete

floors, drywall taping and texturing, painting) must be complete and dry. Then store the wood on location for at least two weeks. A normal humidity level must be maintained during this period (by heating or air conditioning).

Compression set

The wood is too dry to start with and the flooring absorbs excessive moisture after installation. As the wood expands, the pressure will crush fibers at the edge of the boards along tight joints. This is called compression set. When the wood dries out again, it will shrink; the crushed fibers won't completely rebound and a gap will form. Again, the solution is to acclimate the wood to the space, making sure the humidity is kept close to its normal level.

In all cases, put a coat of finish on new floors as soon as possible, as this will slow down moisture movement into and out of the wood floor planks.

ANY SOURCES FOR LOCATING ANTIQUE HARDWARE?

Where can I find hardware such as antique desk lid supports, door hinges and dresser mirror hinges?

Here are a couple of different approaches. Search antiques stores, architectural antiques stores and building reuse (salvage) outfits for the real deal. If you find something suitable but in bad cosmetic shape, you may be able to have it cleaned up and restored. Most large cities have businesses that specialize in metal plating. Look in the Yellow Pages. Replating also adds the option of changing the finish, say, from polished brass to chrome. This also works for light fixtures, locksets and plumbing fixtures.

The other approach is to shop for reproductions of antiques. Check with local home centers and hardware and woodworking stores and see what they stock or what they can order from their suppliers.

Finally, call or go to the Internet for mail-order sources. Here are some catalogs to try:
- Van Dyke's Restorers, (800) 558-1234. www.vandykes.com
- Hershbergers Hardware Ltd., (800) 734-8044.
- Constantine's Woodworkers Catalog, (954) 561-1716. www.constantines.com
- Rockler Woodworking and Hardware, (800) 279-4441. www.rockler.com

HOW CAN I ADD A SWITCH
TO AN EXISTING RECEPTACLE?

None of the outlets in our living room are connected to a switch, so we have to go around the room turning on lamps. Is there an easy way to connect a switch to some of the outlets?

Yes—buy a set of wireless electronic switch modules. You plug your lamp into a receiver module and then into a nearby wall receptacle (shown above). Then mount the battery-operated switch module at any convenient location on the wall. That's it! Each receptacle you want to switch must have a receiver module. A single switch and receiver costs $24 at Radio Shack and some hardware stores and home centers.

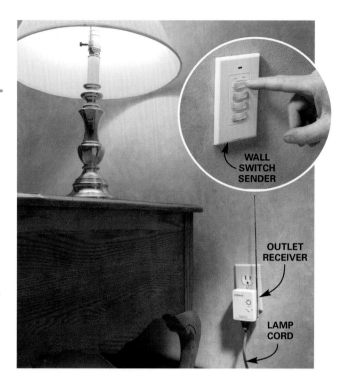

WALL SWITCH SENDER

OUTLET RECEIVER

LAMP CORD

CAN YOU GET ME OUT OF A STICKY PROBLEM?

I've had no success getting paint to stick to my bedroom walls. I've painted them three times over the years with oil and latex paints and primers. I've even tried BIN shellac primer. Within a year or two, it peels again right down to the bare drywall. Do you have any suggestions?

After about 15 calls to drywall manufacturers, professional painters and numerous paint companies, I still can't definitively tell you what the problem is. Considering that adhesion is the No. 1 priority when manufacturers formulate paint, and the fact that you've tried so many brands, obviously there's a problem with the drywall surface.

The (sometimes bizarre) theories I heard include:
- The pH level (level of acidity) in the drywall is too alkaline. Ideally the pH should be between 7 and 8. Surfaces with levels above 11 need to be treated with a product like Gripper made by ICI Corp. (800-984-5444).
- The recycled paper on the drywall surface may contain wax contaminants that prevent the paint or primer from sticking for long.
- Excessive moisture penetrated the drywall either before or after painting.
- Water damage to the drywall (even years before) can leave residues that'll reduce adhesion.
- The room had a high humidity level during painting.

- How about this one? The drywall contains oil residues from the fork trucks that haul it in warehouses!

The bottom line is that since the paint sticks to the taping compound, as your enclosed photo shows, but not to the paper, the drywall surface is obviously contaminated with something. Because only a few walls are affected, the simplest solution is to rough them up with 100-grit sandpaper and trowel on a 1/16-in. thick skim coat of taping compound, sand that smooth, and reprime and paint. Before trying this fix, closely examine the walls to make sure there's not a serious moisture problem, most likely a chronic leaky roof. Look for rusty drywall screws and jab a sharp screwdriver between an electrical box and the drywall into a stud to see if there's any rotten wood. Repair moisture problems first.

If you had a houseful of problem drywall, I'd suggest getting the brand name from the binding tape on the back of a sheet and contacting the manufacturer to have a rep come to your home to investigate. You may be entitled to compensation or at least some free drywall.

HOW CAN I SOUNDPROOF MY HOME OFFICE?

I work from an office in my home, and when my teenagers have their friends over, they drive me crazy with their noise. Often I can barely hear my phone ring. How can I modify the room to cut down the noise?

The solution to this common problem (other than evicting all teenagers) is to block the avenues sound uses to get into your office. Sound transmission reduction is a complex subject, but keep it simple by considering this basic scenario: A massive wall, whether it's concrete or built-up drywall, is a great sound absorber and blocker, but it becomes useless if there's even a tiny hole in it.

The lesson? Start small. First seal openings into your office, and then consider strategies for absorbing more of the sound as it passes through the wall, ceiling, floor and door materials.

Try these solutions in the order shown.

1. Install a solid-core door with vinyl weatherstripping and a bottom sweep and threshold.

2. Caulk around ductwork and electrical boxes where they penetrate the drywall.

3. Glue a layer of acoustic board and then another layer of drywall over the existing interior walls. This is a bigger project. It requires extending or moving electrical boxes, adding jamb extensions to doors, and removing and reinstalling casings and baseboard.

4. If the noise is coming from upstairs, nail 1x2 furring strips on the ceiling with 3/4-in. rigid insulation in between. Run the strips perpendicular to the joists. Screw resilient channel to the furring strips with 3/4-in. screws, then hang 5/8-in. drywall from the resilient channel with 1-1/4 in. drywall screws. Tape, sand and paint the ceiling. Electrical boxes and heating registers will need to be extended or moved downward. Another big job.

5. Glue a layer of acoustic board and drywall inside a stud space that's being used as an air return. This will reduce the amount of return airflow by about one-third. Consult with a heating contractor to ensure that this won't compromise your heating system.

6. Install rigid foam insulation board or fiberglass batts behind and around ductwork and electrical boxes. You have to tear open walls.

7. Fill wall and ceiling cavities with fiberglass insulation batts. If you open a wall for any another reason, add this step.

8. If the noise is coming from below, loose-lay acoustic board under the carpet. This requires pulling up the existing carpet and tack strip, installing new tack strip and restretching the carpet.

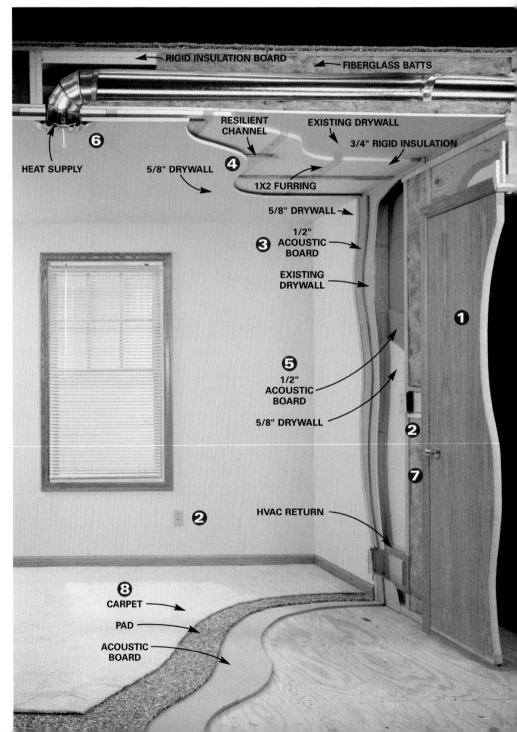

Gallery
of Ideas

FROM NOVEMBER 2001, P. 31

BEADED WAINSCOTING

Wood wainscoting is the perfect project to transform a plain room into an inviting place to read, study or just hang out. Tongue and groove boards, like the ones used in this project, not only look good, but are easy to install with basic carpentry tools. This design lets you go right over your existing drywall, and we show you how to make the shelf and brackets too.

Project Facts:
Cost: $30 per linear foot of wall
Skill level: Intermediate carpentry, simple electrical

Time: 3 or 4 days for an average room
Special tools: Miter box, finish nail gun, table saw

BUILT-IN BOOKCASE

This handsome bookcase features classic elements like curved brackets, columned partitions and crown molding. The project is built from hardwood plywood, 2x6s, hardwood boards and standard moldings available at home centers and lumberyards. You can even preassemble nearly all the parts of this modular-type project in your garage or shop and carry them into your family room for assembly.

Project Facts:
Cost: $420
Skill level: Intermediate
Time: 25 to 30 hours

Special tools: Table saw, 18-gauge air nailer, power miter saw

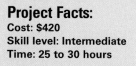

FROM DECEMBER/JANUARY 2002, P. 32

FROM MAY 2002, P. 60

NATURAL CORK FLOOR

Cork flooring, popular decades ago, is regaining lost turf as a primary flooring choice. Why? It's a natural, renewable product; warm comfortable and quiet under foot; and just plain beautiful. Best of all, with basic tools, some patience and persistence, you can enjoy the benefits of a natural cork floor in a weekend. This article takes you every step of the way.

Project Facts:
Cost: $3 to $5 per square foot
Time: 1 weekend (for an average 150-sq.-ft. room)
Skill level: Intermediate
Special tools: Circular saw, soft rubber mallet, 100-lb. floor roller (rented).

To order photocopies of complete plans for the projects shown above, call 715-246-4344 or write to:
Copies, The Family Handyman, 511 Wisconsin Dr., New Richmond, WI 54017.
Many public libraries also carry back issues of The Family Handyman magazine.

THE BEST WAY TO
HANG WALLPAPER

Don't be stymied by tough-to-match patterns, slippery seams and out-of-plumb corners. Our pro shows you how to handle them with ease.

by **Jeff Timm**

If you want to change the entire character of a room fast, hang wallpaper. You can change a dull room into a dramatic personal statement in less than a weekend, and you don't need a bunch of expensive tools to do the job. In fact, you can buy everything you'll need for less than $40.

This kind of transformation does require patience, careful planning and familiarity with key techniques. We asked a professional hanger to demonstrate every technique you'll need, start to finish, and to show you how to save time and avoid a heap of frustration.

The techniques we show in this article apply to 90 percent of papers you'll find at wallpaper stores. We won't cover the specialty papers (such as grass cloth, foil, fabric and ones that require pretrimming). We recommend you master the basics before taking on these papers. Nor will we address how to remove old wallpaper.

With our instructions, you can successfully wallpaper a room even if you haven't done it before. Start with a simple bedroom or dining room, a space that doesn't require a lot of fitting and trimming. With experience, you can tackle tougher rooms like kitchens and baths.

Selecting wallpaper

For your first time papering, we recommend that you buy from a paint and wallcovering store. The staff can advise you on the best primers, paste and tools for the particular paper you select. They'll answer any questions unique to your situation. Tell the salesperson where you'll be using the paper, and ask what features you'll need to meet the demands of the room. Prices average $20 to $50 per roll, but some specialty papers can cost as much as $100 a roll.

Our paper (see style numbers, p. 39) cost $40 a roll and took about three weeks to arrive. We used 11 rolls for our 12 x 12-ft. room.

Selection tips

■ If your room has crooked walls (check them with a level and a long, straight board), consider a paper with a random pattern so the crooked corners aren't so noticeable.

■ Big prints and dark colors will make a room feel cozy, but make sure the room is large enough to view the pattern from a comfortable distance.

■ Small prints and light colors make a room feel larger.

■ Once you get your paper, unroll it and inspect it for flaws. Save the run and dye lot numbers for ordering matching paper in the future.

■ Read and follow the hanging instructions of the paper you've selected. Pros always do. Fail to follow instructions and you could void the paper's warranty. Or worse yet, it could fall off the wall. See p. 39 for more buying details.

Prepare the walls

It's far easier to paper a room if it's empty. If it isn't possible to remove all the furniture in the room, move it to the center and cover it with plastic. Turn off the electrical power to the switches and outlets at the service panel and remove the cover plates. Place a canvas dropcloth over the floor to catch any dripping primer or paste (plastic dropcloths are too slippery). If the ceiling or woodwork needs painting, do it before you hang the wallpaper.

Scan the wall with a utility light to highlight any imperfections, and fill or sand them down. Don't cheat on this step; some papers can actually accentuate cracks and bumps in a wall. If a wall is in really rough shape, ask the salesperson about "liner paper." Hang it like wallpaper over the wall to smooth it out. Then apply your wallpaper over it. Consider a heavyweight vinyl- or fabric-backed commercial paper with a dull background if your walls are lightly textured. Otherwise, skim-coat or sand them smooth.

Wash the walls down with TSP (trisodium phosphate), or a TSP substitute, to dissolve grease, oils and other dirt, then rinse with clean water. Next apply a 100 percent acrylic pre-wallcovering primer/ sizer, which is available at wallpaper stores for about $20 a gallon (**Photo 1**). This gives you

<table>
<tr><td>**Tip**</td><td>If you're hanging a dark paper, have the wallcovering store tint the primer the dominant color of the paper to disguise gaps at the edges or seams.</td></tr>
</table>

more working time to slide the paper into position. The primer also helps control shrinking, which could result in seams opening up, and allows you to remove the paper more easily when it's time for a change. Prewall primer dries fast and is difficult to remove, so wash your brushes quickly and don't get it on your hands.

ELECTRICAL POWER IS OFF

MASKING TAPE

ACRYLIC UNDERCOAT

1 REPAIR any dings or cracks in the walls with joint compound and drywall tape. Sand the repairs smooth. Mask off the trim and apply an acrylic undercoat (sizing) over all the surfaces to be wallpapered. Cut in the edges and corners with a brush. Allow it to dry overnight or the time specified on the label before applying the wallcovering.

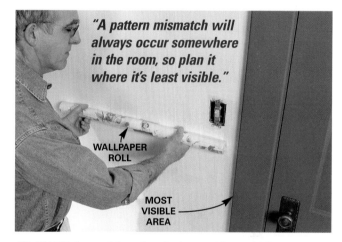

"A pattern mismatch will always occur somewhere in the room, so plan it where it's least visible."

WALLPAPER ROLL

MOST VISIBLE AREA

2 MARK the position of each sheet with a pencil, using the roll of wallpaper as a guide. Start your first sheet in the most visible corner and work in both directions to the least noticeable corner. Adjust your starting point to avoid narrow strips (less than 2 in.) along windows, doors or corners.

Gather your tools and set up your workstation

Pros use a special table made of basswood because it's a good surface to cut on and easy on razor blades. Rent one from a wallpaper store ($20 per day), or substitute a 36-in. hollow-core door or even a 3 x 6-ft. piece of 3/4-in. plywood resting on a pair of sawhorses. Soften the plywood edges with sandpaper so you don't accidentally tear your paper.

You can buy all the specialty tools you need at a specialty wallcovering store or home center. Purchase a vinyl smoother ($2; **Photo 8**), a snap-off razor with an extra pack of blades ($7; **Photo 9**), a seam roller ($2; **Photo 11**) and two 6-in. broad knives ($5 each; **Photo 9**). You may already have the other items you need: a sturdy 6-ft. step-ladder, a 5-gallon bucket, a paint roller and 3/8-in. nap roller cover, a sharp scissors, a 4-ft. level, a 10-ft. or longer tape measure and a sponge.

3 DRAW a light plumb line with a pencil from ceiling to floor at your starting point, using a 4-ft. level as a guide. Measure the height of the wall and add a total of 4 in. for trimming the paper at the top and bottom. Cut strips from the roll to your measurement length with scissors.

Plan carefully to avoid wrestling with tiny strips

Planning the sheet layout will let you visualize all your cuts and allow you to make adjustments to the beginning and end points. Ideally, you would hang your first sheet, come full circle and the pattern would match perfectly. That's not going to happen. Put that final joint where it's least visible. Your goals are to have the patterns match at corners where they're most noticeable and avoid hanging strips less than a few inches wide. Narrow strips can be tricky (and frustrating) to hang, even for a pro.

Start your trial layout at the most visible corner of the room—across from a door in our case—and work around the room in both directions, meeting at the least visible spot. Use a roll of paper to roughly space how the sheets will align on the wall (Photo 2). If your layout leaves strips less than 2 in. wide against a door or into a corner, adjust your starting point by about 6 in. Our first layout left a tiny strip along a door, so we shifted it over to overlap the trim. The sheets now meet in an inconspicuous corner behind the door.

A good level gets you started straight

More often than not, the corners of the room and the door and window molding will be a little crooked or out of plumb. Taking the time to set a plumb line with a level to start your first sheet and near each corner will provide consistent reference points to align the wallpaper on each wall. This makes hanging a whole lot easier (Photo 3).

Pros will cut all the full-length strips needed for a room before they start pasting. For your first time, we recommend cutting only two or three sheets ahead. Measure the height of the wall and add a few inches to the top and bottom, enough extra wallpaper to shift the pattern up and down for the best position.

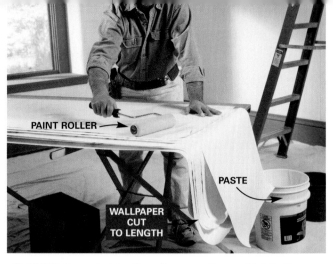

4 PLACE the cut strips face down on the worktable. Paste the bottom half of a sheet evenly with a 3/8-in. nap roller, dipping it in a 5-gallon bucket with paste in it. Cover the edges by laying the upcoming strips under the one you're pasting; excess paste will be rolled onto the upcoming sheets. This will keep your worktable clean.

"Paper needs time to relax. It expands after pasting."

5 "BOOK" the bottom half of the paper by folding the pasted faces together. Align the edges to keep the paste from drying out.

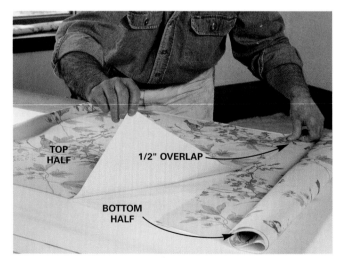

6 ROLL up the bottom half loosely, slide the top half onto the table and spread more paste. Book the top half over so it overlaps the bottom edge by 1/2 in. Roll it up and allow the entire sheet to rest for the time specified by the manufacturer, about 10 minutes.

7 ALIGN the top half of the paper's edge to the plumb line, overlapping the ceiling molding by a few inches. Let the other edge hang loose to make positioning easier.

8 PULL a vinyl smoother across the paper. Move up and down along the plumbed edge, then diagonally away from it, to work out bubbles and wrinkles. Align and flatten the bottom half the same way.

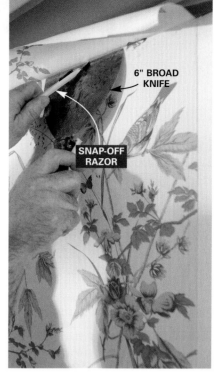

9 TRIM the paper with a sharp razor knife, using a 6-in. broad knife as a guide. Slide the broad knife across while leaving the tip of the razor in the paper till the cut is complete. Press hard enough to cut through the wallcovering, not the drywall.

"To line up sheets, focus your eyes on a dominant element and the rest of the pattern will line up."

10 LOOSELY SET one edge of the second sheet on the wall and align the pattern to the first. Precisely butt the second sheet to the first, leaving the other edge loose.

11 PRESS the edge to the wall with a seam roller, then work out the wrinkles with the smoother. Set the top half first, then unfold and set the bottom half. Wipe off any paste from the surface with a clean, damp sponge.

An even paste job and proper booking ensure tight seams

If your paper requires paste, use the type that's recommended in the instructions or by your supplier. The premixed kind is easiest to use. We're using "clear hang" premixed adhesive for our project. It took 2 gallons of paste for our 12 x 12-ft. room with 9-ft. high walls. Many papers come prepasted. Roll these into a tray of water to activate the paste. Your supplier may recommend a special activator for certain prepasted papers to guarantee they'll stick to the wall and seams won't curl.

Paste the back evenly (**Photo 4**). Roll it perpendicular to the long edge to move paste to the edges, then back and forth the long way again till the paste is evenly spread.

The strips of paper need time to "relax," that is, expand slightly because of the moisture in the paste. Booking the paper (**Photos 5 and 6**) keeps the paste from drying out while the paper adjusts. This is a critical step: If the paper doesn't sit long enough, it could shrink on the wall, resulting in open seams, blisters or curling. Set a timer to remind you when a sheet is ready. You can let a sheet sit for a little longer than the booking time but never less.

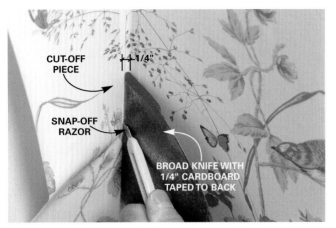

CUT-OFF PIECE

1/4"

SNAP-OFF RAZOR

BROAD KNIFE WITH 1/4" CARDBOARD TAPED TO BACK

12 WRAP the paper around the corner, leaving the wrapped side loose and smoothing out the other. Trim off the paper with a sharp razor knife, leaving 1/4 in. wrapped around the corner. Guide the cut with a broad knife built up on one side with 1/4-in. thick cardboard taped to the knife. Book the cut-off piece for later use.

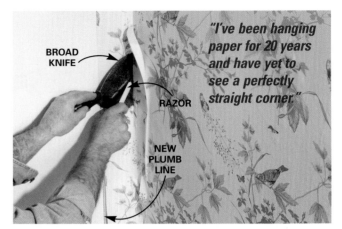

BROAD KNIFE

RAZOR

"I've been hanging paper for 20 years and have yet to see a perfectly straight corner."

NEW PLUMB LINE

13 MEASURE the width of the cut-off piece at its narrowest spot and draw a plumb line with your level at that distance from the corner. (Careful, the corner won't be perfectly plumb or straight.) Hang the cut-off piece along the plumb line, wrapping the excess around the corner. Smooth it out. Trim through the overlapping sheet at the corner so the seam follows the corner.

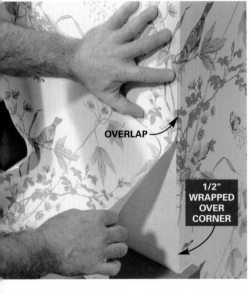

OVERLAP

1/2" WRAPPED OVER CORNER

14 WRAP the paper around an outside corner and trim it off, leaving 1/2 in. wrapped. Set a new plumb line if you're continuing on a long wall. Overlap the next piece, holding it 1/8 in. away from the corner.

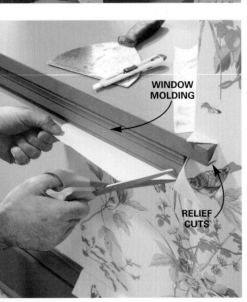

WINDOW MOLDING

RELIEF CUTS

15 TRIM the paper around window and door moldings by pressing it to the edge of the molding and making relief cuts with scissors and a razor until it lies flat to the wall. Using the razor, trim off the excess paper following the contour of the moldings. Guide your cuts with the broad knife on straight sections.

Plan ahead. Paste two or three sheets in a row if you're working on a blank wall that requires full sheets. Paste only one if you're coming up on a tricky window or corner that'll take some time to fit.

The payoff comes when you hang the first sheet

After the booking time is up, unroll your sheet and carry it to the wall. Gently unfold the top half. Standing on a stepladder, align the sheet to your plumb line (**Photo 7**). Leave the bottom half booked to keep the paste from drying out while you're positioning the top. Even though it might seem easier to butt the paper right up to the ceiling, don't try it. You'll get a much better fit and professional look by leaving it long and then trimming it off later (**Photo 9**). Once the paper is aligned, work out wrinkles with a vinyl smoother (**Photo 8**). If you have a wrinkle that's not smoothing out, pull one edge of the paper away from the wall, keeping the plumbed edge in place, and reset. Finish the top half while you're on the ladder, then come down and unfold, align, smooth and trim the bottom half.

Trim the paper in place to ensure a perfect fit

For straight, clean cuts, trim off the overlap by guiding the blade against a broad knife (**Photo 9**). Keep your blade sharp. The most common novice mistake is to try to economize on razor blades. A dull blade will tear the paper. Advance a new blade after every few cuts (after every one if you're using heavyweight paper).

Pick a leaf, branch or other element of the wallpaper pattern to help align the second sheet (**Photo 10**). Gently slide it into position to align the pattern and seam, but don't stretch the paper or it could shrink later. With some papers, the pattern may not perfectly align the full length of the sheet. In this situation align these at eye level where it's most noticeable.

Go over the seam with the smoother, roll it with a seam roller (**Photo 11**), then smooth out the rest of the sheet. Wipe down the paper at the edges with a sponge dampened with clean water after completing each sheet.

Corners

Corners are never perfectly straight. Always end the paper at an inside corner and start the next strip along a new plumb line (**Photos 12 and 13**). A perfectly concealed seam at the corner involves a three-step process:

1. Wrap the first sheet around the corner and trim it off, leaving about 1/4 in.
2. Set the next strip to a new plumb line so it completely overlaps the 1/4-in. wrap.
3. Trim off the paper that wrapped over at the corner. (Cut through the top piece only.)

There will always be a pattern mismatch at the corners. Keep it slight by starting out of the corner with the cut-off piece you came into it with. **Photo 12** shows a way to cut this piece by guiding the razor with a broad knife with cardboard taped to one side to create the 1/4-in. wrap. If the strip you cut off is less than 2 in., discard it and start the wall with a new strip.

Trick: Pete noticed that the pattern repeated twice across the width of our paper. To avoid a mismatched corner, he held up a second sheet, found where the pattern aligned and cut a strip lengthwise. If your paper doesn't allow this, hang a full sheet—only your eyes will notice the mismatch.

If you're using a vinyl-coated or vinyl paper, use a vinyl-to-vinyl adhesive on the overlap. Regular paste won't hold. Use this adhesive any time you're putting a paper over a vinyl-coated or vinyl paper—on borders, for instance.

If an outside corner is perfectly plumb and straight (check it with your level and a long, straight board), you can wrap the paper around it and keep hanging. If not, fit it like an inside corner (**Photo 14**). If the corner is prone to a lot of abuse, install corner protectors ($2 to $3) from a home center.

Cutting around trim and other obstacles

Don't try to cut an opening for a window or door with the wallpaper on your worktable. Instead, align the seam and smooth out as much of the sheet as possible up to the molding. Relief cuts (**Photo 15**) will allow the paper to lie flat on the wall. Make these gradually so you don't overcut. Trim tight against the molding with the razor. Cut freehand along the contours and guide the razor with a broad knife on straight areas. Slit an "X" over electrical boxes and trim off the excess paper. **CAUTION: The power must be off.**

Crucial details for buying wallpaper

The back of the wallpaper sample tells about ordering, durability and the essential hanging details you need to know. If the sample doesn't have this information, ask the salesperson about each of the following categories.

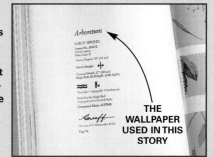

THE WALLPAPER USED IN THIS STORY

Vertical repeat

The repeat is the length of the image before it shows itself again. Repeats can range from none, for a covering without a pattern, to more than 36 in. Order extra paper for repeats more than 24 in.; you'll waste a lot when matching the pattern.

Match

The match is how the patterns align sheet to sheet. Our straight match requires shifting the pattern to have all the birds at the same distance from the ceiling.

With a random match, you don't have to fuss with lining up patterns from sheet to sheet. This is the easiest pattern to hang.

You align the pattern of a drop match halfway down the repeat. With drop matches, plan the dominant elements so you don't slice them off at the ceiling.

Single roll/double roll

Look for the square foot coverage to calculate how many rolls you'll need to cover a room. In double-roll bolts, the paper is twice as long as on a single roll. Compared with a single roll, this provides more usable square footage of paper. Add up the area of the walls (minus doors and windows) and divide by the number of square feet listed on the roll. Round up your calculation to the nearest roll. Order at least one extra roll, two if you've got a lot of tricky cuts or angles. The worst thing that can happen when wallpapering is to run out of paper!

Washable

Washability is the degree of cleaning a paper can take before showing wear. If a paper isn't washable, use it only in areas that aren't subject to a lot of abuse.

Pretrimmed

Most wallpapers are pretrimmed, which means the edges are perfectly cut and all ready for hanging. Don't store or drop pretrimmed papers on the ends because you'll mar the edges. Untrimmed papers require a good straightedge and experience to cut. Stick with a pretrimmed paper for your first hanging experience.

CAULK A
TUB SURROUND

The durability secret: Thoroughly clean out the old caulk before running the new.

by **Rocky Larson**

When the caulking around a bathtub starts to crack and become a cozy home for dark stains that signal mold, it's time to replace it. The caulk is the watertight seal between the bathtub and the wall. Once the caulk's integrity is compromised, water can invade the wall, causing rot in the framing around the tub. Pick up a 5.5-fl.-oz. tube of tub-and-tile caulk ($3) and you can clean and recaulk the tub in less than an hour.

Laying a smooth, clean-looking bead of caulk is tricky. If it doesn't go right, you can wind up with sticky caulk all over the place and a sloppy-looking job. It takes a little technique and practice to lay a caulk bead like a pro, but this article will set you on the right path.

Before you recaulk your bathtub, you must completely remove the old caulk. Clean the joint so the new caulk will bond properly, creating a watertight seal (**Photos 1 – 3**).

Cutting the right size opening at the tip of the caulk tube is critical for a clean, smooth bead. A large opening will spread too much caulk into the joint and you'll wind up getting it all over the place. Cut the tip too small at first because you can always recut it if necessary. Cut the caulk tip so the opening is about the diameter of a wire coat hanger.

Fill the bathtub with water before caulking. The water weight will maximize the width of the tub/wall joint and prevent future stress and cracking. Once your caulk bead is dry, you can drain the water.

USE a utility knife to cut the tip of the caulk tube at a 45-degree angle so the opening is about the diameter of a wire coat hanger.

Laying a uniform bead of caulk requires constant pressure on the caulk tube. The bead should be sized so only a slight amount wipes off when you drag your finger over it. As the caulk tube empties, you'll find it increasingly difficult to keep constant pressure on the tube and lay a uniform bead. **Photo 4** shows the size of the caulk bead and how to repressurize a partially spent caulk tube. Finish the bead and clean off any excess caulk as shown in **Photo 5**. If you're having trouble smoothing the bead of caulk, try rewetting your finger or using a different one. The tile corner joint is just as important as the tub joint. Caulk it as shown in **Photo 6**. Allow the caulk to dry for 24 hours before using the bathtub. ⌂

TWO COOL CAULKING TIPS

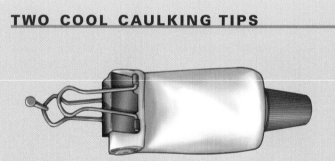

Caulking extender

If you have to get caulk into a tight spot, just tape a flexible drinking straw to the tip of your caulking gun and you'll be ready to caulk into any nook the straw will reach.

Caulk clips

Use paper binder clips to keep the empty portion of tube glues and caulks (and even toothpaste!) rolled up. The handles can be used to hang the tubes for neat, visible storage and flipped alongside the tube to help you squeeze 'em.

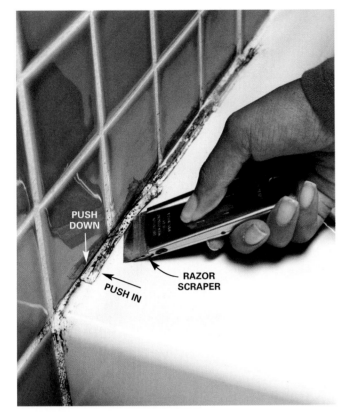

1 PUSH a razor scraper in all the way under both edges of the old caulk bead to release its grip. Don't pry the caulk with the scraper because you could break off the razor blade.

2 SCRAPE the loosened caulk out of the joint with the pointed end of a can opener or putty knife. Take care not to scratch the tile or tub.

3 REMOVE any remaining caulking residue and grime with a tub-and-tile cleaner (available at home centers and tile stores) and a non-abrasive sponge.

4 PULL the caulk tube down the tub/wall joint from the inside corner of the tub. Keep even pressure on the tube by pushing the caulk forward and folding over the empty portion.

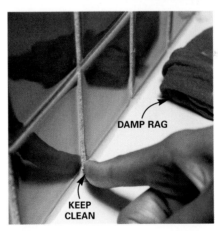

5 DAMPEN your finger in the tub and drag it over the freshly laid bead of caulk. Press the caulk into the joint with the tip of your finger and scrape away the excess with the sides of your finger (it may take a few swipes). Wipe excess caulk off your finger with a damp rag.

6 APPLY a bead of caulk along the tile corner joint if the old caulk or grout has cracked or deteriorated.

Great Goofs™

True tales by real readers!

Cat'll call

After living in our old house for years, we decided to go all out and remodel the bathroom. Our dream was to install a Jacuzzi tub with a beautiful tile surround. After all the backbreaking work, we finally got to the fun part—setting the tile. We did a flawless job! Later that evening, we realized our cat was missing. After looking everywhere, we heard a distinct meow coming from the bathroom.

Realizing that the sound was coming from the new tub surround, we carefully cut through the tile and cement board and found our cat alive and well. We made the best of a bad situation—our rescue hole became a maintenance access panel that we probably should have installed in the first place.

A few socks short of a load

Space is at a premium in our house, so we make use of every square foot. Last year I decided to build a shelf in the laundry room to store all the detergents, prewash additives and bleach bottles. I carefully measured the space between the washer and ceiling and calculated the number of shelves to fit the space. I got right to work. After finishing my shelving project, I stepped back to admire my space-saving genius just as my wife entered the room and lifted the washer lid. It hit the lower shelf and would only open halfway!

Litter-box Olympics

We keep our cat's litter box in the basement. Much to my annoyance, the door to the basement often gets closed unintentionally and the cat can't get downstairs to do her business. To make life easier for the cat and us, I decided to cut a little archway in the bottom of the door so my cat could find her way to the basement and back even if the door was closed. After removing the door, hauling it to the work-shop and cutting the archway, I brought the door back into the house to install it. Well, now I've got two choices: teach my cat to pole-vault, or go and buy a new door and start over. Yes, I cut the archway on the top of the door!

Over, under, sideways, down

My bathroom-remodeling project was going to be first class. I ordered a solid granite vanity top with a cutout for an undermount sink. I flipped the granite top over, carefully marked the sink and epoxied it to the granite. I taped it to keep it from moving while the epoxy set overnight. The next day I flipped the top with sink attached onto the vanity. I was horrified. The sink was glued in backward! I tugged and tugged to pull it loose, then I got out the pry bar. Still no luck. I ran to the shop and got my heat gun and went to work. Whew! Fortunately the epoxy wasn't completely cured and I was able to work it loose and clean up both surfaces. Yes, this time I got it right.

42

Wordless™
Workshop

by **Roy Doty**

FLIP-UP SHELF

TAPING WITH A
DRYWALL BANJO

Speedy, trouble-free taping is easy with this pro tool.

by **Jeff Gorton**

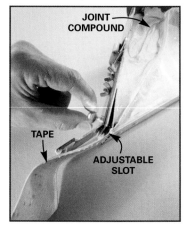

Taping drywall isn't for everyone. It takes patience and a fair amount of skill to do a good job. But if you're like me and enjoy the challenge, here's a tool you've gotta try out. It's called a banjo and it makes short work of covering drywall seams with paper tape. But speed isn't the only advantage a banjo offers. It practically eliminates the common problem of loose or bubbling tape that plagues many beginning tapers.

In this article, we'll show you how to use a banjo to apply the first coat of paper tape to drywall seams. For complete information on how to tape, start to finish, see "Drywall Taping," April '01, p. 35. To order a copy, see p. 220.

A banjo like the one we're using costs $75 to $100, a big investment for the occasional taping job. Fortunately, most full-service rental stores and some home centers rent banjos for about $10 per day—plenty of time to get a coat of tape on one or two rooms.

Thinned mud is the key to success

You'll find ready-mixed joint compound (called "mud" in drywall taping lingo) in plastic buckets or boxes at home centers, lumberyards and drywall suppliers. Buy all-purpose lightweight joint compound (one type is USG's Plus-3) and use it for embedding the tape as well as covering the tape with the second and third coats. You'll have to thin the mud with water, up to about 4 cups per pail, before you pour it into the banjo. If you're only taping one or two rooms, transfer a few gallons of joint compound to another bucket.

Then you'll still be able to use the remaining thicker mud for troweling on the second coat. First mix the joint compound with either a potato masher– type mixer like we're using (**Photo 1**) or a mixing paddle and heavy-duty 1/2-in. electric drill (mashers or paddles are available for about $11 at home centers and drywall suppliers). Then mix in water a little at a time until the joint compound drips in large blobs from the mixer (**Photo 1**).

The true test of proper mud consistency is how well it works in the banjo. Too thick and you'll struggle to pull out the tape. Too thin and the mud will leak from every nook and cranny. When you get the mix just right, the tape will pull out smoothly, be evenly coated and flatten easily with your taping knife (**Photo 4**).

Adjust the banjo to let out just enough mud

Load the banjo with a roll of paper tape and thinned joint compound (**Photos 2 and 3**). Then with the nose of the banjo angled toward the floor, pull out a few feet of tape and inspect the compound on the back. A properly adjusted banjo should leave an even 1/8-in. thick layer of joint compound. On most banjos, the width of the slot where the tape comes out is adjustable by either turning a thumbscrew or loosening Wing-Nuts and sliding the tape cutter up or down (**photo at right**). Test the setup by applying strips of tape to a scrap of drywall and flattening them with your taping knife. If very little joint compound oozes out from under the tape as you embed it, widen the gap to deposit more mud on the back of the tape. If there's so much joint compound that it's difficult to embed the tape and a large amount of mud piles up under your knife, reduce the size of the opening.

Tip

When you're embedding drywall tape, the compound should be fairly runny, especially if you're using a banjo. A soup ladle is the perfect no-mess, scooping device. It'll clean up just fine for tonight's cabbage soup.

A layer of mud on the top and bottom of the tape ensures success

Photos 4 – 8 show how to apply the tape to seams. To ensure trouble-free results, prefill the gaps between sheets of drywall with a setting-type joint compound and allow it to harden. Be careful to wipe off all excess compound flush to the drywall as you apply it, and scrape off any dried lumps with your taping knife before you start taping. As you pull the tape from the banjo, the topside may be dry or have very little joint compound. This isn't a problem as long as you trowel a thin layer of joint compound over the tape before you embed it to lubricate your knife. If friction from your knife is leaving the tape fuzzy or causing it to buckle up into little ridges, you'll know you need to trowel on a thin layer of mud before you trowel the tape flat. Transfer the mud that oozes out from under the tape back onto the surface of the tape as you go.

As the mud in the banjo runs low, it will no longer cover the bottom of the tape and the tape will be very easy to pull out. These are clues to refill the banjo. Open the cover and reposition the tape (**Photo 2**) before you refill the compartment. Joint compound often thickens as it sits. You may have to mix in a little more water.

Follow this sequence for the best results

The pros we talked to suggested applying tape in this order: (1) the vertical seams, (2) the horizontal seams and (3) the inside corners. It's OK to overlap the tape where one seam meets another. Divide long horizontal wall seams or seams that run across an entire ceiling into smaller sections by cutting the tape at an intersection with another seam (it's difficult to embed a section much over 10 ft. long). Always start at the center of each section and work toward the ends when you're embedding the tape (**Photo 6**). It's OK

1 MIX the joint compound to determine its consistency. Then mix in water until the joint compound is thin enough to drip slowly from your mixer. Add small amounts of water by squeezing it from a sponge.

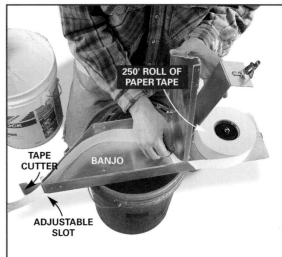

2 THREAD paper drywall tape through the banjo as shown in the photo. Clamp the metal cover over the 250-ft. roll of tape to secure it.

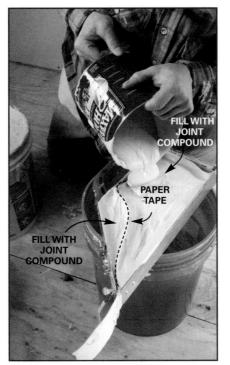

3 POUR the thinned joint compound into the banjo. Pull a section of tape away from the banjo wall and pour joint compound into the space to help cover the topside of the tape with joint compound when you pull it from the banjo (see photo). Completely fill the compartment and clamp the lid shut. Tip the banjo down and pull the tape until joint compound is visible on both the front and back sides. Cut this piece of tape loose and throw it away.

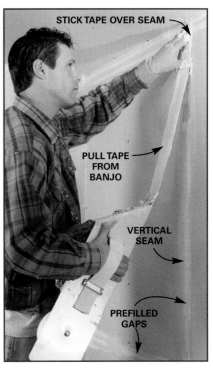

4 GRAB the tape and pull out about 12 in. Starting at the top of a vertical seam, center the tape and stick it to the wall. Hold the tape in this position while you pull the banjo with the other arm to release more tape. Slide your hand down the tape to press it to the wall and repeat the process as you work the length of the seam.

to tape a number of seams before returning to embed the tape as long as the joint compound doesn't start to dry out. Working with a partner who follows closely behind to embed the tape is a good way to speed up the job.

Keep the tools clean to avoid lumps

Taping is a messy job. It's a good idea to keep the banjo, mud pan and taping knife free of dried joint compound. I like to keep a 5-gallon pail of warm water and a sponge handy to clean my hands and wipe off the tools. Otherwise, little chunks of dried mud will cause all kinds of trouble as they get stuck under the tape or create streaks in the joint compound when your taping knife drags them along. When you're through for the day, scrape excess mud into a garbage bag and scrub the banjo and tools with a stiff-bristle brush to remove joint compound before it hardens. 🏠

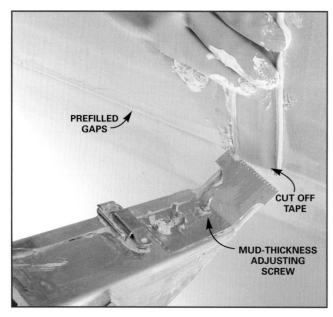

PREFILLED GAPS

CUT OFF TAPE

MUD-THICKNESS ADJUSTING SCREW

5 USING a slight twist, snap the tape with the blade at the nose of the banjo. If this doesn't work for you, grab the tape and pull it across the nose to tear it. After the tape is cut, quickly point the nose of the banjo toward the floor to prevent the tape from being pulled back into the banjo by the weight of the joint compound.

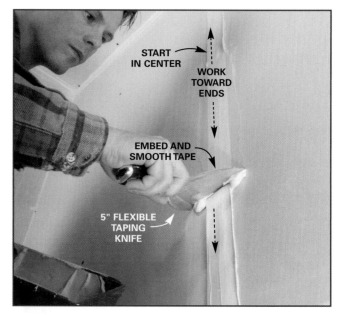

START IN CENTER

WORK TOWARD ENDS

EMBED AND SMOOTH TAPE

5" FLEXIBLE TAPING KNIFE

6 EMBED the tape and smooth it by dragging a 5- or 6-in. flexible taping knife over the tape. Apply just enough pressure to flatten the tape to the wall. Start at the middle and work in both directions to the ends.

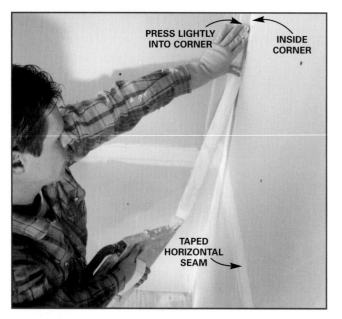

PRESS LIGHTLY INTO CORNER

INSIDE CORNER

TAPED HORIZONTAL SEAM

7 CENTER the tape on inside corner seams and press it lightly into place with your hand.

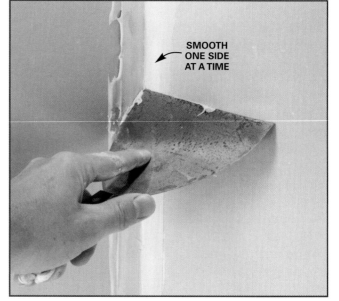

SMOOTH ONE SIDE AT A TIME

8 SMOOTH one side and then the other with your flexible taping knife. Run the side of the knife against the adjacent wall to guide it and create a straight, square corner.

WHICH JOINT COMPOUND SHOULD I BUY?

I'm a novice do-it-yourselfer who just finished hanging drywall in our basement. Now I'm going to tackle the taping. My home center offers a dozen types of joint compound—which should I buy?

When I see the word "novice" and "drywall" in the same sentence, two images pop into my head. The first is of drywall with hefty gaps between sheets, in the corners and around electrical boxes. The second image is of lots and lots of sanding. Our recommendations aim to minimize those headaches.

For starters, buy a bag of 45-minute setting compound; you'll find it in 30-lb. bags (and sometimes smaller boxes), with names like Durabond or Sheetrock 45. It comes as a powder—mostly plaster of Paris—you mix with water as you need it. It hardens quickly (you guessed it, in 45 minutes), shrinks very little and dries hard as a rock. This makes it ideal for filling oversize cutouts around electrical boxes, nail and screw dimples and cracks in areas where drywall sheets don't butt tightly. And since it dries quickly, you can move on to the "real" taping without waiting. Buy an "easy-sand" variety; the standard stuff dries so hard you can spend hours sanding ridges left behind by your trowel. Make sure to clean your tools off pronto when you're done unless you want a sculpture titled "Drywall Knife Stuck in Pan."

For embedding the tape and the subsequent layers, buy lightweight, all-purpose joint compound in the familiar (and ever-so-useful) 5-gallon bucket. This drying compound hardens through evaporation—which means waiting up to 24 hours between coats. Apply it full strength across the joints and at corners for bedding the tape. Then use it full strength or slightly thinned for the top layers. Try to avoid ridges and bumps. But if you get them, don't worry; the lightweight compound sands easily. It also scratches easily, so get a coat of primer on it as soon as you can. It's worth the extra buck per 5 gallons you'll pay for it. A 5-gallon bucket will finish about 450 sq. ft. of drywall, the equivalent of fifteen 4x8 sheets.

What's all the other stuff on the shelves? Topping compounds are "soupy" and contain less adhesive than all-purpose compounds. This makes them easy to feather and sand and thus ideal for the final coat or coats. Some pros are fond of this stuff, but for small jobs, all-purpose is fine. The five- and 20-minute setting compounds are used by pros for filling gaps, bedding tape, sometimes even for topcoats. Time is money for these folks; they can get away with using fast-setting compounds because they know how to apply them quickly and smoothly with very little sanding. But if you're a rookie, stay clear of these; they'll harden before you can walk across the room!

SLOW-, MEDIUM- AND FAST-SETTING COMPOUNDS

TOPPING COMPOUND

45-MINUTE SETTING COMPOUND

5-MINUTE SETTING COMPOUND (WOW!)

LIGHTWEIGHT, ALL-PURPOSE COMPOUND

3-1/2 HOUR SETTING COMPOUND

20-MINUTE SETTING COMPOUND

90-MINUTE SETTING COMPOUND

ALL-PURPOSE COMPOUND

Lightweight "all-purpose" compound and "easy-sand" 45-minute setting compound are the two items novices should load into their carts. You'll find uses for all that other stuff as your projects get bigger—and you get faster and better.

Which
Should I buy?

NATURAL OR SYNTHETIC BRUSH?

I'm painting my house with an oil-based primer and a latex paint. Is there one brush that can handle both tasks?

If you're using one brush for both tasks, buy a synthetic one. Natural-bristle brushes, commonly called China brushes, are made from animal hair, usually hog. Since natural bristles are hollow or have split ends, they hold lots of paint, finish or stain—then release it evenly. The best ones have bristles of varying lengths so they release the paint evenly and smoothly, not all at once. But latex paint eventually causes natural bristles to swell, leaving you with a floppy, fluffy brush that's harder to control.

Synthetic-bristle brushes, usually made from nylon, polyester or both, arguably don't hold as much paint or primer, but won't become distorted in water- or oil-based finishes. Buy good ones with flagged or split ends; they'll hold more paint than the cheaper, blunt-end brushes.

NATURAL CHINA BRISTLE BRUSH

NYLON BRUSH WITH BLUNT ENDS

SYNTHETIC BRISTLE BRUSH WITH FLAGGED ENDS

WHICH NAIL HOLE PUTTY?

We're installing oak trim in a room we've converted into a home office. What kind of putty should we use to fill the nail holes?

It depends on how and where you do the staining and finishing. I strongly suggest you prestain your trim then give it the first coat of polyurethane or clear finish before installing it; you'll save time and mess. If you go this route, use one of the colored oil-based putties in the little jars. They come in a wide range of colors; you can even knead different shades together to get just the right color where the grain is darker or lighter. But it's critical that you stain and seal your wood before using oil-based putty. Don't use it on bare wood because the oils in it soak into the wood surrounding the nail holes, and stain and finish will absorb differently and look blotchy. It's equally important to apply a coat of polyurethane over the putty after it's applied; the stuff remains soft and the clear finish will help protect it. Also because of its softness, don't use it on floors or to fill large holes or gaps.

Sandable putty hardens after it's applied and needs to be sanded smooth for best results. It's the best choice for filling large holes in wood. But I've had horrible luck using it for filling nail holes in unstained wood. It can unevenly absorb the stain applied over them. And, since sandable putty doesn't flex with the wood as it expands and contracts, it can crack and fall out.

SANDABLE PUTTY

SOFT, OIL-BASED PUTTY

If you've prestained and prefinished your trim, use the oil-based putty on the right. If you're sanding and finishing your wood after it's up (boy, is THAT a lot of extra work!), you can use the stuff on the left, but the results will be less predictable.

SHOULD WE USE WATER-BASED OR OIL-BASED POLY?

We're installing tongue-and-groove maple flooring in our newly remodeled master bedroom. We love the natural look of the maple but want a finish that will protect it. Is water- or oil-based polyurethane better?

Both offer good protection; the biggest difference is in appearance. If you love the natural look of maple, apply a water-based (waterborne) polyurethane. They appear milky in the can, but go on clear and remain clear. They'll slightly accent the character of your wood without giving it the amber tint of an oil-based poly. (However, some woods, like the oak shown, cry out for that amber tint.) Water-based finishes dry fast—most within two hours—so you can apply several coats in a day and use the room that night. They have minimal odor and clean up with water too.

WATER-BASED FINISH

NO FINISH

FINNISH

OIL-BASED FINISH

WATER-BASED POLYURETHANES provide a clear finish and have low odor. You can recoat them in two hours and clean your tools with water. If you start early enough in the day, you can apply the recommended four coats and sleep in the room that night.

OIL-BASED POLYURETHANES leave an amber glow and require fewer coats. But the five-hour wait between coats and 12-hour wait after the last coat will put a bedroom out of commission for a few days—and you'll have to put up with a strong odor.

But water-based polys have their tradeoffs. They cost twice as much as oil-based polys. They won't give wood the rich glow that oil-based polys impart; some even consider them cold looking. When I applied waterborne poly recently, I found that it went on so clear I had to use a bottle cap to mark each 8-in. wide swath of finish as I went.

Most water-based polys contain only 30 to 35 percent solids, compared with the 45 to 50 percent solids in oil-based products. Since these solids create the protective finish, you need to apply four coats, as opposed to two or three. And you may need to apply additional coats every two years or so.

There's debate over which finish is harder, but some experts maintain that hardness isn't necessarily a good attribute of a floor finish. You want a finish that will flex along with the floor. And a super-hard finish shows scratches more readily.

You'll prolong the protective life of any finish by eliminating its No. 1 enemies: dirt and grit. Sweep or vacuum the floor often and put throw rugs in high-traffic areas.

SHOULD I REPLACE MY HOLLOW-CORE ENTRY DOOR?

I just bought a house that has a hollow-core entry door. Should I replace it?

Yes, you should replace it with a steel, fiberglass or solid-core wood door. Although no codes specify that an exterior door can't have a hollow core, there are at least four reasons why you should replace the door: security, insulation, noise and aesthetics.

Hollow-core doors are a security risk. Most consist

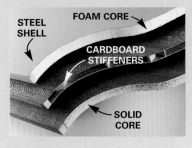

STEEL SHELL

FOAM CORE

CARDBOARD STIFFENERS

SOLID CORE

of two layers of 1/8-in. plywood held apart by cardboard stiffeners (though they're beefed up where the lockset is installed). A deter-

mined person can put a pry bar or even a fist right through them and open your door.

Hollow-core doors are also poor insulators. If you live in a cold climate, a much better choice is a steel or fiberglass door that has a rigid core of insulation. This extra insulation will also help block traffic noise (assuming you also have quality windows).

The sound of a hollow-core door shutting just doesn't make you feel like you walked into a well-built, solid home, even if it is. This can become a real issue when you're ready to sell your home.

Solid-core doors are also a type of fire-rated door. One place you must have one is between an attached garage and the home.

THE RIGHT WAY TO
ELIMINATE MOLD

If left unchecked, a major mold infestation can ruin your home—and your health! Here's how to get rid of it.

by **Bruce Clark**

Mold is a major-league nuisance. It blackens the grout lines in your shower, discolors drywall, shows up as black spots on siding, darkens decks, and grows on and rots damp wood everywhere. Even worse, it can be bad for your health. It releases microscopic spores into the air that cause allergic reactions, runny noses and sneezing, as well as irritating, even injurious, odors.

Almost every home gets mold infestations. The trick is to stop them before they get big and harm both you and your home. In this article, we'll show you how to identify mold and eliminate the small infestations as well as the big ones that have gotten out of hand.

You can easily remove minor mold with ordinary household cleaning products (see p. 52). But disturbing big infestations can be bad for your health, particularly if you are an allergy sufferer or have a weakened immune system. When you discover an extensive mold problem, we recommend that you use the rigorous protective measures we show in **Photos 1 – 6**, or consider calling in a professional to handle the problem. (Look under "Industrial Hygiene Consultants" or "Environmental and Ecological Consultants" in your Yellow Pages. Or call your local public health department.) And even if you hire pros, read through this article and make sure they follow similar precautions to keep the mold from spreading throughout your house.

How to identify mold

Mold is everywhere. It's a type of fungus that grows from tiny spores that float in the air. It can grow almost anywhere that spores land and find moisture and a comfortable temperature, between 40 and 100 degrees F. Typically that includes about every damp place in your home.

You can easily spot the most visible type of mold, called mildew, which begins as tiny, usually black spots but often grows into larger colonies. It's the black stuff you see in the grout lines in your shower, on damp walls, and outdoors on the surfaces of deck boards and painted siding, especially in damp and shady areas. A mildewed surface is often difficult to distinguish from a dirty one. To test for mildew, simply dab

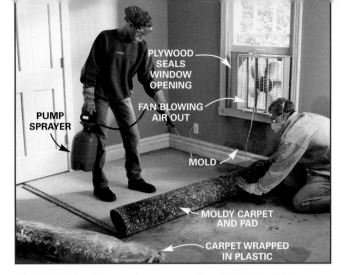

1 CUT stained or musty carpet and pads into 6 x 8-ft. sections with a utility knife. Using a pump sprayer, mist the surfaces with water to control the spread of spores, and roll up the sections. Double-wrap them in 6-mil plastic and tape them with duct tape for disposal. Wear protective clothing (see text) and run an exhaust fan in the window.

> **CAUTION: A few types of mold are highly toxic. If you have an allergic reaction to mold or a heavy infestation inside your home, call in a pro to analyze the types. or call your local public health department and ask for mold-testing advice.**

a few drops of household bleach on the blackened area. If it lightens after one to two minutes, you have mildew. If the area remains dark, you probably have dirt.

Mildew is a surface type of mold that won't damage your home's structure. But other types of mold cause rot. Probe the suspect area with a screwdriver or other sharp tool (**Photo 3**). If the wood is soft or crumbles, the fungi have taken hold and rot has begun.

If you have a high concentration of mold, you may smell it. If you detect the typical musty odor, check for mold on damp carpets, damp walls, damp crawlspaces and wet wood under your floors, wet roof sheathing and other damp areas. Clean up these infestations right away before they get worse, and see below for prevention measures.

2 SEAL the room from the rest of the house. Cover the doorway with a barrier made of overlapping plastic sheeting and tape it to the wall and floor. Cover all air ducts in the room with plastic and tape.

Removing large infestations requires precautions—and work!

You can scrub away the surface mold common to bathrooms, decks and siding in a matter of minutes with a 1-to-8 bleach/water solution. (See p. 52 for techniques.) But often

Tips for mold prevention

The key to stopping most mold is to control dampness. The worst infestations usually occur in damp crawlspaces, in attics and walls where water has leaked in from the outside, and in basements with poor foundation drainage. Stopping leaks, ensuring good ventilation in attics, keeping crawlspaces dry and routing water away from the foundation are the best defenses.

Mildewcide in paint is usually effective for controlling surface mold in damp rooms like bathrooms and outside in shady areas. Many paints already have mildewcide in them. Check with your paint dealer to be sure. You can add mildewcide, although you might void the paint warranty.

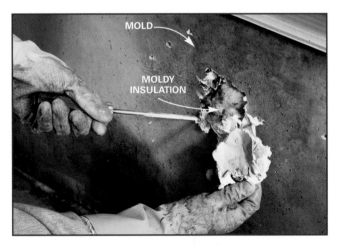

3 PRY OFF baseboards and trim from contaminated areas with a pry bar and block of wood. Probe heavily stained or moisture-swollen walls using a screwdriver to discover and open up moisture damage and hidden mold in the insulation and wall framing.

MOLDY INSULATION

HEAVY-DUTY TRASH BAG

4 TURN off the electrical power to the room and cut open the damaged wall with a reciprocating saw, drywall saw or utility knife. Mist the moldy drywall and insulation with the pump sprayer to avoid spreading mold spores. Double-bag moldy material in heavy-duty plastic bags and tie them shut.

WET/DRY VACUUM

5 VACUUM up moldy debris with a standard wet/dry vacuum. Buy an extra length of hose and run it out the window so you can keep the vacuum outside to avoid further spore spread.

mold grows and spreads in places you don't notice, until you spot surface staining, feel mushy drywall or detect that musty smell. If you have to remove mold concentrations covering more than a few square feet, where the musty odor is strong or where you find extensive water damage, we recommend that you take special precautions. You want to not only avoid contaminating the rest of the house but also protect yourself from breathing high concentrations of spores and VOCs.

- Wear old clothes and shoes that you can launder or throw away after the cleanup work.
- Wear special N-95 or P-100 respirators, in addition to goggles and gloves. See the Buyer's Guide, p. 53, for a source.
- Set an old box fan or a cheap new one in a window to ventilate the room while working. Throw it out when you're done cleaning, because the spores are almost impossible to clean off. Tape plywood or cardboard around the window openings so the spores can't blow back in (**Photo 1**).
- Wrap and tape moldy carpeting in 6-mil plastic, and double-bag mold-infested debris in garbage bags for disposal (**Photos 1 and 4**).
- To control airborne spores, moisten moldy areas with a garden sprayer while you work (**Photo 1**).
- Turn off your furnace and air conditioner and cover ducts and doors to contain spores.
- Keep your wet/dry vacuum outside when you vacuum (**Photo 5**).

Moisture damage and large mold infestations go hand in hand. **Photos 1 – 7** demonstrate cleaning under an old leaky window where wind-driven rain frequently got into the wall and gave mold a foothold.

You have to open up the wall to get at the mold growing inside (**Photo 4**). Since you have to repair the wall anyway,

Techniques for cleaning surface mold

Surface molds grow in just about any damp location, such as the grout lines of a ceramic tiled shower (see photo). They're easy to scrub away with a mixture of 1/2 cup bleach, 1 qt. water and a little detergent. The bleach in the cleaning mixture kills the mold, and the detergent helps lift it off the surface so you can rinse it away so it won't return as fast. You can also buy a mildew cleaner at hardware stores, paint stores and most home centers.

MILDEW

BLEACH

BLEACH, DETERGENT AND WATER MIXTURE

Even for simple cleaning, protect yourself from contact with mold and the bleach solution by wearing a long-sleeve shirt and long pants as well as plastic or rubber gloves and goggles.

TIP: Special gloves made of nitrile are as tough as latex but thinner and more protective. See the Buyer's Guide for a source.

If the mold doesn't disappear after light scrubbing, reapply the cleaning mix and let it sit for a minute or two. Then lightly scrub again.

Seal the clean surfaces when they're thoroughly dry to slow future moisture penetration. Apply a grout sealer ($5 to $25 per quart from tile shops and home centers) to tile joints.

CAUTION: Don't mix ammonia or any detergent containing ammonia with bleach. The combination forms a poisonous gas.

don't hesitate to cut the drywall back beyond the obvious damage to find all the mold and let the wall dry out. To avoid cutting electrical wires, poke a hole through the damaged section and locate the wires first. Turn off the power to the outlets before you cut.

If the moisture damage has been neglected or gone unnoticed for long, you're likely to find rot. Where possible, remove and replace soft, spongy studs and wall sheathing. Where removal is difficult, treat the affected areas with a wood preservative (available at home centers), after cleaning the wood and allowing it to dry. Then double up rotted members with pressure-treated wood.

Complete the initial cleanup by vacuuming up the debris (**Photo 5**). Thoroughly clean the wet/ dry vac afterward by disposing of the filter and washing out the tank, hose and attachments with the bleach-and-water solution.

After scrubbing the surfaces (**Photo 6**), simply allow the bleach solution to continue to penetrate the surfaces and dry. Wash concrete floors with TSP, automatic dishwasher detergent or a chlorinated cleaner such as Comet.

Set out dehumidifiers and new fans to dry the now-cleaned areas for at least three days, then check them (by sight and smell) for mold. If you discover more mold, clean again with bleach.

When you're sure the mold has been eliminated, seal the wood surfaces with pigmented shellac like BIN or an oil-based primer like KILZ (**Photo 7**). Repaint cleaned wall surfaces with a regular latex paint that contains a mildewcide to help stop future mold growth. And keep in mind that if the moisture returns, mold will return.

For More Information

"How a House Works," "Combating Mold and Mildew," March '00, p. 89. For information on how to order copies of past articles, see p. 220. 🏠

Buyer's Guide

■ For local sources of safety gear, see "Safety Equipment and Clothing" in your Yellow Pages.

■ Direct Safety Inc.: (800) 528-7405. www.directsafety.com. Source for N-95 particulate respirator masks (item No. 03-017, about $24 for box of 10), unlined 13-in. nitrile gloves (item No. 07-121, about $2 a pair) and anti-fog goggles (item No. 02-709, about $4).

6 SCRUB the surface mold stains from walls and wood trim with a mixture of 1 qt. water and 1/2 cup bleach to kill the mold. Use a soft brush and work until signs of the mold disappear. Wipe off, but DO NOT RINSE these surfaces. Set trim in direct sunlight to dry. Scrub concrete with TSP or automatic dishwasher detergent.

COVERED HOSE HOLE

SOLID BUT MOLDY DRYWALL

MOLDY WOOD

7 ALLOW to dry, then seal all previously infested areas with a pigmented shellac- or oil-based primer. Then install new insulation and drywall and nail the trim back on.

EXTERIOR WALL SHEATHING

13 common breeding grounds for mold and mildew

1 Leaky air-conditioning duct joints, especially those running through a hot attic, create a moist environment for mildew to flourish.
■ **Solution:** Seal all duct joints with the special flexible mastic available at heating and cooling supply stores.

2 In warm environments, impermeable vinyl wallcoverings can trap moisture-laden air as it moves from the warm exterior to the cooler interior. Mold degrades the drywall and adhesive behind the vinyl wallcovering.
■ **Solution:** Use paint or apply wallcoverings with permeable paper backings that don't trap moisture on exterior walls.

3 When washing machines in a room without a floor drain overflow or hose connections burst, water with no point of exit will soak into adjacent carpet, drywall and insulation.
■ **Solution:** Always provide a floor drain near the washing machine. Install an overflow pan directly under the machine or install a 1-in. lip at the doorway to contain overflows in main-level or second-story laundry rooms. (An overflow pan is available for about $125 plus shipping from AMI, 800-929-9269.)

4 Water-resistant drywall used as a tile backer quickly degrades once subjected to moisture.
■ **Solution:** Install cement backer board, which will remain structurally sound even if repeatedly subjected to moisture.

5 Poorly ventilated bathrooms allow surface mold to grow.
■ **Solution:** Install a bathroom fan (or at least, open a window) to exhaust moisture. Remove surface mildew by scrubbing the area with a bleach solution (see "Techniques for Cleaning Surface Mold," p. 52). When the area is dry, prime it with an alcohol-based, white pigmented shellac, such as Zinsser Bullseye, and use a paint containing mildewcide.

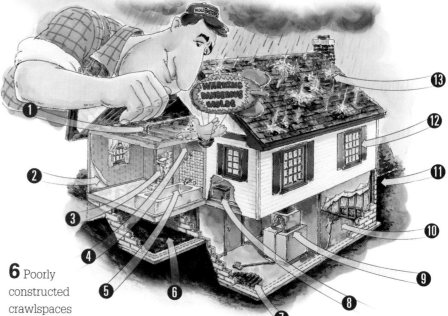

6 Poorly constructed crawlspaces promote mildew growth. Bare earth floors transmit huge amounts of moisture.
■ **Solution:** There are many regional differences and solutions. Cover bare earth with 6-mil poly sheeting. Heat, cool and humidify the area the same as the rest of the house.

7 Freshly cut firewood stored indoors emits huge amounts of moisture.
■ **Solution:** Store it outside.

8 Humidifiers (especially reservoir-type central units and portable units) provide both a growth medium and a distribution system for mold and mildew.
■ **Solution:** Clean and treat the reservoir often with an antimicrobial solution, available at most hardware stores.

9 The condensation pan directly under the coil of your central air conditioner can harbor mold.
■ **Solution:** Before each cooling season, clean the pan with a 1/2 percent bleach solution and make sure the continuous drain is working.

10 Finished concrete basements that haven't been thoroughly waterproofed from the outside are problematic. When moisture migrates through the earth and non-waterproofed concrete walls, it can get trapped behind vapor barriers, carpet, insulation and drywall.
■ **Solution:** Thoroughly waterproof the exterior of concrete walls before backfilling. Install 6 in. of gravel under concrete floors during construction to prevent moisture from wicking up through concrete floors and into floor coverings.

11 Yards that slope toward foundations invite water into basements.
■ **Solution:** Regrade yard so it slopes away at a rate of 1 in. per foot.

12 Improperly flashed or caulked windows (and those with large amounts of surface condensation) let moisture seep into the surrounding wood, drywall or plaster and insulation.
■ **Solution:** Properly flash and caulk windows during installation; minimize condensation with good ventilation.

13 Leaky flashings and shingles allow rain to infiltrate attics, insulation, eaves and other areas that can trap moisture.
■ **Solution:** Perform yearly roof inspections—even if you do it from the ground with binoculars.

2

It's hard to beat outdoor projects. You get sunshine and fresh air, the fruits of your labor are out there for all the world to see and the mess stays outside. Here are some favorites.

Outdoor Projects
& IMPROVEMENTS

DURABLE
HARDBOARD SIDING

All siding installations are not created equal. Here's how to do it right!

by **Duane Johnson**

Hardboard siding, essentially highly compressed wood fiber and adhesive, is less expensive than solid wood. But it has to be installed correctly for it to last.

Hardboard siding that's swollen won't hold paint. When water seeps into raw hardboard, the wood fibers swell and crack the painted surface, allowing yet more water to seep

Failed hardboard siding

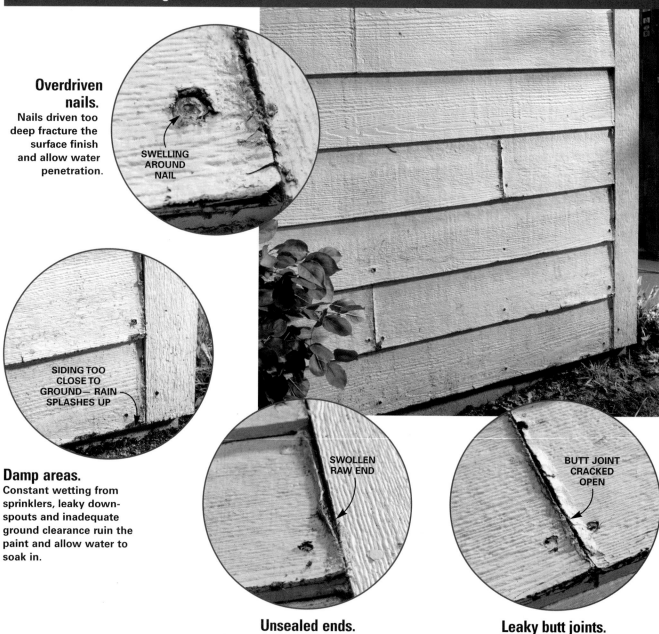

Overdriven nails.
Nails driven too deep fracture the surface finish and allow water penetration.

SWELLING AROUND NAIL

SIDING TOO CLOSE TO GROUND— RAIN SPLASHES UP

Damp areas.
Constant wetting from sprinklers, leaky downspouts and inadequate ground clearance ruin the paint and allow water to soak in.

SWOLLEN RAW END

BUTT JOINT CRACKED OPEN

Unsealed ends.
Sawn ends swell when caulk fails.

Leaky butt joints.
Caulked butt joints eventually crack open, allowing water to seep in.

in. The process is the same with solid wood siding too, except that solid wood shrinks back to its original size when it dries. Hardboard doesn't—once it swells, it stays swollen. Unless you quickly caulk gaps and reseal exposed fibers with paint, the damage will spread.

When it comes to installing hardboard, durability and longevity are dictated by the details. If you take the time to do the job right so water won't penetrate the hardboard, your siding will last for decades. If you cut corners during installation, your hardboard will fail. The photos show the most common mistakes and the ways to get those details right. When you buy hardboard, pick up a set of manufacturer's directions from the retailer and make sure you follow all the installation steps. ⌂

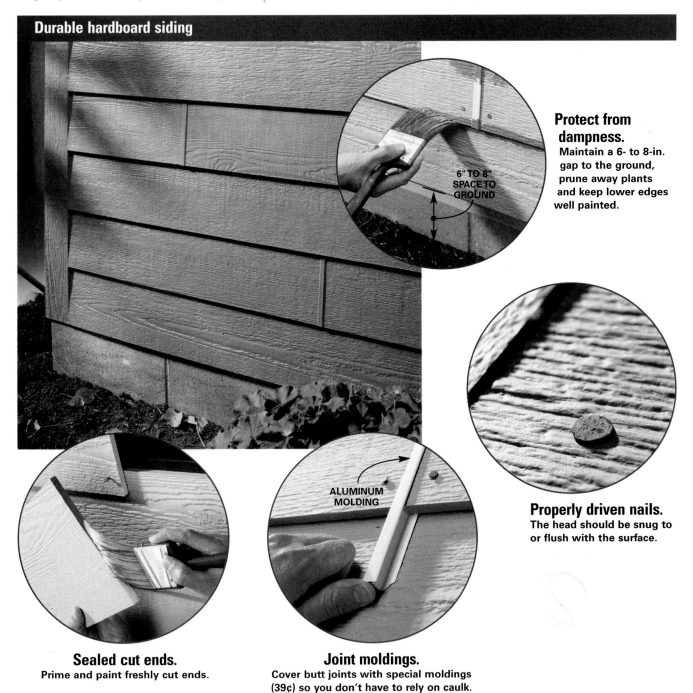

Durable hardboard siding

6" TO 8" SPACE TO GROUND

Protect from dampness.
Maintain a 6- to 8-in. gap to the ground, prune away plants and keep lower edges well painted.

Properly driven nails.
The head should be snug to or flush with the surface.

Sealed cut ends.
Prime and paint freshly cut ends.

ALUMINUM MOLDING

Joint moldings.
Cover butt joints with special moldings (39¢) so you don't have to rely on caulk.

Handy hints® from our readers...

JOIST LEVELER

When you're building a deck or other structure solo, it's pretty hard to level long joists and beams, then hold them in place while you secure them. Here's one way to do it. Secure one end of the joist or beam, then support it with a car scissors jack. Crank the jack up or down to level as necessary, then secure or support the other end at just the right position.

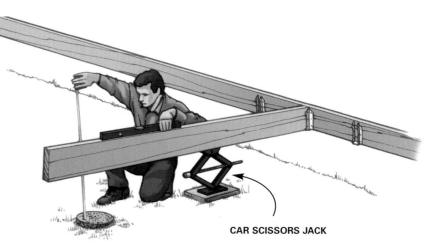

CAR SCISSORS JACK

INSTANT ANTIQUITY

Give a new concrete planter that stylish patina of age by applying stain specially formulated to look like moss-covered stone. We used Mason's Select Transparent Concrete Stain, which is made with 100 percent acrylic binders for excellent adhesion and durability. It's also mildew resistant. (Look for it at full-service hardware stores or contact Duckback Products at 800-825-5382 or www.superdeck.com.)

Prepare the planter by cleaning it with a stiff brush. Then dilute the stain with water according to the label directions. Test for color intensity on an inconspicuous place first. The

stain will dry to a lighter shade. If you want a deeper tone, let the first coat dry and apply a second coat. When satisfied with your test, simply brush on the stain. Choose from eight stain finishes, including patina green (for the mossy look), terra cotta, fieldstone, sandstone and slate.

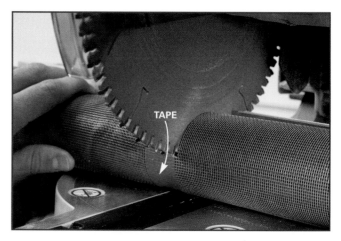

TAPE

SPEED SCREENING

Here's how to rough-cut long lengths of screen for full-screen storm doors or identical windows in an instant. Wrap a piece of tape around the screen to mark the cutting width and to keep the roll tight. Then use a power miter saw to cut through the entire roll. The saw will ensure an even cut, and all that's left is trimming off the excess.

RUST IMMUNIZATION

To keep your table saw, drill press and radial arm saw from rusting, rub auto wax on all the large, flat steel surfaces. The tools remain rust free, and the wax greatly reduces drag and friction when you're cutting.

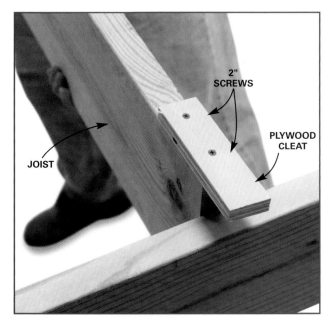

A SMALL PLYWOOD CLEAT

A plywood cleat screwed to the top of a joist will hold it up while you nail the opposite end. Plus, it will hold the tops flush while you nail on the joist hanger. Use scraps of 3/4-in. plywood rather than boards for small cleats. Plywood won't split when you drive screws into it.

DECK BOARD SPACERS

Sixteen-penny nails work great as spacers when you're installing deck boards, but they often fall through the cracks. Keep the nails in place by pounding them through plastic jar covers. They're easier to move and will stay up on the deck instead of falling on the ground.

STAIN SPRAYER

Here's an easier way to stain or seal chairs, lattice or anything with numerous tight recesses. Pour the stain into a clean, empty spray bottle ($3). Spray the stain onto the project and wipe up the excess with a brush or rag. The sprayer will squirt stain into all those tight, hard-to-reach cracks and joints.

CLEANER SCREENS

Revive dirty window screens with automotive plastic and vinyl protector (Armor All, for example). A light wiping on both sides of the screen will leave it looking like new.

BUILD A
BACKYARD BIRDHOUSE

Even our fine feathered friends need a quaint little place to call home.
Here's a fun-to-build project made with simple tools.

by **David Radtke**

This is a fun project—so fun that it's hard to say who benefits more from it: the bird or the builder. You can let your imagination run and experiment with a variety of materials, shapes and designs. You only need to follow a few parameters (see chart on p. 86) that are specific to the bird species you're trying to attract. Follow the clear how-to photos and study the drawing and the cutting list to build our project exactly, or personalize it with the details you want: a stone chimney, some shutters or cedar shingles.

Most any softwood (pine, cedar, cypress, redwood, fir) will work for your birdhouse. We used pine for the walls and base, exterior fir plywood for the roof, and birch square dowels (available at home centers or hobby shops) as well as

birch dowel pins for porch balusters.

We used simple tools to build this project. You'll notice the 1x8 pine boards are actually 7-1/4 in. wide but need to be 7 in. wide for this project. If you don't have a table saw to rip them to this narrower width, have the lumberyard rip them for you and then cut the lengths at home with the simple tools shown.

Attracting the right birds

Just as with people, one house doesn't fit all. In fact, many bird species don't use houses at all but nest on branches or groundcover. Birds that use hollowed-out cliffs, tree trunks or birdhouses, however, are called cavity dwellers. They come in all sizes.

The size of the entry hole and size of the interior room can make a huge difference in the type of bird your house will attract. We've sized this birdhouse to fit a variety of smaller bird species. To attract very small birds like nuthatches, bluebirds or chickadees, you may want to make the floor area a bit smaller by gluing an extra piece of wood to the front interior wall of the birdhouse and another on one side. A smaller interior is not as hard for a bird to fill with nesting material.

Keep in mind that you'll also need to maintain your birdhouse by cleaning it after the nesting season. To make this as easy as possible, we've included a sliding rear door held in place with small hook-and-eye latches. Just lift the latch and slide the door to the side to remove the nest and wipe out the inside.

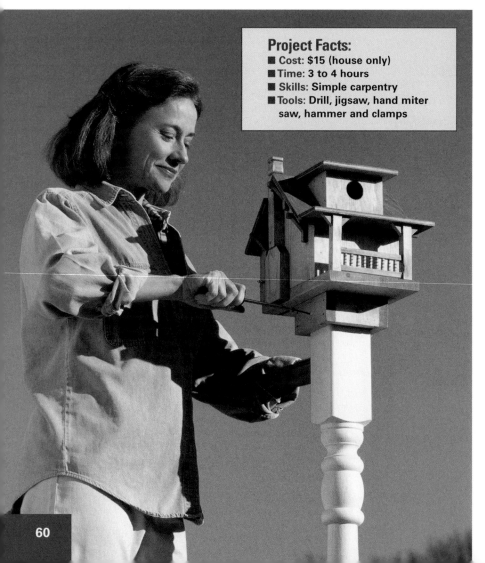

Project Facts:
- Cost: $15 (house only)
- Time: 3 to 4 hours
- Skills: Simple carpentry
- Tools: Drill, jigsaw, hand miter saw, hammer and clamps

Backyard birdhouse

FIG. A

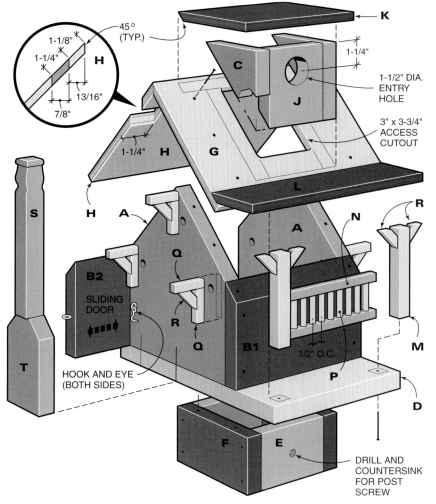

45° (TYP.)

1-1/8"
1-1/4"
H
13/16"
7/8"

1-1/4" **H**

S

T

C

J

G

H **A**

Q

B2
SLIDING DOOR
⬅️▰▰▰▰

HOOK AND EYE (BOTH SIDES)

R

Q

B1

A

N

R

M

1/2" O.C.

P

D

F **E**

DRILL AND COUNTERSINK FOR POST SCREW

K

1-1/4"

1-1/2" DIA. ENTRY HOLE

3" x 3-3/4" ACCESS CUTOUT

L

FIG. B

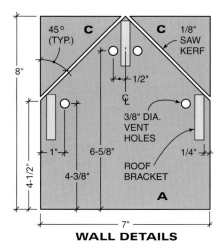

45° (TYP.) **C** **C** 1/8" SAW KERF

8"

4-1/2"

1/2"

C̵L

3/8" DIA. VENT HOLES

ROOF BRACKET

1"

6-5/8"

4-3/8"

1/4"

A

7"

WALL DETAILS

FIG. C

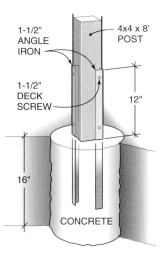

1-1/2" ANGLE IRON

4x4 x 8' POST

1-1/2" DECK SCREW

12"

16"

CONCRETE

CUTTING LIST

KEY	QTY.	SIZE & DESCRIPTION
A	2	3/4" x 7" x 8" gable end wall (rough cut)
B1	1	3/4" x 7" x 4-1/2" front wall
B2	1	3/4" x 7" x 4-3/8" back wall
C	2	3/4" x 3-3/8" x 3-3/8" dormer side wall
D	1	3/4" x 7" x 11" floor
E	2	3/4" x 2-1/2" x 3-1/2" front flange pieces
F	2	3/4" x 2-1/2" x 5" side flange pieces
G	1	3/8" x 9-1/2" x 6-1/4" front roof plywood
H	1	3/8" x 9-1/2" x 6-3/4" rear roof plywood
J	1	3/4" x 3" x 3-3/8" front dormer wall
K	1	3/8" x 6" x 4-3/4" dormer roof
L	1	3/8" x 9-1/2" x 2-3/4" plywood porch roof
M	2	5/8" x 5/8" x 4" porch columns
N	2	3/8" x 3/8" x 4-7/8" railings
P	9	1/4" x 1-1/4" wood dowel balusters
Q	12	3/8" x 3/8" x 1-1/2" roof brackets
R	10	3/8" x 3/8" x 1-1/8" diagonal roof brackets
S	1	7/8" x 7/8" x 6-3/4" chimney (corner castle block)
T	1	3/4" x 2-1/2" x 4" chimney base

SHOPPING LIST

ITEM	QTY.
1x8 x 4' pine	1
1x4 x2' pine	1
3/8" exterior fir plywood	1/4 sheet
1-5/8" x 36" square dowel	1
3/8" x 36" square dowel	1
1/4" x 1" spiral dowels	1 pkg.
7/8" x 6-6/4" corner castle block (specialty trim; purchase at home center in specialty trim)	1
4d galvanized finish nails	1/4 lb.
6d galvanized finish nails	1/4 lb.
Outdoor carpenter's glue	1/2 pint

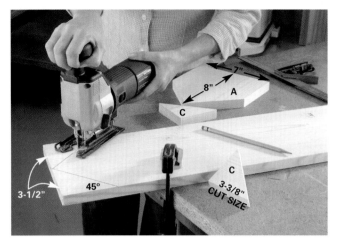

1 CUT all the pieces with a jigsaw or circular saw. Rip the solid pine board to 7 in. wide (see text) before cutting parts A, B and D.

2 NAIL the wood flange assembly together with 6d galvanized finish nails. Next, glue and nail the base to this assembly. Use outdoor carpenter's glue for a stable, water-resistant bond.

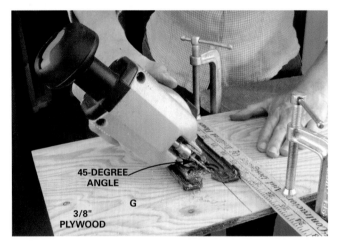

3 SET your jigsaw base at 45 degrees and cut miter joints for the plywood roof pieces G and H. Use a straightedge clamped to the workpiece to guide your saw for a perfectly even and straight cut.

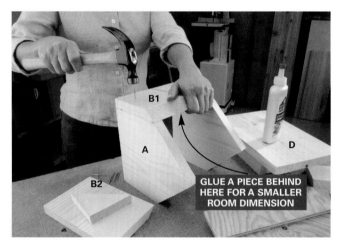

4 GLUE AND NAIL the front piece (B1) to the side pieces (A). Use 4d galvanized finish nails. Don't glue and nail the backside (B2). The back piece is 1/8 in. shorter so it can slide in place once the roof is in place. This back panel is removable for cleaning.

5 CUT an opening into the front roof panel (G) for access through the dormer. Drill a 3/8-in. starter hole in two opposite corners to start the cut easily. Cut the chimney opening in the rear roof panel with the blade set at a 45-degree angle.

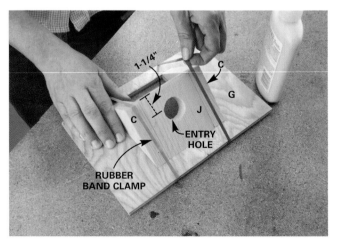

6 GLUE AND NAIL parts C to the center entry panel (J) once you've drilled the entry hole. Glue this assembly to the front plywood roof panel. Use rubber bands as clamps to hold the dormer assembly in place until the glue dries.

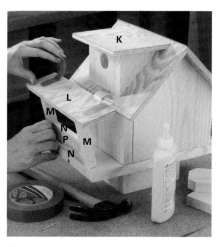

7 NAIL the roof panels to the side walls with 4d galvanized nails. Use glue along the mitered seam at the top.

8 ASSEMBLE the porch railing and nail it to the posts. Then nail the porch roof (L) to the posts. Glue the seam along the roof and hold it in place with masking tape. Once the glue is dry, nail (use 4d finish nails and predrill a pilot hole) up from the underside of the base into each column.

9 CUT the small roof bracket pieces (Q and R) and assemble them using exterior wood glue. Once they're assembled, glue them to the sides of the birdhouse. Next, drill the vent holes to keep the birdhouse cool, and finally, select and apply an exterior finish.

Protect your birdhouse with an exterior oil finish

Birds would just as soon not have a finish on the exterior, but to make it last you'll need a coat of oil finish every few years. You can also paint your birdhouse, but keep in mind that birds are color sensitive and may be repelled by certain colors. Try using colors found in natural surroundings and avoid bright and flashy colors. Never stain or paint the inside of the birdhouse. The odor may keep them from moving in. Let the exterior stain dry thoroughly (two to three weeks) before mounting the birdhouse outside.

Mount the birdhouse to a 4x4 post or a tree limb

We made a wood flange (**Photo 2**) to secure the birdhouse to a 4x4 fence post or decorative porch post anchored to a concrete base (see **Fig. C**). You can also mount your birdhouse in a tree; just eliminate the mounting flange and put screw eyes through the roof into the wall, then attach a chain hung from a tree limb. Keep in mind that some bird species like to nest in houses in the open while others feel more protected near buildings or in a wooded area. See "For More Information" for books about birdhouses.

EASTERN BLUEBIRD	TREE SWALLOW	WHITE-BREASTED NUTHATCH	CAROLINA WREN	RED-BELLIED WOODPECKER

Basic Birdhouse Dimensions (for Common Cavity Dwellers)*

Bird	Entry hole size (inches)	Hole above floor (inches)	Floor dimensions (inches)	Height above ground (feet)
Bluebird	1-1/2	6-7	4 x 4 to 5 x 5	3-6
Chickadee, Nuthatch, Swallow, Wren, Downy Woodpecker, Warbler	1-1/8 to 1-1/2	6-7	4 x 4 to 5 x 5	4-15
Red-Bellied Woodpecker, Northern Flicker, Red-headed Woodpecker, Starling, Fly-catcher, Sparrow	1-1/2 to 3	7-9	6 x 6 to 8 x 8	9-15

*Keep in mind that these measurements are estimates only, and unwanted birds may take over the nest as they do in natural settings.

For More Information
- "Birdhouse Book" by Donald and Lillian Stokes. Little, Brown and Co. www.stokesbooks.com. $13.
- "The Ultimate Birdhouse Book" by Deborah Morgenthal. Sterling Publishing Co. www.cambiumbooks.com. $14.95.
- "The Best Birdhouses for Your Backyard" by Michael Berger. Popular Woodworking Books. www.popularwoodworking.com. $38.99 plus shipping.

Which
Should I buy?

CEDAR VS. PRESSURE-TREATED VS. COMPOSITE DECKING

We'll be building a 12 x 16-ft. deck this spring. We love the look of radius-edged cedar deck boards, but the guy at the lumber desk told us we'd be crazy to use anything but pressure-treated or composite material. Got any advice?

All three choices—5/4 x 6-in. radius-edged cedar, pressure-treated and composite decking—share similarities. They're all rot resistant to varying degrees, require 16-in. joist spacing for proper support, bleach out to a silvery gray, and can all be cut and installed using conventional tools and fasteners.

But alas, there's no perfect choice. All have tradeoffs. Figure out what characteristics are most important to you, then make your selection based on that.

If the natural look of wood is tops on your list, use cedar. The heartwood of the tree (the deeper-colored red part, not the white sap part) is rot resistant. Cedar doesn't readily absorb moisture—and, since moisture is what creates twisting and splitting, cedar decking tends to lie flat and straight. Most carpenters figure a lifespan of 15 to 20 years for cedar deck boards, but it can deteriorate faster when used for ground-level decks and for shaded decks that are slow to dry out.

To retain the color, you have to clean it and reseal it every year or two, and even then it's a losing battle. I've never seen a 10-year-old cedar deck that still had that warm, rich look of new wood. Cedar is also soft; when used for stairs or for decks where furniture gets dragged around a lot, the edges in particular can get beat up. Finally, the cost of the cedar for your 12 x 16-ft. deck (based on a price of $1 per linear foot for twenty-six 16-ft. deck boards) would be about $400.

If economy and longevity are your bag, go with pressure-treated wood. It's stainable, hard enough to resist abuse, and many brands carry a lifetime (though limited) warranty. But beware, not all treated woods are created equal. The standard treated decking at my local lumberyard costs 55¢ per linear foot, meaning your decking would only cost $225. But inexpensive treated wood is often full of moisture and will shrink unevenly and twist when it dries. One homeowner told me, "Yeah, my treated deck may last

forever—but it's going to look BAD forever too."

We suggest you buy "choice," "premium" or "select" treated boards. At 80¢ per linear foot, you'll pay $100 more, but the boards have fewer knots and straighter grain. And, since many of the higher-grade choices are kiln-dried both before and after pressure treatment, they have less tendency to warp and twist.

If near-zero maintenance is your goal, buy composite decking. Most is made from recycled plastic and wood chips or sawdust. It costs about $1.50 per linear foot, which amounts to about $625 for your 12 x 16-ft. deck. But once it's down, it won't rot, splinter or twist. The color change is even (though in shady, damp areas it can turn dark, like the example in the photo). You can even stain most types after four to six months. Since the material is defect free, you can use every inch. Maintenance involves spraying it off with a hose. Some people don't like the look of the stuff and it's cold on bare feet. But if you want to relax on your deck instead of work on it, bite the bullet and spend the extra cash.

These pairs show the contrast between new deck boards (right sides) and those that have been exposed to the elements for about two years (left sides). Each has tradeoffs in terms of cost, maintenance and appearance.

"PREMIUM" TREATED WOOD (80¢/LIN. FT.)

CEDAR ($1/LIN. FT.)

COMPOSITE ($1.50/LIN. FT.)

WHICH BAGGED CONCRETE?

The walkway up to my house is starting to deteriorate. One of the sections heaved and cracked over the winter. Does it matter what kind of concrete mix I use when I replace that section this spring?

Use "high early strength" concrete for your walkway. This type of concrete has a higher percentage of cement in the blend (or more finely ground cement in it), which gives it certain advantages.

1.High early strength concrete sets up faster and generates more heat than standard bagged concrete mix. This means you can tackle your project this spring, in temperatures as low as 35 degrees F, with less chance of setting and hardening problems.

2. You can walk on it in 10 to 12 hours instead of waiting several days as you would with standard concrete mix.

3. Though not all our experts concurred, high early strength concrete may stand up better to the salt you spread during the winter to melt ice in cold climates and help minimize scaling.

4. After a 28-day curing period, high early strength concrete can withstand 5,000 lbs. per square inch (psi) compared with the 3,500 psi of standard mix. This isn't a factor for sidewalks but would be if you were pouring a garage apron or making a driveway repair.

Other products? Fiber-reinforced concrete mix has thousands of little plastic fibers mixed in. This makes it more resistant to shrinkage cracks and to impact damage and chipping. For this reason, it's a good choice for stairs or landings with exposed edges.

Fast-setting concrete can harden in as little as 20 minutes and is a good choice for setting swing-set, lamp or mailbox posts, and for other projects where you need to work quickly. It's just as strong as or stronger than standard concrete mix, but it's expensive. The $3 to $4 more you pay per bag would make something like a large fence project appreciably more expensive.

CAN I BUY MORE DURABLE, BETTER LOOKING SOFFIT AND FASCIA MATERIAL?

My house is gray and I'd like to install aluminum soffit and fascia to match. Where the heck do I find colored material?

Aluminum soffits come in a lot of different colors, but you'll probably find only brown and white at most home centers and lumberyards. If you'd like a greater selection and usually higher-quality materials, look under "Siding Materials" in the Yellow Pages to find out where the pros shop. Most suppliers will sell to the public. Rollex, Alcoa and Reynolds are three manufacturers that offer top-notch products. Manufacturers of premium-grade aluminum use thicker metal with sturdier edges, so the soffits are more resistant to kinking and denting. Their color finishes are less likely to scratch or wear off and they hold color tones better over time. They also supply complementary colors in siding, corner pieces and window trim if you decide to go the next step and make your whole house maintenance free.

RENEW YOUR
WOOD FENCE

Make your fence look better and last longer in three easy steps.

by **Carl Hines**

When did your cedar fence lose its rich, warm glow? Who invited that discolored, shabby-looking impostor into the neighborhood? Don't worry—underneath that thin gray skin, the glow still remains. All you have to do is remove the surface layer of aged wood cells to expose a fresh layer of wood. With a power washer, it's as easy as washing your car. Then apply an exterior wood oil stain to preserve this new layer of wood. It'll prolong the life of your fence to boot.

Power washing makes the huge cleaning task easy

Power washers are aggressive. They'll strip the wood as well as clean off the dirt and grime, but you can also erode the wood too deeply and ruin it. The key is to use the right sprayer tip and technique. In any case, the power washer's spray will slightly raise and roughen the grain on smooth wood. That's actually good—it allows more sealer to soak in and improves the finish.

Wash

Repair

Stain

Power washers cost about $40 to rent for four hours. Rent one that operates at 1,500 or 2,000 psi and avoid more powerful 3,000 or 3,500 psi units. Be sure to get both 15- and 25-degree spray tips. Have the rental people demonstrate the washer's use. It's an easy machine to run.

SPRAYER TIP

To avoid damaging the pump, don't run the power washer without first filling the pump and hoses with water. To do this, attach both hoses (**Photo 1**), snap in a 25-degree tip, turn on the garden hose spigot and hold down the trigger on the wand until water squirts out. Release the wand trigger and start the engine. If it's hard to pull the start cord, pull the wand trigger to release the water pressure.

Clear the area along the fence by tying back plants that are growing alongside it. Wear water-repellent clothing—you will get wet from the spray.

Start spraying with the wand tip 18 in. from the wood surface. Move in closer as you swing the tip slowly along the length of the board (**Photo 2**). Keep the width of the fan spray aligned across the boards. The wood's color will brighten as the surface is stripped away. Watch closely and stop stripping when no more color change occurs. You don't have to remove too much surface to expose fresh wood, and continuing to spray won't improve the color.

It takes a little practice to arrive at the proper tip distance and speed of movement, but you'll catch on fast. It's better to make two or three passes than to risk gouging the surface trying to accomplish this job in one pass. As you gain experience, you can switch to a 15-degree tip. This tip cuts more aggressively and works faster than the 25-degree tip.

Simple repairs add years to the life of your fence

With the fence clean, it's time to fix or replace damaged boards, refasten loose boards and countersink any protruding nails. Use waterproof glue to repair any split and broken boards. Drive corrosion-resistant screws instead of nails to pull loose pieces tightly together. If a gate is sagging, straighten it with a turnbuckle support. Also coat the posts (**Photo 3**) where they emerge from the ground or concrete with a wood preservative. This is the area that rots first.

Stain makes the fence look brand new

To preserve the natural color of the wood, use an exterior semitransparent oil stain. It seals the wood while allowing the grain and color variations to show through. And its pigments add an overall color tone. Make sure the stain contains ultraviolet inhibitors, which will slow down bleaching by sunlight, and a mildewcide to slow fungal growth. Look for samples on cedar at the paint store, or bring in your own

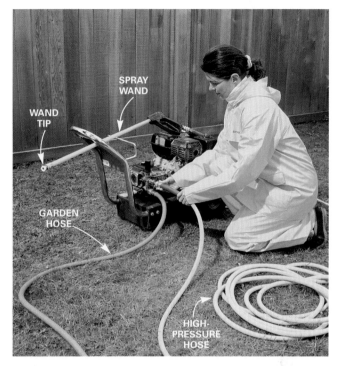

1 CONNECT a garden hose and the power washer hose to the machine. Snap a 25-degree tip onto the end of the wand. Turn on the water to the garden hose and pull the trigger on the spray wand until water squirts out. Now start up the power washer's engine.

2 HOLD the tip of the wand about 18 in. from the fence and move it the length of the boards. Pull the trigger and keep the sprayer tip moving to avoid gouging the wood. Use a variety of attack angles to strip inside corners.

piece of wood to test. A test sample is the best way to ensure a satisfactory result.

Before applying the stain, be certain the fence is dry. Allow at least 24 hours. If it's cool and humid, allow an additional 24 hours.

Use a paint roller with a "medium nap" cover (**Photo 4**) to apply a soaking coat to the wood. Let the wood absorb as much sealer as it can. Roll about a 3-ft. section of fence and then brush (**Photo 5**) the sealer into the wood. If the wood still appears dry, roll on additional sealer. Work the sealer into all recesses and corners. The roller applies the stain, but you

need the brush to work it well into the wood's surface. Coat detailed areas with a trim roller and smaller brush (**Photo 6**). Keep wet edges to prevent lap marks.

Most semitransparent oil stains are guaranteed to last two to five years. (Solid-color stains last longer but are more difficult to renew.) Fences usually face severe weathering, so expect the finish to last no more than three years. Recoat the fence within this time frame to keep it looking fresh. Before recoating, wash the fence with a garden hose sprayer and use a bristle brush on stubborn dirt and stains. Let the fence dry and stain it using the same method. ⌂

3 BRUSH a wood preservative into the posts around the base to help prevent rot at this vulnerable area.

4 ROLL into the dry wood a soaking coat of semitransparent stain. Coat about 3 ft. of fence, then proceed to the step shown in Photo 6.

5 BRUSH the stain (backbrush) into the wood grain and all corners and gaps. Brush out any runs or drips.

6 WORK the stain into tight areas with a trim roller and a 2-in. brush. One generous coat should be enough.

FROM JUNE 2002, P. 34

COVERED PATIO

You can easily double your time in the great outdoors with this beautiful pavillion. Just think—no more baking in the hot sun or getting rained out during your next barbecue. Don't be intimidated by the design. If you have basic power tools and a bit of remodeling experience, you have the moxie to pull off this project.

Project Facts:
Cost: About $3,500
Skill level: Intermediate to advanced
Time: 8 to 10 days

Special tools: Circular saw, jigsaw

CLASSIC PERGOLA

You can create this low-maintenance outdoor retreat with treated lumber, composite columns and simple framing techniques. The overhead lattice works just like a big shade tree to keep you cool and comfortable. And it can stand alone or be attached to your house.

Project Facts:
Cost: About $2,500
Skill level: Intermediate
Time: 5 to 7 days

Special tools: Post hole digger, jigsaw, circular saw

FROM JUNE 2002, P. 70

FROM SEPTEMBER 2002, P. 44

STORAGE SHED

Who says backyard storage has to look bad to be good? This 10 x 12-ft. shed has tons of storage space, requires minimal maintenance and is built to last. Big windows provide plenty of light and a special garage door creates a quaint look while providing easy access to all your stuff.

Project Facts:
Cost: $4,000–$5,000
Skill level: Intermediate
Time: 10 to 12 days

Special tools: Portable table saw, concrete finishing tools, roof jacks

To order photocopies of complete plans for the projects shown above, call 715-246-4344 or write to:
Copies, The Family Handyman, 511 Wisconsin Dr., New Richmond, WI 54017.
Many public libraries also carry back issues of The Family Handyman magazine.

ANY TRICKS TO REMOVING OLD, DRY GLAZING COMPOUND?

I've been digging out the old cracked and hardened putty from around my old window glass, but some of it is stuck and I'm gouging the wood frames. Is there a better way to remove it?

First soften the putty with heat. A heat gun works best. Set it on low and direct the heat back and forth along the putty, slowly warming it. Be careful. If you hold the heat in one place on or near the glass, the glass will crack and you'll have an even bigger job on your hands! As the glazing compound softens, scrape it out with a stiff putty knife.

WHAT'S THE BEST WAY TO REINFORCE CONCRETE?

I'm pouring a concrete patio slab and am wondering how I should reinforce the concrete. Is the new fiber-reinforced concrete an OK substitute for the welded wire mesh that's been around for years? I want to do the job right so my slab lasts.

The real question is whether or not you even need reinforcement. It really isn't required on a slab that just gets foot traffic. For slabs that get automobile traffic, reinforcing rod (often called rebar) is a better way to buttress the concrete than fiber or welded wire.

Concrete cracks will develop. The best you can hope for is to direct them with purposely placed "control" joints tooled into the slab. The joints should be at least one-fourth the thickness of the slab. For sidewalks, the control joints should be placed as far apart as the sidewalk is wide (for example, space joints 4 ft. apart for a 4-ft. wide sidewalk). For slabs, multiply the thickness by 24 to get a rough idea of the spacing. Then divide the slab equally within a range of 8 to 12 ft. (For example, a 4-in. thick slab times 24 in. equals 96-in., or 8-ft., spacing between joints.)

To prevent cracks in a typical patio, you just need to follow a few simple guidelines while ordering, pouring and curing the new slab. That's much more important than using any reinforcement.

For your best shot at a crack-free slab, follow these tips:

- If at all possible, pour concrete on a cool, windless, cloudy day.
- Order at least 3,500-psi concrete and don't ask the operator to add any extra water to the mix.
- Order "air-entrained" concrete, especially important because you live in a region that freezes.
- If you have poor-draining soil under the slab, remove 4 in. of earth and replace it with well-compacted gravel.
- After the slab hardens overnight, keep it moist for at least three days by occasionally running a misting-type sprinkler over it.

WHAT TYPE OF GLUE
SHOULD I USE FOR
EXTERIOR WORK?

*What's the best type of glue to use for out-
door projects? Specifically, I'm repairing my
deck rail post that has a piece broken off it.
Can I get away with yellow woodworking
glue or do I need something else?*

An exterior-grade yellow woodworking glue
may work fine, especially if it's protected by a
coat of paint, but it's not my first choice. I would
use a polyurethane-based glue; it's fully waterproof and bonds wood and other materials well.
It's not gap-filling, so be sure to get a good fit
and clamp it.

PLANS FOR PVC PATIO FURNITURE

*Are there plans available for making lawn furniture with
PVC piping and fittings? I'm particularly interested in a
pattern for a chaise lounge.*

A company called PTG (Patios To Go) Plastics sells supplies for
PVC furniture and has free plans available on its Web site.
Some of the plans are complex and require heat bending, but
even a beginner can handle others.

The PVC pipe offered at home centers for plumbing isn't
the best to use
for furniture
because it's
brittle, ugly and
can't stand up
to the sun.
Specially formu-
lated, furniture-
grade PVC fit-
tings and piping
are worth
investing in for
long-lasting fur-
niture. They're

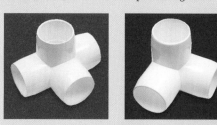

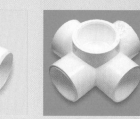

sleeker, colorfast (in white, beige and gray), impact resistant
and UV resistant, and they don't have any unsightly printing
or stampings.

You can visit PTG's Web site at www.patiostogo. com or
call (352) 243-3220. The company is located at 307 N. Hwy. 27,
Clermont, FL 34711.

SPLIT A NUT

*I need to sharpen my lawn mower blade, but the
nut holding it in place is rusted tight. Now what
do I do?*

A nut splitter will crack any no-go nut without damaging
the threads of the bolt or stem that it's screwed onto.
Just slip the ring over the nut and use a wrench to turn
the tooth into the nut until it breaks. Find it at Sears
(part No. 94772) and other tool stores. Cost: about $15.

DECK
LIGHTING

Low-voltage systems make deck lighting fast and safer. With the simple techniques we show, you can install it in a weekend.

by **Carl Hines**

If the night is calling you, pull up a lounge chair and enjoy it from your back yard. Your deck can be the setting for many relaxing evenings. The key is to add lighting that casts a nice glow over sitting areas, highlights features and illuminates steps and walks.

Low-voltage systems do this well and they're safe and easy to work with. Unlike with standard household voltage, the transformer that powers them simply plugs into a receptacle. In this article, we'll show you how to plan a system for your deck and how to install the transformer and fixtures.

Draw your deck and plan the light positions

There are several types of low-voltage fixtures, each designed for special uses. To decide on which light fixtures to use where, first draw a rough plan of your deck (**Fig. A**). On the plan, note the following key features: stairs, sitting and congregating areas, features such as railings and plantings and traffic paths. Also note the location of nearby receptacles that can be used to plug in your transformer.

Take your deck plan to a lighting showroom to select specific fixtures to light each feature. Ask a salesperson to help. Mark the selected fixtures on the plan. Note that a single fixture can sometimes handle several tasks. Next position the transformer on the drawing next to an existing receptacle. If no receptacle is nearby, you'll have to install one. (See "Add an Outlet," p. 158, and "How do I run underground cable," p. 188.) A receptacle controlled by an inside switch is the most convenient setup.

Draw lines to connect the fixtures to the transformer. Minimize the amount of wire you'll need by connecting multiple fixtures to a single circuit wire. (This may affect the size wire you need. See "Sizing Circuit Cables," p. 73.)

Next, add up the total wattage for all the fixtures you plan to install (see "Sizing the Transformer," p. 73). Select a transformer size that provides at least 25 percent excess capacity. Also decide what features you want with the transformer (**bottom photo**, p. 73).

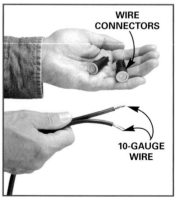

WATERPROOF WIRE CONNECTORS are ideal for exterior low-voltage wiring. Strip 3/4 in. of insulation from each wire end. Hold all the ends flush together and twist on a connector. You can get waterproof connectors at home centers, electrical supply houses and irrigation supply houses. If you need help finding a local dealer, call King Safety Products at (800) 633-0232, or visit its Web site at www.kingsafety.com.

WIRE CONNECTORS

10-GAUGE WIRE

Fig. A: Lighting plan

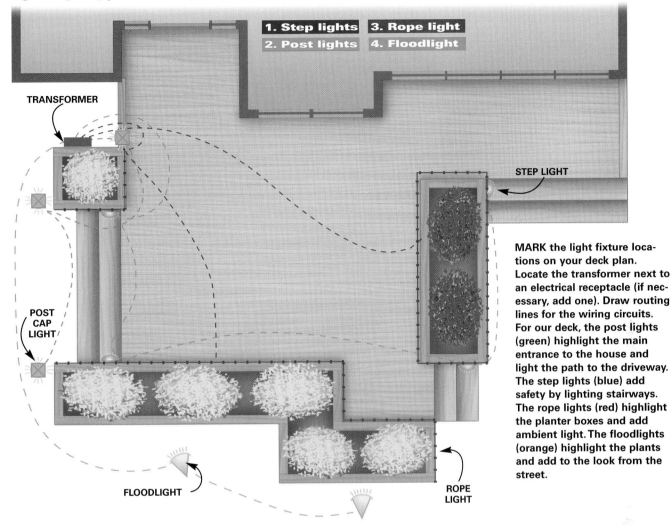

| 1. Step lights | 3. Rope light |
| 2. Post lights | 4. Floodlight |

TRANSFORMER

STEP LIGHT

POST CAP LIGHT

FLOODLIGHT

ROPE LIGHT

MARK the light fixture locations on your deck plan. Locate the transformer next to an electrical receptacle (if necessary, add one). Draw routing lines for the wiring circuits. For our deck, the post lights (green) highlight the main entrance to the house and light the path to the driveway. The step lights (blue) add safety by lighting stairways. The rope lights (red) highlight the planter boxes and add ambient light. The floodlights (orange) highlight the plants and add to the look from the street.

Running the wiring

Each circuit requires a cable that is made up of a pair of wires. Calculate the total length of cable needed and buy it as one piece. Plan on cutting specific lengths on the job.

Always try to route wires out of sight. You don't have to worry about safety. Low-voltage wiring isn't dangerous. Run the cables under the decking. If a cable must be visible, staple it into a corner or on the least conspicuous surface.

Use insulated staples to fasten the cables to wood members at 2-ft. intervals. The low-voltage wire and the waterproof wire connectors must be buried 6 in. deep into the ground.

Sizing the transformer
Add the wattage of each fixture to determine the total load. Our deck:

4 step lights x 12 watts	48 watts
3 post lights x 20 watts	60 watts
60 ft. of rope light	
x 5.45 watts per foot	327 watts
2 floodlights x 20 watts	40 watts
Total	**475 watts**
Add 25 percent excess:	
475 x 1.25	**594 watts**

Transformer size: at least 594 watts

Sizing circuit cables
(Allows for connecting fixtures with a maximum total of 150 watts)

LENGTH OF CABLE	WIRE SIZE
0 to 50 ft.	Use 12-gauge
50 to 100 ft.	Use 10-gauge
100-plus ft.	Use 8-gauge

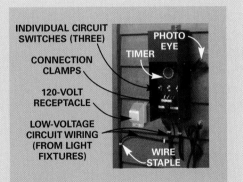

INDIVIDUAL CIRCUIT SWITCHES (THREE)

PHOTO EYE

TIMER

CONNECTION CLAMPS

120-VOLT RECEPTACLE

LOW-VOLTAGE CIRCUIT WIRING (FROM LIGHT FIXTURES)

WIRE STAPLE

The power center
Optional features:
- Timer switch, which automatically turns the lights on and off at preset times.
- Photo eye, which turns the lights on at dusk and off at dawn.
- Individually switched circuits, which allow different groups of lights (scenes) to be independently controlled.

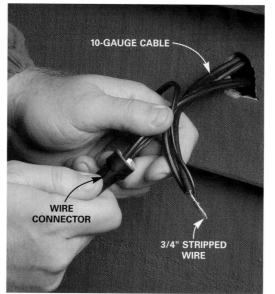

10-GAUGE CABLE

WIRE CONNECTOR

3/4" STRIPPED WIRE

1 BORE a 1-1/2 in. hole from the front side and pull a loop of the cable through. Cut the cable and rejoin the ends along with the light fixture leads with waterproof wire connectors.

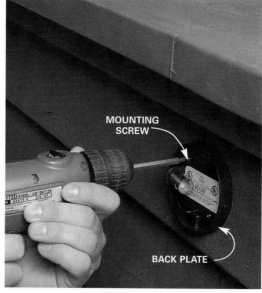

MOUNTING SCREW

BACK PLATE

2 PUSH the wires back through the hole and screw the back plate to the planter siding.

Stair and post lighting

Most **step lights** have to be connected through the back. Drill a hole through the planter wall behind the fixture and feed the wires through (**Photo 1**). Connect the wires with waterproof wire connectors and push the wires back into the hole. Fasten the back plate to the siding (**Photo 2**) and then install the cover (**Photo 3**).

The wires for the **post cap lights** come from below. Again, try to find a hidden route. In our case, we drilled partially through the length of the existing rail post (**Photos 4 – 6**). After feeding the wire through the rail post, we drilled through the center of an additional post section (**Photo 4**) and screwed it to the top rail (**Photo 7**).

3 INSTALL the cover plate and tighten the set screws. Staple the wires somewhere on the backside to anchor them.

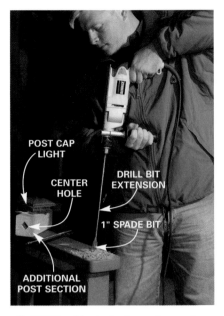

4 BORE a 1-in. hole down the center of the rail post. Drill deep enough to get below the second horizontal rail.

5 DRILL a 1/2-in. hole from below the rail. Angle up to intercept the 1-in. hole bored in Photo 4.

6 FEED a heavy wire or electrician's fish tape through the holes in the post. Tape the circuit cable to the wire and pull it back through the holes. Connect the cable to the post cap light's feed wires with twist connectors.

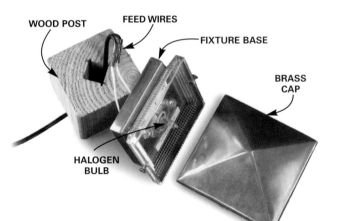

New-post technique

For the new posts, we first cut them in half lengthwise with a circular saw, then cut V-shaped grooves lengthwise in each half for the wire. We then reglued the halves together with ure-thane glue. You can use a tablesaw, if available, to cut the posts in half and to cut the grooves. Feed the circuit wires through the post before connecting the fixture (**Photo 8**). Dig a hole 18 to 24 in. deep with a posthole digger to set the post. Adjust the length of the post to the hole's depth.

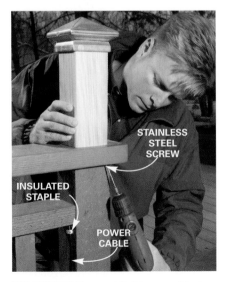

7 SCREW the post light assembly to the rail. Use four corrosion-resistant wood screws, one near each corner.

8 FEED the circuit wires through the post, connect them to the fixture wires with the wire connectors, and push the wire back into the post. Screw the post light to the top of the post, and drop the post into the hole. Par-tially fill the hole with dirt, plumb the post with a carpenter's level and tamp the dirt around the post. Continue add-ing dirt, checking for plumb and tamp-ing until the hole is completely filled. Cover the circuit wires with 6 in. of dirt.

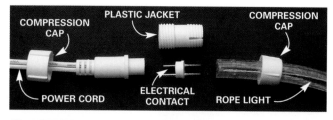

COMPRESSION CAP — PLASTIC JACKET — COMPRESSION CAP — POWER CORD — ELECTRICAL CONTACT — ROPE LIGHT

9 CONNECT the power cord to the end of the rope light by inserting the contact pins with pliers. Then assemble the rest of the connector.

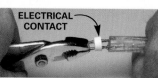

ELECTRICAL CONTACT

Rope lighting

Rope lighting is unique. It's a flexible, solid plastic rod with a series of tiny bulbs embedded in it. Calculate the total length needed, add 10 percent and buy one long piece (it's available in 250-ft. rolls) and cut it on the job.

Attach a power connector to one end of the rope lighting (Photo 9). The cord on the power connector then attaches to the circuit wire with twist connectors. You can connect multiple pieces of rope light with straight and 90-degree connectors, but it's quite flexible and we were able to bend it around 90-degree corners without the 90-degree connector.

While you can install the rope with clips that mount every foot or so, the best system is a plastic rope light track. Cut the track to length and then mount it with nails or screws. We found that predrilling the back of the track and fastening with 3/4-in. corrosion-resistant screws worked best (Photo 10).

Round up a helper and stretch the rope light along the installed track, then cut it to length (Photo 11) at one of the cutting marks. Start with the end with the connected power cord and push it into the track, working to the other end (Photo 12).

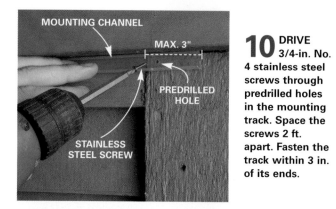

MOUNTING CHANNEL — MAX. 3" — PREDRILLED HOLE — STAINLESS STEEL SCREW

10 DRIVE 3/4-in. No. 4 stainless steel screws through predrilled holes in the mounting track. Space the screws 2 ft. apart. Fasten the track within 3 in. of its ends.

Connecting the floodlights

Floodlights provide a wash that highlights features. Be careful not to direct the light into people's eyes when they're on the deck. Some floodlights come with a hood to reduce glare. A ground stake attached to the bottom of the fixture makes installation a snap (Photo 13). Bury the wire 6 in. deep.

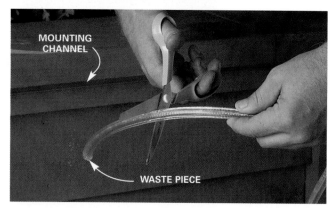

MOUNTING CHANNEL — WASTE PIECE

11 CUT the rope light to length with a scissors at a marked cutting point; these are spaced every 6 in.

10-GAUGE POWER WIRE — WATERPROOF WIRE CONNECTOR

13 INSTALL the floodlight by pushing the stake into the ground. Cover the wire and waterproof connectors with 6 in. of dirt.

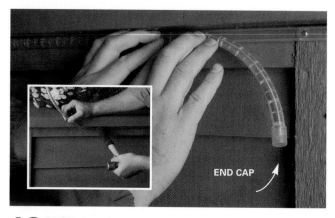

END CAP

12 PUSH the rope light into the channel. A hammer handle or a piece of wood works well as a push tool and is easier on the fingers. Slide on an end cap.

Buyer's Guide

Here is one manufacturer of high-quality 12-volt rope light. Call if you need help finding a local dealer. WAC: (800) 526-2588. www.waclighting.com. Catalog available on-line.

ALIGN A PATIO SCREEN DOOR

There you are, balancing a tray full of burgers fresh from the grill, struggling to open the sticking patio screen door. Badly aligned rollers cause the screen door to bind and stick when it's opened or closed. Eventually this stresses the corner joints of the door, and if they open or loosen up, the door is shot. But you can adjust the door to run smoothly in minutes with just a screwdriver.

You'll find two adjustment screws at the bottom of the door, one at each end, that lift and lower separate rollers. (Inspect the rollers for damage. Get new ones at home centers or by calling Blaine Window Hardware at 800-678-1919.) First lower the door to the track (**Photo 1**), then raise it evenly (**Photo 2**).

Still runs rough? Clean the track. Chances are, leaves, grit or other debris is clogging it.

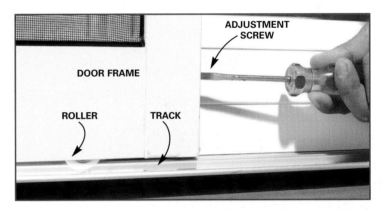

1 TURN the adjustment screws counterclockwise and lower the door frame until it rests on the track.

2 RAISE one roller until it lifts the door off the track approximately 1/4 in. Slowly raise the second roller on the other end until the gap between the bottom of the door and the track is even. Make sure there's a gap between the top of the screen frame and the upper track as well.

HANDS-FREE SCREEN DOOR CLOSER

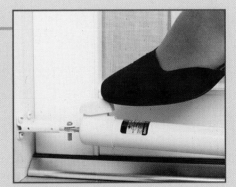

No more wrestling with that screen door or sliding that goofy little washer along the closer arm to hold it open. With a touch of a finger (or foot or elbow or cane) the Touch N Hold keeps the door wide open while you carry in groceries, babies and drywall. It's a sturdy little workhorse, available in heavy- and medium-duty models and carrying a lifetime warranty. It will even self-close in high winds to protect your door from damage.

To install it, you simply pop out the two pins that hold your old closer, insert the Touch N Hold between the existing brackets and reinsert the pins. It's available in seven colors and ranges in price from $13 to $19 at home centers and hardware stores. Find a dealer near you on the Web site. National Manufacturing, One First Ave., Sterling, IL 61081; (815) 625-1320. www.natman.com

STRONGER
DECKS

Build a deck the correct way right from the start and you can relax on it for 20 years or more!

by **The Editors of Family Handyman**

Whenever we travel around the country, we make it a point to talk to carpenters, electricians, masons and other construction pros to learn their favorite techniques. Sometimes their methods differ from ours, but they've all been proved by the test of time. Here we've collected the best tips from carpenters who build decks to last. Remember, decks take more abuse than almost any other part of your home. Foot traffic, rain, sun, snow and dragged furniture all take their toll. Build it right, right from the start.

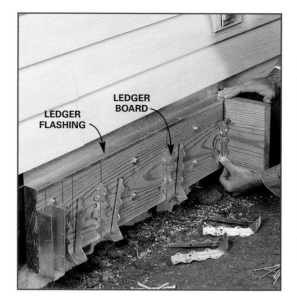

LEDGER FLASHING

LEDGER BOARD

INSTALL LEDGER FLASHING along the house to keep water from soaking into the siding and framing and causing rot. Skip this step and you'll soon face premature deck failure and expensive repair bills on the house itself. The bent metal flange ($2 per 10-ft. strip at home centers and lumberyards) routes water to the outside of the ledger, where it drips away or dries. It's a few bucks well spent.

Splice decking with a single seam

The typical way to handle a deck that is wider than the deck boards is to randomly butt the ends together and split them over a deck joist. Cutting and fitting all these joints takes a lot of time and forces you to butt two boards tightly together to share the 1-1/2 in. thickness of a floor joist. Nailing close to the ends makes wood split and rot prematurely because moisture gets into the splice and doesn't dry out for long periods of time.

A more elegant, longer-lasting way is to create a single seam with a dogeared length of decking perpendicular to the deck itself. Then toe-nail in another floor joist for nailing the ends of the next section. Having a full 1-1/2 in. of joist for nailing each deck board allows for a space between the end of the decking board and the splice board for drying, and helps keep nails away from the splitting zone.

CUT notches in a piece of decking so that it protrudes above the joists 1-1/4 in. (flush with the top of the decking), away from the deck edge and even with the decking overhang.

NAIL the notched piece to the side of the joist. Nail a second joist against it and toe-nail the joist into the rims. Nail the decking, leaving a gap between the splice board and the end of the decking.

DECK JOISTS

JOIST HANGERS

BOLTS

SEMI-TRANSPARENT STAIN

CLEANED DECKING

INCREASE JOIST DEPTH one size above the minimum (for example, 2x10 instead of 2x8). Decks built to the minimum requirements often feel like a trampoline. Wider joists are stronger and stiffer, so they'll eliminate that bounce. This will add $50 to $100 to your lumber costs, but the solid feel underfoot is worth it.

BOLT RAILING POSTS to the frame with 3/8-in. minimum-size carriage or hex bolts with nuts and washers. Don't rely on deck screws or nails. In addition, you can retighten the bolts later if the post or framing lumber shrinks.

APPLY A DECK SEALER, water repellent or semi-transparent stain every year or two to keep deck boards and railings from cracking, splitting and warping. Keep in mind that all unstained wood soon weathers to a silvery gray. Use cleaning and brightening products only if you prefer the freshly milled look.

DRIVE SCREWS to keep your deck boards solidly fastened. Nails will pop up from periodic wood expansion and contraction. Screws won't. The downside? Screws take about twice as long to drive and cost more.

Buy special coated deck screws (5¢ each) for most applications. Buy stainless steel deck screws (10¢ each) for highly corrosive environments such as you'd find around saltwater. If you can find them, buy self-tapping deck screws so you don't have to predrill board ends.

STAINLESS STEEL DECK SCREWS

SELF-TAPPING POINT

Tip

If the deck boards you're installing are wet, drive the screws slightly below the surface so the heads won't stick up when the boards dry out.

COATED DECK SCREWS

More Tips for Durability

■ Make sure overhanging roofs have **gutters** so water from the roof doesn't dump down on the deck.

■ **Clean leaves** and other debris from between deck boards annually to prevent rot.

■ When using nails, choose **double-dipped** galvanized nails rather than other types of galvanized nails for greatest durability. Ask for them at your local lumberyard. (One source is Maze Nails, 800-435-5949, www.mazenails.com.)

■ Consider **composite decking** (a combination of wood fiber and plastic) in damp climates, because it won't rot, warp or split.

■ **Slope** entire deck away from the house slightly (1/8 in. per foot) to help drain water away. ⌂

Stained with guilt

My father and I decided it was time to stain the 7-ft. high fence in my back yard. To speed up the job, we used a sprayer and hit the tough areas with a brush. Well, all went fine until the guy next door came over steaming mad. All over his car were specks that seemed to match the color of the fence. Red-faced with embarrassment, we realized the wind had carried our stain over and through the fence, depositing tiny droplets all over his car. The good news is, we didn't have to pay for a new paint job—a local body shop removed the damage for a reasonable $150!

The tar 'pits'

Last winter, my roof developed some leaks. As soon as the snow melted, I went up to pinpoint the problem. The section of roof in question had damaged roll roofing, so I decided to get a bucket of roofing tar and fix it. The cool, 50-degree day was great for working but the tar seemed a bit too stiff to spread thinly. I worked the tar in along the edge of the roof over the leak. All was fine until we got our first day of 80-degree heat. My dog came into the house with tar all over his feet. I went out to investigate and saw melted tar dripping all over the siding and windows.

Grand Slam

The wind can really howl around our house. I've often come home to see the front storm door flapping in the wind and the hydraulic closer broken. Tired of making repairs to this system, I'd given up hope until a co-worker suggested what sounded like a brilliant solution. He suggested mounting a heavy-duty spring from the jamb to the door. I went to the hardware store, and, thinking about how strong the wind blows, I grabbed a beefy-looking spring and some strong eyebolts and mounted them to the door. Now for the test and the moment of truth. I opened the door all the way and let go. The door slammed so hard the glass shattered all over the front steps. I'm now considering less "heavy duty" measures.

A watchful eye

Last November we decided to have a new concrete sidewalk and driveway poured. We live on a busy street right near a school, and my husband was determined to keep the schoolkids from writing their initials in the fresh cement. Wearing a winter coat and a blanket to ward off the fall chill, he sat on the front lawn and kept watch over the cement. He even went to the trouble of barricading the area with wire and "Caution" tape. After several hours, he set an old garbage can with a "Keep Off" sign in it at the end of the driveway so no one would mistakenly drive on it.

After two days, his mission seemed to be a success. My husband was pleased that his watchful eye had prevented any sabotage—that is, until he lifted the garbage can off the end of the driveway. There, plain as day, was a 3-ft. dia. permanent rust ring that seeped deeply into the new driveway. The prospect of a few initials doesn't seem so bad now.

A/C for the road

Many years ago in our first home, my husband decided to install a new window air conditioner. The window was a couple of inches too small, so he framed a new opening below it for the air conditioner. The installation looked great! A while later, I had to drive to the store. I got in the car and backed down the driveway (which is right next to the house). All of a sudden, I heard this loud noise, looked out the passenger window and saw a gaping hole in the side of the house. I'd knocked the air conditioner right out of the wall. I've yet to live this one down!

CIRCULAR
PATIO

Build a great-looking patio, without cutting a single paver.

by Jeff Timm

There may be circles, angles and curves everywhere, but if you think this patio is difficult to build, you're wrong. In fact, this is as simple as landscape construction gets. The free-floating circular patio is built from specially designed pavers that fit together like a simple puzzle.

While the step-by-step process is straightforward, this project entails a lot of hard work. You'll never have to lift more than 60 lbs. at a time, but you'll be handling literally tons of material. So you could probably skip your weight training while you're building it!

We'll show you everything you need to know to install this circular patio. Once you complete the "groundwork," the pavers go in surprisingly quickly. Allow at least two long, sweaty weekends of labor, one for the prep work and one for laying the pavers. When you're finished, you'll have the satisfaction of having an attractive patio that'll last for generations.

Project Facts: (main patio only)
Cost: About $600 for all the patio materials and rental equipment
Time: 2 weekends (at least!)
Skills: Leveling and physical fitness
Special Tools: Bobcat and plate compactor (rented), hand tamper

NOTE: This patio was built in conjunction with the curved retaining wall. For a copy of the complete story, see p. 220.

GETTING STARTED: Design your space and estimate the material

Use garden hoses to represent the patio and wall, and move them around until you find a design and size you like. Use marking paint to establish the outlines (**Photo 1**).

To order the patio pavers, just provide your supplier with the diameter; they'll put together a package containing the right quantity of each stone shape. At first glance it might look complicated, but the manufacturer has directions telling how many of each shape to put in each ring. Ask for the paver layout plan when you order; it's not packaged with the pavers. We selected a "cobble" style paver we ordered through a local landscape supply company. Check your Yellow Pages or the Buyer's Guide on p. 87 for more information..

Tools (and the perfect excuse to rent a Bobcat)

You'll need several heavy-duty tools to do the job right. You'll have to rent a plate compactor (**Photo 4**). This 200-lb. beast is the secret of a long-lasting patio. Rent it for $60 a day and move it around with a dolly. You'll need it for two days: one day to pack the gravel footing for the retaining wall and a second day for the patio.

For excavating, you've got two choices: a good shovel and strong back, or a skid-steer loader (commonly called a Bobcat; see **Photo 2**). If you're just doing the patio, dig it by hand. But for cutting into a hill like we did, a skid-steer is the only way to go. If you're a tool junkie, you can rent one. Bear in mind, though—by the time you're done hauling it, learning how to operate it, using it and replacing the neighbor's hedge you destroyed, you can probably get the job done cheaper and faster by hiring a contractor (about $60 an hour). A skid-steer loader will rut your lawn, so plan on filling in the path with topsoil and grass seed when you're done.

To get rid of the excavated soil, you can rent a trash container, ask the contractor to haul it away, fill in a low spot or persuade a neighbor to take it. If you rent a trash container, keep it until you're finished so you can throw in any extra gravel or sand.

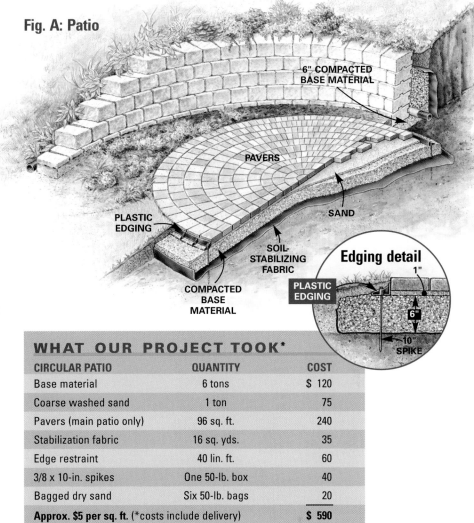

Fig. A: Patio

6" COMPACTED BASE MATERIAL

PAVERS

PLASTIC EDGING

SAND

SOIL-STABILIZING FABRIC

COMPACTED BASE MATERIAL

Edging detail

1"

PLASTIC EDGING

6"

10" SPIKE

WHAT OUR PROJECT TOOK*

CIRCULAR PATIO	QUANTITY	COST
Base material	6 tons	$ 120
Coarse washed sand	1 ton	75
Pavers (main patio only)	96 sq. ft.	240
Stabilization fabric	16 sq. yds.	35
Edge restraint	40 lin. ft.	60
3/8 x 10-in. spikes	One 50-lb. box	40
Bagged dry sand	Six 50-lb. bags	20
Approx. $5 per sq. ft. (*costs include delivery)		**$ 590**

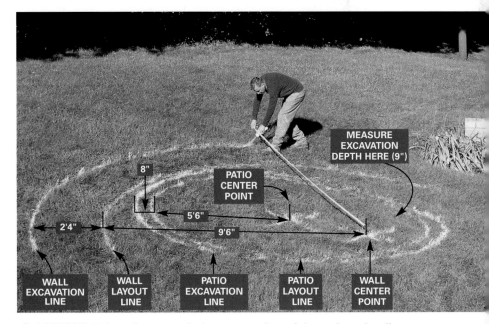

8"

PATIO CENTER POINT

MEASURE EXCAVATION DEPTH HERE (9")

5'6"

2'4"

9'6"

WALL EXCAVATION LINE

WALL LAYOUT LINE

PATIO EXCAVATION LINE

PATIO LAYOUT LINE

WALL CENTER POINT

1 POSITION 10-in. spikes to mark the center points of the patio and wall. Swing a tape measure hooked on the spikes and spray-paint arcs to mark the actual face of the wall and edge of the patio. Paint a second set of arcs to indicate outer excavation lines, adding 2 ft. 4 in. to the wall radius and 8 in. to the patio radius.

2 DIG into the hill to create a flat area for the patio and wall. Dig 9 in. below the sod, using a point 3 ft. in from the lowest edge of the patio as a reference point. Hire or rent a skidsteer loader to remove the bulk of the material. Clean up the perimeter and flatten the bottom with a shovel.

3 CHECK your patio area using a straight 10-ft. 2x4 and 4-ft. level. It should have a slight slope (about 1/4 in. every 4 ft.) away from the wall and be level side to side. Use a plate compactor to compact any soil you've added or loosened.

4 RESET a spike at the center point of the patio and spray an arc 8 in. larger than the radius of the patio. Spread two 2-in. layers of base material over the stabilization fabric, compacting each layer with the plate compactor. Build up the perimeter with soil to keep the base material from spreading outward as you compact.

Rent or buy (about $25) a hand tamper for compacting the gravel behind the wall, and get a sturdy contractor's wheelbarrow for moving those 300-lb. loads of gravel.

Dig in

Spray-paint the "footprints" of your wall and patio (**Photo 1**), dig just inside the outer layout lines and then reestablish the center points of your arcs after excavation. Dig about 9 in. below the patio's center point to provide room for the gravel, sand and pavers. **Photo 1** shows you where to measure your depth. Because of the sloping hill, the front edge of the patio will be a little high compared with the lawn. (You won't dig out as much soil here.) Add soil when you're done to blend the elevations. The bottom of the excavation has to be flat and slightly sloping (**Photo 3**). Be sure you compact any loose soil. If you don't, it will settle over time and the patio will end up with a dip.

PATIO CONSTRUCTION: Laying the base

After excavating, we laid a special woven "ground stabilization fabric" over the patio area (**Photo 4**). It's cut off a roll from the landscape supplier and sells for less than $2 per square yard (a total of $32 for our patio). You don't need it in stable sandy or gravelly soils, but in other soils it's cheap insurance for a flat patio for years to come.

Reestablish the patio's center point. Keep the spike in until you start laying the pavers; it'll mark the starting point for the paver circle. Mark out the patio perimeter plus an extra 8 in. with marking paint. Add and compact two layers of base material in 2-in. layers (**Photo 4**). Position and slope the screed pipes so the patio will drain water away from the wall (**Photos 5 and 6**). The third layer should be no more than 3 in. below the sod at any point. A few inches higher than the sod is better. Add more base material to raise the entire patio if necessary. Slide the 2x4 side to side along the pipes to distribute the base material and create a flat surface. Compact this final layer four times, changing direction each time—north to south, then east to west (**inset, Photo 6**).

Lay the sand bed

Leave enough time—at least one half day—to set the sand bed and lay the pavers. Leave your meticulously screeded sand overnight and the neighbor's cat, a stray dog and a rain shower are guaranteed to disrupt your hard work.

Lay the pipes on the compacted base (the pipe diameter provides for 1 in. of sand). If you spot gaps larger than 1/2 in. anywhere under the pipe, add base material in the depression and compact. Pour a few wheelbarrows of coarse washed sand between the pipes, spread it out with a shovel, and screed it the same way you did the base (**Photo 6**). Work your way out from the wall so you have room to work. You won't compact the sand layer until after the pavers are laid.

Planning, paperwork and materials

We carved our patio into a gradual hill, using the retaining wall to hold back the slope. The main wall is a 30-ft. long arc, 30 in. high. The patio is 11 ft. in diameter. This combination creates a cozy area for a couple to enjoy a cup of coffee or read a book and creates a nice space for flowerbeds and plantings. If you plan to entertain, or want room for the kids to cruise around with the Big Wheel, you can easily stretch the patio's diameter to 16 ft. without complicating the job. Increase the wall diameter accordingly.

Most communities don't require a building permit for patios or for retaining walls under 4 ft. high. They can usually be placed anywhere on your property, which makes them a great alternative to a deck in small yards. But keep them out of easements, which are bands of property left open for drainage or for access to buried utilities. Your local building or planning department can tell you, or your survey will show you, if there are any on your property. Review your plans with them to be safe. Also call the local utilities and have them mark their underground lines, even if you don't think there are any in the area. The service is free and it could save you from an injury or from having to dig up your patio later.

Don't locate a patio beneath a mature tree. Even though the tree makes for a nice shady spot and nothing will grow under it anyway, the patio can damage the roots (and vice versa). Locate it outside the tree's canopy; anything closer, consult a tree specialist.

Our expenses came to about half what a contractor would charge. The material costs listed on p. 50 may vary substantially depending on your location and delivery costs.

We suggest buying all your materials from a landscape supplier (see "Landscape Materials" in the Yellow Pages) and having them delivered. A landscape supplier will have a better selection than a home center and you can see the different styles of pavers and retaining wall block firsthand at the displays in their yard. Plus they can provide expert advice for any questions you might have.

Fig. B: Bird's-eye view of completed project

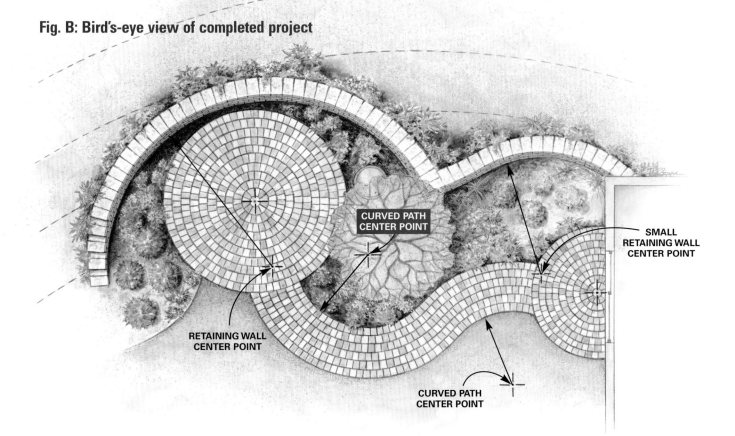

CURVED PATH CENTER POINT

SMALL RETAINING WALL CENTER POINT

RETAINING WALL CENTER POINT

CURVED PATH CENTER POINT

Selecting patio pavers

Circular patio systems are available in a wide range of colors, mostly earth tones. We chose a color called "autumn blend," which has red, brown and tan tones. The blend gives more depth and character than a single color. A blend will also help disguise weathering. On small areas, the manufacturer will recommend a two-color blend over a three-color because one pallet might not represent the entire range of color. We went against that advice with the understanding that our order could be heavy on one color—but we loved the "depth" of our finished patio. Use brochures to narrow your color choices.

Bring home four or five pavers representing the full color range from your selection. Set them in the future patio area to be sure you're satisfied with the color before you place your order. Returning 3 tons of pavers isn't an economical proposition. Manufacturers vary by region. They'll offer slightly different style and color variations.

5 SET two 1-in. steel pipes about 6 ft. apart on top of the compacted base material. Orient them in the direction of drainage, away from the wall. Slip base material under the pipe until a 4-ft. level with a 3/4-in. block slipped under the low side reads level. Set the other pipe level and parallel to the first.

6 SHUFFLE a 10-ft. 2x4 side to side along the pipes as you level the final layer of base material and pull it away from the wall. Fill in any depressions and remove any high spots as you work. Remove the pipes and fill the troughs with gravel. Compact this last layer (inset), making certain the soil is built up on the sides and the base material is perfectly flat.

7 PLACE the pipes in the same location as shown in Photo 5. No leveling should be needed, since the slope is established from the gravel layer. Repeat the procedure shown in Photo 6, using sand instead of base material. Remove the pipes, fill the troughs with sand and trowel the area smooth. Fill in your footprints as you back out. Remove the center spike.

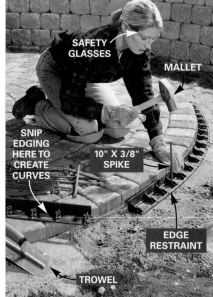

8 POSITION the center pavers (see opposite page), then install the outer rings using the manufacturer's plan. Stagger the joints. Disturb the sand as little as possible. Stand on the pavers once you have a few rings placed and have a helper pass you the next half-dozen rings. Add sand and trowel out the footprints when you reach them. Work out to the final size.

9 PULL the sand away from the perimeter of the patio with a steel trowel until you reach the base material. Snip the backside of the edging with garden pruners to bend it to the arc of the patio. Hold the edge restraint tight to the pavers, then drive 10-in. long, 3/8-in. spikes every foot through holes in the edging. Connect the edging, leaving no gaps between the pieces.

10 RUN the plate compactor on top of the pavers. Pass over the patio four times, switching direction after each pass. Compact around the outer edge after each pass.

Laying the pavers—the fun part

Laying the pavers (Photo 8) is the easiest and most rewarding part of the project. And as you can see from the photos on the right, they go down fast. The manufacturer's chart tells you how many of each of the five shapes to put into each ring. Alternate the shapes if a ring has more than one paver shape.

Tip

Wear kneepads to protect your knees from hard paver edges.

Since you start in the center and work out, you'll have to disrupt that flat sand layer with a few footprints. Minimize the damage by staying in the same footprints, then trowel them flat when the paver rings get close. After you've laid three or four rings, stand on the pavers and have a helper pass you the next pavers. Don't step on the very edge or you'll create a dip. Once you get the first five rings in, it's pretty methodical and will go quickly.

If you end up with a gap where a ring comes together, distribute it by spacing several bricks up to 1/8 in. apart. To get an even color mix throughout the patio, draw the pavers from more than one pallet. If you're just using one pallet, you can blend the colors well by drawing from opposite sides; one half is usually darker than the other.

The final details

To contain the pavers and sand, install a paver edging around the perimeter (Photo 9). We used Snap-Edge ($1.50 per foot; see Buyer's Guide, below). It costs a little more, but it installs easier and offers better support than less expensive alternatives. Before installing the edging, be sure to scrape the sand away to expose the base material. Conceal the edge with soil or mulch when you're finished.

Run the compactor over the patio to set the pavers, compact the sand and vibrate sand up into the joints, locking the pavers together (Photo 10). The steel plate won't hurt the pavers, but it will make your ears ring. Wear hearing protection. (If a paver does break or chip during this step, gently wiggle it out with a pair of flat screwdrivers and replace it.) Spread coarse, dry sand over the patio to fill the joints and repeat the compacting. *The sand has to be thoroughly dry to jiggle into the joints.* Don't try to save money on a tamper rental by skipping this step. The last tamping will vibrate the sand into the joints, locking all the bricks together.

No maintenance!

This type of patio and wall requires little to no maintenance. Don't let dirt build up on them or you'll provide a home for weeds, and be sure to wash the patio down periodically. Sealers are available for enhancing the paver color, but once you apply them, you need to repeat the process every few years. I prefer to skip the sealer. ⌂

Buyer's Guide

■ **RETAINING WALL BLOCK AND PAVERS**

Anchor Block Co., 8201 Brooklyn Blvd., Brooklyn Park, MN 55445; (763) 425-9779. www.anchorblock.com

Visit the Interlocking Concrete Pavement institute web site at www.icpi.org to find a paver supplier near you.

■ **EDGING**

Snap-Edge Corp., 3925 Stern Ave., St. Charles, IL 60174. (800) 932-3343. www.snapedgeusa.com

Pave Tech Inc., P.O. Box 576, Prior Lake, MN 55372; (800) 728-3832. www.pavetech.com

CENTER PAVERS

1:30 p.m.

TAPERED PAVERS

1:45 p.m.

FILL IN FOOTPRINT

1:55 p.m.

2:20 p.m.

2:45 p.m.

3:00 p.m.

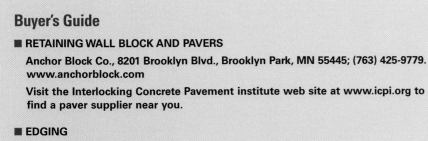

THE RIGHT WAY TO
INSTALL WINDOWS

You can spend as much as you want on good windows, but if you don't install them right, you're asking for trouble.

by **Jeff Gorton**

Leaks, rot and moisture are high on everyone's list of annoying and destructive problems when it comes to their windows.

Wind-driven rain sneaks through cracks and gaps and runs down the wall behind the siding until it hits a window or door opening. Properly installed and flashed windows simply divert the water around and out, where it exits harmlessly to the outdoors. Traditional wood-trimmed windows combined with a metal drip cap and building paper–covered walls usually have held up well. But the advent of modern vinyl and aluminum windows, attached to the building with flimsy nailing fins and installed by untrained workers, has led to a rash of problems and prompted manufacturers and installers to come up with tougher installation methods.

The failed window (opposite page, left side) was simply nailed into the opening and covered with siding, a recipe for disaster. The one on the right is carefully flashed to prevent water from leaking in. Modern materials, like the 4-in. wide self-sticking window flashing material, make it easy to do a top-notch job. The key is to lap each layer of material over the one below, in a shingle-like fashion, so that water will be shed to the outside. Use caulk only as an extra precaution and to seal out drafts, not as a primary defense against leaks.

When you buy windows, ask for complete installation instructions and follow them to the letter, or your warranty will be void. Spend a few extra minutes installing your window the right way and you could save thousands of dollars in repair bills later. ⌂

ANSWERS TO 2 BIG QUESTIONS ABOUT WINDOWS

How do I compare windows to see which are the most energy-efficient?

Many window manufacturers voluntarily have their windows tested and then apply a sticker stating its overall efficiency (see photo at left). This system, using U-value instead of R-value, was developed by the National Fenestration Rating Council ("fenestration" is a fancy word for window applications). The U-value takes into account the infiltration and conduction for the entire window: the glass, the wood around the glass (sash), the frame (the portion fastened to your walls), and the weatherstripping and any sealing gaskets. The lower the rating

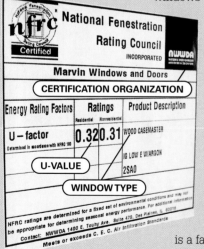

number, the better the thermal performance and the less you'll spend on utility bills.

Lower U-values are also achieved by using a thermal break, such as wood, between the interior and the exterior of the window. The thermal break acts as a road block for conduction. Note: An all-aluminum window without thermal breaks isn't the best choice. The aluminum runs continuously from the outside to the inside, so if there's frost on the outside of the window sash, you can bet it'll show up on the inside as well.

Along with a thermal break, good weatherstripping and an efficient glass panel (double or triple pane) will really help lower U-values for better overall window performance and energy efficiency.

Is a warranty important?

You bet it is! Even though new windows are manufactured to exacting standards, window parts can fail. For your protection, a comprehensive warranty can save repair dollars down the road. But warranties vary—read the fine print, even of the name brands. The coverage should include weatherstrip failure, bad gaskets, broken glass, loose joints and any mechanical defects.

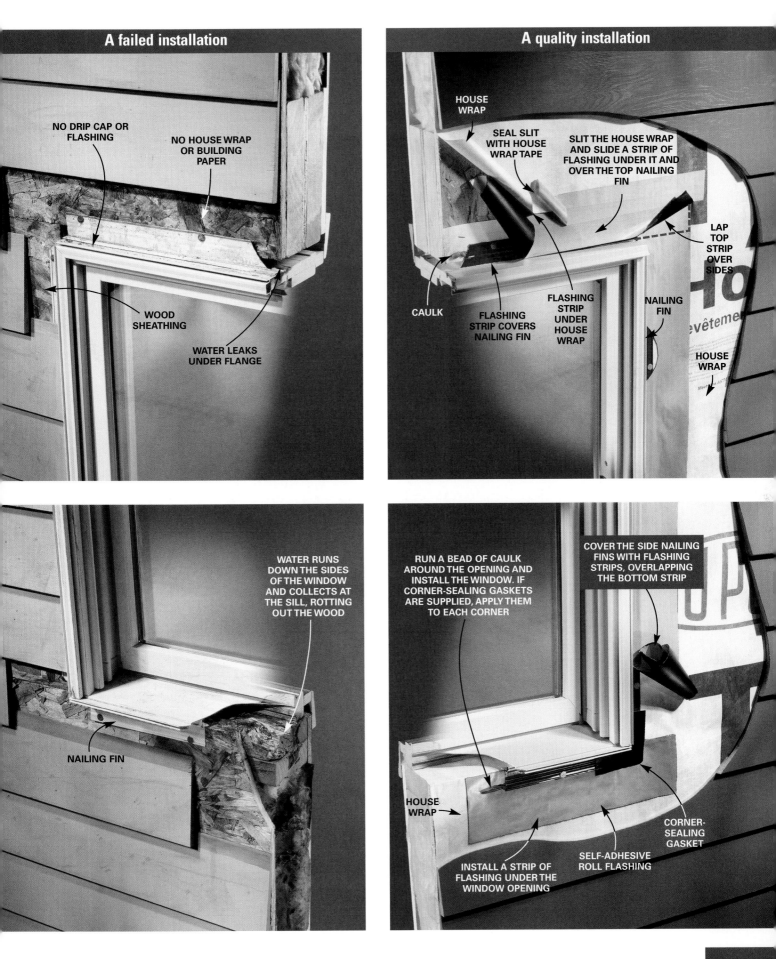

A failed installation

NO DRIP CAP OR FLASHING

NO HOUSE WRAP OR BUILDING PAPER

WOOD SHEATHING

WATER LEAKS UNDER FLANGE

A quality installation

HOUSE WRAP

SEAL SLIT WITH HOUSE WRAP TAPE

SLIT THE HOUSE WRAP AND SLIDE A STRIP OF FLASHING UNDER IT AND OVER THE TOP NAILING FIN

LAP TOP STRIP OVER SIDES

CAULK

FLASHING STRIP COVERS NAILING FIN

FLASHING STRIP UNDER HOUSE WRAP

NAILING FIN

HOUSE WRAP

WATER RUNS DOWN THE SIDES OF THE WINDOW AND COLLECTS AT THE SILL, ROTTING OUT THE WOOD

NAILING FIN

RUN A BEAD OF CAULK AROUND THE OPENING AND INSTALL THE WINDOW. IF CORNER-SEALING GASKETS ARE SUPPLIED, APPLY THEM TO EACH CORNER

COVER THE SIDE NAILING FINS WITH FLASHING STRIPS, OVERLAPPING THE BOTTOM STRIP

HOUSE WRAP

INSTALL A STRIP OF FLASHING UNDER THE WINDOW OPENING

SELF-ADHESIVE ROLL FLASHING

CORNER-SEALING GASKET

Which Should I buy?

STORE-BOUGHT GUTTERS VS. SEAMLESS GUTTERS?

Our gutters are sagging and leaking all over the place. What are the pros and cons of installing sectional gutters myself as opposed to hiring one of those seamless gutter companies?

As a do-it-yourself magazine, we find our first instinct is always to say, "Do it yourself!" But seamless metal gutters have certain advantages that you simply can't get with 10-ft. sectional gutters:

Color variety. Seamless gutters are available in gray, almond, tan and at least two dozen other baked-on colors. If you want gutters in something other than "home center" white or brown, you have to go with seamless.

Strength. Aluminum seamless gutters are normally .032 in. thick, while off-the-shelf gutters are about .019 in. thick, even a little less if they're steel. That's a considerable difference. Most seamless gutter companies also use extremely strong mounting brackets. This rigidity can be crucial for withstanding ice dams and leaning ladders. Most seamless gutters are warranted for 20 years for materials (but often only one year for labor).

Performance. Continuous gutter sections as long as 45 ft. can be formed and installed on site. No seams (except at corners and downspouts) means less chance of leaks. Since the flow is unimpeded by splices, water and debris have a straighter shot to the downspout.

The hassle factor. You still need to clean your gutters, but if you're in your "low maintenance" stage of life, choose seamless gutters. They'll require less recaulking and upkeep over the years.

Plus, watching workers extrude the gutters right in your driveway is incredibly cool. A monstrous 1,500-lb. machine on one end converts a roll of flat metal into a continuous, fully formed gutter on the other.

But you pay for these advantages. On a typical house with 120 linear ft. of gutter, the average price for store-bought materials (including downspouts, brackets, corners, splices and other connectors) is about $2 to $2.50 per foot. Installed seamless gutters average anywhere from $6 to $7 per foot—all told, about $500 more than the do-it-yourself approach.

Bear in mind, you can get a bad seamless gutter installation. Many installers get paid by the job or by each lineal foot of installed gutter; the faster they work, the more money they make. This doesn't always result in a top-notch job. Ask for references, make sure the company has been around for at least three years and that the work is guaranteed.

SEAMLESS GUTTER COLOR CHOICES

Best of both worlds

Some seamless gutter companies will form gutters on site, then let you install them. You'll pay about half the installed price, yet get all the benefits of a seamless system. But you'll have to call around; most companies make their profit on installation, not materials. Not all will do it.

STORE-BOUGHT FITTINGS

DECK STRIPPERS VS. DECK CLEANERS

My home center carries deck strippers and deck cleaners. Is there a real difference between the two products?

A deck stripper is used to remove old loose stain and deck sealers, before cleaning and brightening. It breaks the finish loose from the wood like a furniture stripper does. Several brand names are Wolman DeckStrip, Flood Powerlift and Superdeck Wood Stripper. These products also enable you to get rid of an old color and apply a new stain color. The deck stripper products are most effective on oil-based finishes. New products that remove latex stains and finishes will be on the market soon.

There are basically two types of deck cleaners: One type (liquid oxalic acid or powdered hydrogen peroxide) removes a thin layer of gray, dead wood fibers from the surface and exposes the fresh wood beneath. Several brand names are Wolman Deck and Siding Brightener and Rejuvenator, Flood Dekswood and Superdeck Wood Cleaner. The other type has a bleach base that removes unsightly black and green stains on the surface such as mildew. If you notice this condition, clean off the mildew first and rinse, then use one of the standard deck cleaners mentioned above. Most home centers carry a wide variety of cleaners.

For the best buy, pay attention to the concentration of cleaner in the 1-gallon plastic jug. Some of the cleaners appear to cost more, but on inspection, you'll see that the gallon container mixes with water to make 5 gallons of cleaning solution (enough for a large deck).

1 SPRAY the deck surface with deck cleaner the day after you've completed the railing. Also apply the deck cleaner to the railing with a sprayer, because the stripper may have darkened the wood. The cleaner will bring the stripped surfaces back to a fresh, bright wood look.

2 SCRUB away the loose wood fibers and residue 15 minutes after you've applied the cleaner. Work the brush deeply into the wood in the direction of the grain. As soon as you're finished, rinse the deck thoroughly with a firm spray from your garden hose and let the surface dry for at least two days.

DO ASPHALT SEALERS REALLY WORK?

I apply asphalt sealer to my driveway every spring. My neighbor laughs at me and tells me it's nothing but black paint. Do sealers actually help a driveway last longer, or do they just make it look better?

Well, in some ways your neighbor is right—but comparing asphalt sealer to paint isn't necessarily bad! Both products protect outdoor surfaces from sun and moisture damage and therefore, while surely cosmetic, prolong the surfaces' life. But just as paint won't fix rotted siding, sealers won't save a crumbling driveway.

When asphalt is new, it's flexible. As it ages, the oils in it oxidize and degrade, making it brittle and more prone to crazing. Asphalt is also porous. In cold climates, moisture works into these pores as well as the mini-cracks that have formed, expanding and widening them and popping out the surrounding material. Rain, also, can seep through cracks and wash out the supporting base material. This sets up a vicious cycle of ever-widening cracks. Sealers fill these cracks and pores, speed water runoff and help slow the cycle.

Not all asphalt sealers are created equal. You can buy thin sealers that are mostly cosmetic, or choose heavy-duty sealers that fill cracks and create a durable topcoat. Like good paint, good sealers contain less water (which simply evaporates) and more solids, which form the actual protective coat. Good sealers have more additives, often latex, which increase flexibility, and often more sand, which helps traction and adhesion. The two-, four- or six-year protection claims on labels are good for comparing products within a product line, but don't take them literally. A Midwest driveway that gets plowed, covered with road salt and subjected to freeze/thaw cycles will need more frequent sealing than one in a moderate climate.

There are different formulations too. Coal tar emulsion sealers do a better job than asphalt emulsion sealers of resisting gas, oil, brake fluid and other petroleum products that "melt" asphalt. But depending on where you live, you

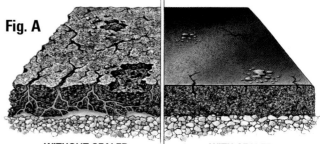

Fig. A

WITHOUT SEALER   **WITH SEALER**

A vicious circle can form as an asphalt driveway ages. Small cracks form, allowing in water, which then freezes and expands, creating ever-widening cracks. In severe cases, water can even erode the underlying subbase. Asphalt sealers keep out water, oils and salt, helping a driveway last longer.

may not have much choice. Coal tar reigns in the East, asphalt emulsion in the West.

Sealers labeled "easy stir" are better in that they keep the solids suspended longer so the application is more uniform. Inadequate stirring is the No. 1 cause of a lousy job.

With the best stuff at $20 per 5 gallons and the cheapest at $10, the price difference is less than $30 for a 15 x 60-ft. driveway. Buy the good stuff. For more details, contact the National Pavement Contractors Association (www.pavementpro.org or 940-327-8041).

Tip

You can overdo a good thing. Too many coats of sealer can crack and peel—just like too many layers of paint.

Tips for a top-notch job

1. **Fill cracks wider than a pencil lead with pourable or caulkable crack filler. Fill potholes with blacktop patching material.**
2. **Sweep your driveway, scrub it with soapy water, then rinse it. If you have fresh oil spots, hit them with an asphalt primer.**
3. **Apply two thin coats instead of one thick one. The sealer will bond better and dry faster.**

3

Whether you're looking for plans for a
harvest table or tablesaw tips, you'll find
what you need right here!

In the Workshop

KNOCKDOWN
WORKBENCHES

For sawing, sewing and sorting you need a sturdy, convenient place to spread out. Here are four space-saving designs that set up in seconds.

by **Travis Larson**

ABC BOXES

Assembling parts is easiest when you can work at a comfortable height. But the height of that working surface depends on the size of the project. These ABC boxes, so called because they're made with sides of three different dimensions, make a variable-height assembly table base. By rotating the boxes or standing them on end, you'll get three different working heights. For stability, you'll need three boxes; it's best to fasten them to the top. All three boxes can be made from one 4x8 sheet of 3/4-in. plywood.

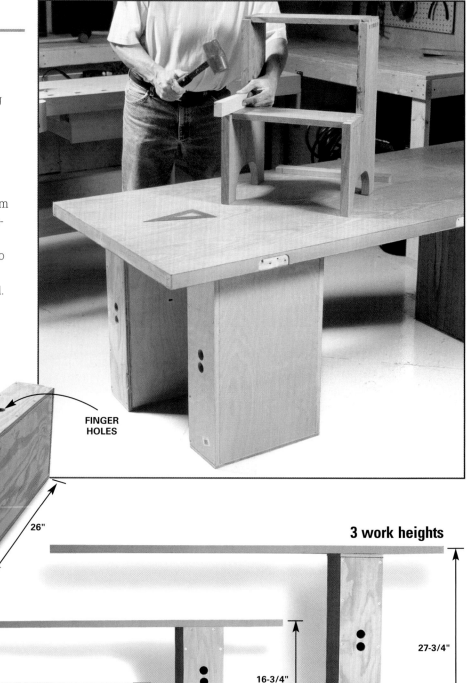

FINGER HOLES

B

A C

15"

26"

6"

PLYWOOD CUTTING LENGTHS
A—6" X 15"
B—6" X 24-1/2"
C—13-1/2" X 24-1/2"

3 work heights

27-3/4"

16-3/4"

7-3/4"

KNOCK-APART UTILITY TABLE

This table is made from a full sheet of 5/8-in. plywood for the interlocking base stand and a sheet of 3/4-in. plywood for the work surface and shelves. You'll also need four 10-ft. lengths of 1x3 pine for the edge banding and cleats.

Cut two 30-in. high by 48-in. long pieces from the 5/8-in. plywood for the base pieces. Then cut a slightly oversize 5/8-in. wide slot in the bottom half of one base and in the top half of the other. Make both slots about 15-1/2 in. long. Assemble the base and position the top so the corners are aligned with the legs. Screw loose-fitting 12-in. long 1x3s along each side of each leg to hold everything stable.

The table is more stable if you use the 3/4-in. waste from the top to make triangular braces (which also act as shelves) with 20-in. long sides. Using 1-1/4 in. drywall screws, attach 1x2s to the base 12 in. up from the floor and screw on shelves.

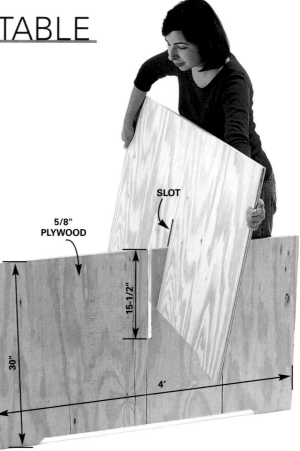

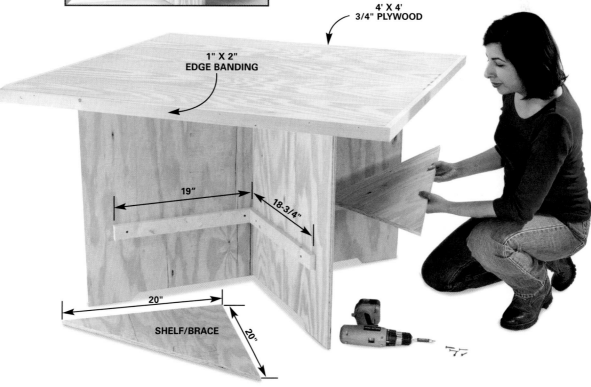

OLD-DOOR WORKBENCH

This space-saving design is made from a salvaged prehung door. Not only does it take zero floor space because it's mounted against a wall but it also has built-in Peg-Board tool storage so your tools are right at hand when you fold open the door.

You can often find damaged prehung doors at the lumberyard for cheap. Look for a flush, solid-core door with the jamb attached. A heavy, sturdy solid-core door provides a strong attachment base for the bench legs and is tough enough to take a pounding.

Reinforce the jamb corners with 1-5/8 in. drywall screws and add a board across the bottom where the threshold would normally be. Screw a 1 x 4-in. flange onto the back edges of the jamb with 2-in. drywall screws. The jamb is hung on the wall with 3-in. drywall screws. For a comfortable working height, hang it at 36 in. for stand-up or barstool work. Screw Peg-Board to the overhanging flange that's inside the opening. Make two legs from 3/4-in. threaded pipe and screw them into two 3/4-in. pipe flanges to support the workbench when it's down. Support the bottom jamb with angle brackets and add a hasp to hold the door shut and keep it from falling open.

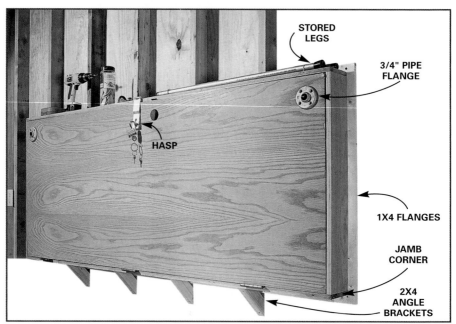

STORED LEGS

3/4" PIPE FLANGE

HASP

1X4 FLANGES

JAMB CORNER

2X4 ANGLE BRACKETS

LIGHT-DUTY WORK TABLE

If you ever need a light-duty work surface anywhere in the house for sewing, painting or school projects, this one's for you. Get to the home center and buy a hollow-core door; four toilet flanges; a 10-ft. length of 3-in. PVC pipe; 16 No. 10, 1-1/4 in. long screws and a tube of construction adhesive (total cost about $40). Inside of a half hour, you'll have the flanges glued and screwed to the door and be ready to slip in the 30-in. long PVC legs. ⌂

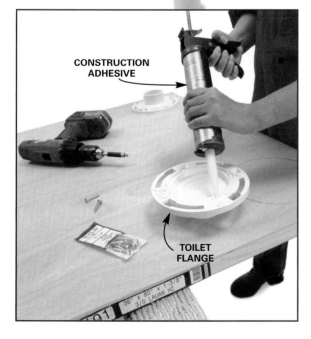

CONSTRUCTION ADHESIVE

TOILET FLANGE

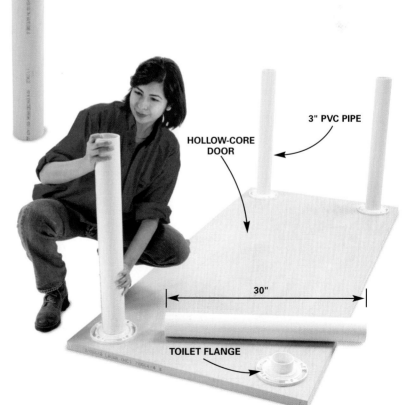

3" PVC PIPE

HOLLOW-CORE DOOR

30"

TOILET FLANGE

Workshop™ tips

HOW TO MEASURE FLOPPY MOLDINGS

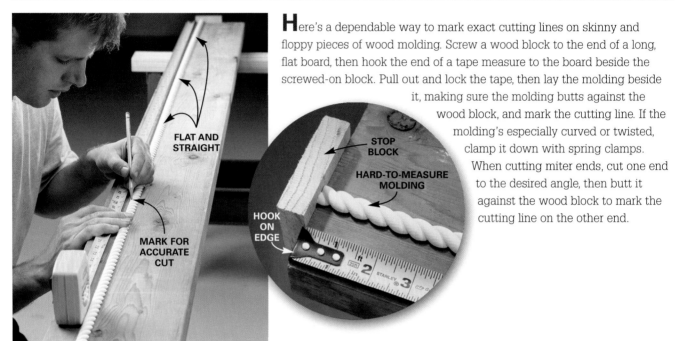

Here's a dependable way to mark exact cutting lines on skinny and floppy pieces of wood molding. Screw a wood block to the end of a long, flat board, then hook the end of a tape measure to the board beside the screwed-on block. Pull out and lock the tape, then lay the molding beside it, making sure the molding butts against the wood block, and mark the cutting line. If the molding's especially curved or twisted, clamp it down with spring clamps. When cutting miter ends, cut one end to the desired angle, then butt it against the wood block to mark the cutting line on the other end.

FLAT AND STRAIGHT

STOP BLOCK

HARD-TO-MEASURE MOLDING

HOOK ON EDGE

MARK FOR ACCURATE CUT

VACUUM EXTENSION TUBE

Don't throw away the cardboard tube from wrapping paper! Tape the tube to the end of a vacuum cleaner wand to reach cobwebs in corners of your workshop or dust freeloading on fans. Reach all the way under beds and furniture, or flatten the roll to vacuum narrow crevices. Make it a permanent dusting wand by wrapping it with duct tape, and it'll stand up to years of use.

WRAPPING PAPER ROLL

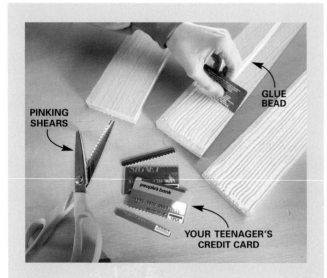

PINKING SHEARS

GLUE BEAD

YOUR TEENAGER'S CREDIT CARD

FAST GLUE SPREADER

When face-gluing boards, use a credit card snipped along its wide edge with a pinking shears. The serrated "pinked" edge spreads the glue like a serrated trowel spreads mastic on floors.

CHISEL SHARPENING BASICS

Old chisels with nicked or rounded tips will need to be reshaped. Use a belt sander or grinder to remove nicks and shape the chisel to a 25-degree angle. If you're using a grinder, dip the chisel in water every two or three seconds to prevent the tip from overheating and turning blue. If this happens, the chisel won't hold an edge for long.

Next, polish the back of the chisel by rubbing it back and forth over progressively finer wet/dry sandpaper, pressing the back perfectly flat to the paper. For all sharpening, a good progression of paper is 120, 220, 400 and 600 grit.

Finally, use a honing guide to hold the chisel at a 30-degree angle to create a "secondary bevel" and run through the grits, starting at 220. Roll the chisel back and forth over the sandpaper until a burr forms on the back of the blade. Turn the chisel over and stroke it flat on the sandpaper to remove the burr. Then move to a finer-grit paper and repeat the process.

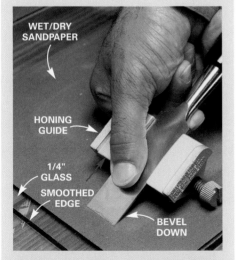

WET/DRY SANDPAPER

HONING GUIDE

1/4" GLASS

SMOOTHED EDGE

BEVEL DOWN

Sharpen your chisels on wet/dry sandpaper that's lightly glued with spray adhesive to a piece of 1/4-in. glass with smoothed edges. Use a honing guide to maintain the correct angle and speed up the sharpening process.

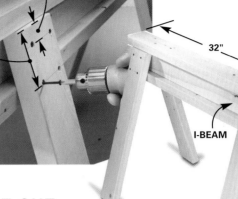

3-1/2" TO BOTTOM SCREWS

1" TO TOP SCREWS

32"

I-BEAM

26-1/4"

STRAIGHT-CUT SAWHORSES

Need sawhorses right now? You can make a pair from five 8-ft. 2x4s cut into six 32-in. lengths and eight 26-1/4 in. lengths.

Nail or screw the 32-in. pieces into I-beam shapes and, after drilling pilot holes, attach the legs to the I-beams with 3-in. drywall screws. These screws, along with the upper edge of the I-beam, stabilize the legs. They're the perfect horses for holding a heavy load of boards and sheet goods. And when you need another workbench, screw a piece of plywood on the sawhorses and you'll have a stable table.

SPIN-OUT PLUG REMOVAL

If you've ever tried to remove the cutout lodged in your hole saw, you know how challenging it can be. To get it out easily, just drive a screw into the plug and turn it counterclockwise until the plug comes free.

CLYDESDALE-STRONG SAWHORSES KNOCK APART IN SECONDS

These easy-to-make sawhorses carry a heavy load without a creak or a whinny, and when you're done with 'em, they knock apart in seconds for flat storage. For two horses you'll need:

- Two sheets of 2 x 4-ft. 3/4-in. plywood (or a half sheet)
- Two 30-in. long 2x6s

Using the dimensions marked, cut out the plywood legs and support blocks with a circular saw and jigsaw. Glue and screw the support blocks to the 2x6, leaving 3/4-in. wide slots for the notched plywood leg to slide into. Fit the legs into the slots, tap them home and put your horses to work.

1. Cut the wood

MARK AND CUT ONE; TRACE THREE MORE

27"
6"
15"
5"
10 DEGREES
5-3/4"
5"

(CUT EIGHT AS SHOWN HERE)

3-1/4"
4-3/4"
2-1/4"

30"
2X6

2. Glue the supports

GLUE, THEN SCREW

2-3/4"

SCROUNGED GLUE DISPENSERS

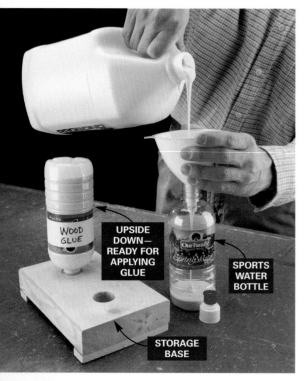

WOOD GLUE

UPSIDE DOWN—READY FOR APPLYING GLUE

SPORTS WATER BOTTLE

STORAGE BASE

Here's a nifty tip—with a nifty tip. Fill snap-capped sports water bottles with glue and stick them upside down in a hunk of 2x6. Now you don't have to wait for the glue to run into the neck of the bottle, and the cap will control glue flow (and never get lost!). To holster the bottle, cut holes in the base with a spade bit that's a smidgen larger than the cap's diameter.

P.S. Be sure to snap the lid closed before returning the bottle to the base. Otherwise the whole bottleful of glue will run out!

SNAP-CAP MAKES AIRTIGHT SEAL AND CONTROLS BEAD SIZE WHEN YOU SQUEEZE

EDGE-GLUING MADE EASY

When you're gluing boards into a panel, do your cushion strips flop out of alignment? Here's an easy fix: Screw some 1/4-in. or 3/8-in. thick by 3-in. wide Peg-Board or plywood strips on the top side of the cushion strips. This will:

1. Ensure the cushion strips remain level with the project boards.
2. Lift the pipe above the project boards so they can't touch squeezed-out glue and stain the workpiece.
3. Help center the pipe clamp's jaw face on the board edge.

1/4" SCRAP MATERIAL

SCREWS

3/4" CUSHION STRIPS

PIVOT TO CENTER THE CLAMP JAW

PIPE CLAMP LIFTERS

EDGE-GLUED BOARDS

PLYWOOD TRAY REST

1/2" PLYWOOD TOTE

MUFFIN TIN STORAGE BIN

Rescue those blackened, neglected muffin tins from a dark cupboard corner and put them to work holding small fasteners, nails, eyescrews, washers, electrical parts and more. Screw together a tote from three pieces of 1/2-in. thick plywood cut to fit the width and height of your trays. Screw plywood strips on the inside to act as drawer runners for the tins, and glue or screw on a thin plywood back. Our tote holds four tins, but you can build it higher for even more storage capacity. Cut the plywood sides long enough so there's room to add a 3/4-in. dia. dowel handle.

SCREW-LUBE STICK

Wood screws will occasionally heat up and break off when you're driving them in hardwoods like oak and maple. To help prevent snapped-off screws in your projects, try this slick tip from a loyal reader: Keep a tube of lip balm handy to lube the screws before driving. It's fast to apply and the wax in it lets you drive screws fast and easy.

TWIRL AND DRIVE

SPOUSE'S CHAPSTICK

SEAT-OF-THE-PANTS RADIAL ARM SAW

You'll forget all about that expensive new radial arm saw once you see how this simple jig produces perfect 90-degree cuts. Careful construction is a must. First, use a base platform with truly parallel sides. We glued and screwed two 3/4-in. plywood pieces together and ripped them to width on a table saw. Second, screw the base sides to the base. Third, rout rabbets on one side of each runner. Finally, screw one runner to the base sides at exactly 90 degrees and then align the other runner parallel to the first and just far enough apart so the saw's baseplate slides perfectly inside the rabbets.

You can take this jig with you and screw it to your sawhorses or to your workbench for a rock-solid cutting platform.

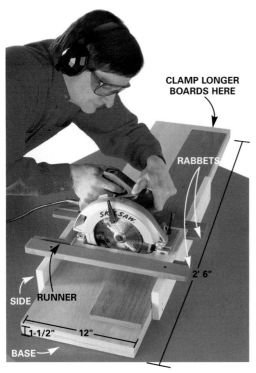

CLAMP LONGER BOARDS HERE

RABBETS

2' 6"

SIDE RUNNER

1-1/2" 12"

BASE

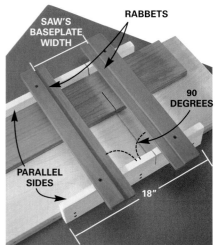

SAW'S BASEPLATE WIDTH

RABBETS

90 DEGREES

PARALLEL SIDES

18"

FREE DUSTPAN FOR SHOP BROOMS

If your broom is too wide for a dustpan, try this tip from a Family Handyman reader. Tape the long edge of a piece of newspaper to the floor and sweep dust and shavings aboard over the taped edge. When you're done, pull up the tape, wad up the paper and toss the whole thing. With this tip, you won't have to bend over to hold the dustpan while you sweep up the pile.

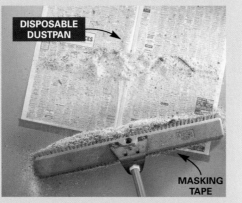

DISPOSABLE DUSTPAN

MASKING TAPE

BOBBY-PIN BRAD GRIPPER

SMALL BRAD

BOBBY PIN

You now have another easy way to pound in little nails without pounding on your fingernails, thanks to another faithful reader. Push the nail brad into a bobby pin—the kind with one wavy side. Tap lightly to set the brad, then pull away the bobby pin, and hammer the brad all the way in.

LARGE WASHER

METAL-CUTTING OIL

OIL-DRILLING RIG

Next time you're drilling holes in a hunk of steel, try this slick tip. Find a washer with an inner diameter larger than the diameter of the drill bit, firmly tape it to the workpiece and squirt cutting oil in the washer's eye. As you drill, the pool of oil keeps the drill bit lubricated. Use a new or freshly sharpened drill bit and you'll be surprised how quickly you can drill the hole applying only light pressure on the drill.

TAPE CADDY

Keep your tape rolls in one place and easy to use with this plywood dispenser. When you run out of tape, just lift the dowel out of the notches, reload and slide it back in the notches. You'll need:

- Two 5-in. x 6-in. side pieces of 3/4-in. plywood
- One 5-in. x 12-in. plywood base
- One 1-in. x 13-1/2 in. hacksaw blade support
- One 14-in. x 1-1/2 in. dia. dowel rod
- An 18-tooth, 12-in. hacksaw blade

Notch the sides to the dimensions shown and screw them to the base along with the hacksaw blade support. Saw the dowel ends to fit in the notched sides and screw the hacksaw blade on the support, positioning it so the saw teeth extend a little beyond the edge of the plywood. That's it. Load up with tape and you'll never go hunting for stray rolls again.

P.S. You may want to screw the dispenser to your workbench to aid in pulling tape (especially duct tape) off the roll.

13-1/2"

14" X 1-1/2" DIAMETER DOWEL

5"

6"

5" X 12" BASE

3-3/4"

1"

TRIM OFF WHEN WORN

EMERY BOARD MINI-SANDERS

Here's a detail sander for delicate work that costs only $1.50 for a pack of five. It offers fine and finer grits plus an easily renewed edge. As the end you're using gets clogged, just snip it off to expose fresh sandpaper.

SANDPAPER WITH A THICK HIDE

A reader who's a woodcarver offered this advice. To prevent rips, tears, rough edges and holes in the sandpaper when using a clamp-style finish or orbital sander, apply strips of wide masking tape, duct tape or clear self-adhesive shelf paper to the backside for reinforcement. With the clear paper, you can still read the grit size, so you can cover several sheets in advance.

NEAT NAIL ORGANIZER

Bleach bottles make great nail organizers, once you cut out a section of the top. When the bottles are stored on their sides, the weight of the nails keeps them from rolling. The handles make for easy carrying, and they can stand upright when off the shelves.

SHAKER-STYLE
COAT AND MITTEN RACK

Build this handsome, handy project in just a few hours using everyday tools and materials—you won't believe you got along without it!

by **David Radtke**

Whenever it was time to leave the house, my brother Gary used to delay everyone while he searched for his misplaced jacket and baseball cap. Not anymore!

Not since I built him this simple coat rack. The design is easy to build with butt joints connected by screws that get hidden by wooden screw-hole buttons and wood plugs. The rack mounts easily to the wall with screws driven through the hidden hanging strip on the back. The five large Shaker pegs are great for holding hats, umbrellas and coats, and the hinged-hatch door at the top keeps the clutter of gloves and scarves from view.

You can build this project in a few hours, with an additional hour to apply a finish. Maple is an ideal wood for Shaker-style pieces, but any hardwood will do. Figure on spending about $60 for wood, hardware and varnish.

Cutting the pieces

Using a compass, transfer the pattern measurements in **Fig. A**, above, and then cut the sides (A) with a jigsaw (**Photo 1**). Next cut the top (D) to length and rip the shelf (B) to the width given in the Cutting List, at left. Cut the hanging strip (F) and the peg strip (C) to the same length as the shelf (B). Now, using your spade bit, drill the 3/8-in. counterbore holes for the screw-hole buttons 3/16 in. deep into the outside of parts A (**Fig. A and Photo 2**). Also drill the 3/8-in. counterbore holes in the top. These holes must be 3/8 in. deep.

Mark and drill the 1/2-in. holes for the Shaker pegs in the peg strip. Drill the holes for the Shaker pegs perfectly perpendicular to the peg strip to ensure they all project evenly when glued in place.

Fig. A: Shaker rack details

PROJECT DIMENSIONS:
14-3/4" H X 36" W X 7-1/4" D

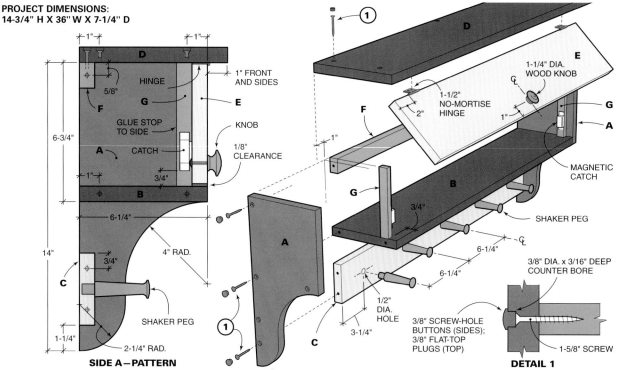

SIDE A—PATTERN

DETAIL 1

Assembly

Lay the pieces on your workbench, as shown in **Photo 3**. Align the hanging strip (F), the shelf (B), and the peg strip (C) as shown and clamp the sides (A) to these parts. Predrill the holes with a combination pilot hole/countersink bit using the center of the counterbore holes as a guide. Next, screw the sides to B, C and F. Mark and drill hinge mounting holes in the top (D), then fasten the top to the sides in the same manner.

Glue and clamp the hatch stops to the inside of parts A, as shown in **Fig. A**, p. 104. To finish the assembly, cut the hatch (E) to size and install the hinges on the underside of part D and the top of the hatch. Now glue the buttons and plugs into their corresponding holes. Use only a small drop of glue for the buttons but be sure to apply a thin layer of glue completely around the plugs. This will swell the plugs for a tight fit. After the glue is dry, trim the wood plugs flush with the top.

Finishing

After assembly, lightly sand the entire piece with 220-grit sandpaper. Apply two coats of clear Danish oil or polyurethane to all the surfaces (remove the hinges and knobs). Once the finish is dry, add two magnetic catches to the hatch stop (G).

NOTE: Be sure this project is screwed to the wall studs. Drill two holes into the hanging strip at stud locations and use 2-1/2 in. or longer wood screws.

SHOPPING LIST

ITEM	QUANTITY
1x8 x 12' maple (A, B, D, E)	1
1x4 x 6' maple (C, F, G)	1
1-1/2" no-mortise hinges*	1 pair
1-1/4" beech knob*	1
Narrow magnetic catch*	2
3-3/8" long Shaker pegs*	5
3/8" screw-hole buttons*	10
3/8" plugs*	5
3/8" spade bit	1
1/2" spade bit	1
1-5/8" wood screws	15
Carpenter's glue	1 pint
Danish oil	1 pint
150- and 220-grit sandpaper	

* Available from home centers or Rockler Woodworking and Hardware, 4365 Willow Dr., Medina, MN 55340; (800) 279-4441, www.rockler.com.

CUTTING LIST

KEY	PCS.	SIZE & DESCRIPTION
A	2	3/4" x 6-1/4" x 14" maple sides
B	1	3/4" x 6-1/4" x 32-1/2" maple shelf
C	1	3/4" x 3-1/2" x 32-1/2" maple peg strip
D	1	3/4" x 7-1/4" x 36" maple top
E	1	3/4" x 5-13/16" x 32-5/16" maple hatch
F	1	3/4" x 1-1/4" x 32-1/2" maple hanging strip
G	2	3/4" x 1/2" x 6" maple hatch stops

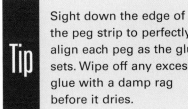

Tip Sight down the edge of the peg strip to perfectly align each peg as the glue sets. Wipe off any excess glue with a damp rag before it dries.

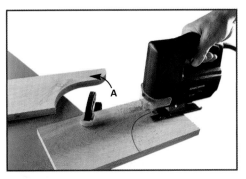

1 CUT the side pieces (A) using a jigsaw or band saw. Sand the curved edges smooth with a 1-1/2 in. drum sander attached to a drill.

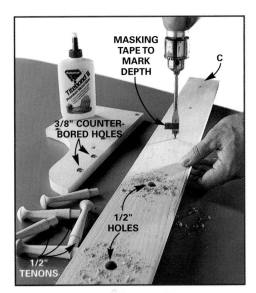

2 DRILL the 1/2-in. holes 5/8 in. deep for the 3-3/8 in. Shaker pegs and the 3/8-in. counterbore holes 3/16 in. deep for the screw-hole buttons in parts A.

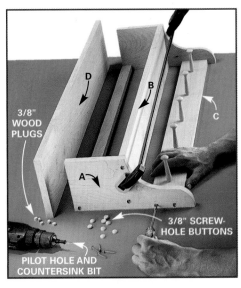

3 ASSEMBLE the shelf by clamping parts C, F and B to the sides. Drill pilot holes and screw the pieces together. The screws will be covered by the buttons and plugs.

Which
Should I buy?

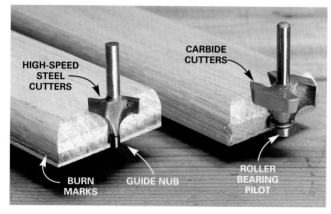

HIGH-SPEED STEEL CUTTERS

CARBIDE CUTTERS

BURN MARKS

GUIDE NUB

ROLLER BEARING PILOT

The $30 ball-bearing piloted bit on the right may cost four times as much as the high-speed steel piloted bit on the left, but it'll still be cutting long after you've gone through 10 of the cheaper ones. And your projects won't have burn marks along the edges.

ARE EXPENSIVE ROUTER BITS WORTH THE MONEY?

I'm amazed that some bits cost almost as much as the router itself! Is there really $25 worth of difference between bits with roller bearings and those without?

First, most bits with roller bearings (above, right) have cutters made of carbide, a material that—depending on whom you believe—lasts 6 to 50 times longer than high-speed steel. Second, cheaper bits made of high-speed steel are guided by a nub that rotates with the bit; the damage this guide nub inflicts is the other big difference.

Most routers operate at 20,000 rpm, which means the guide nub on a high-speed steel bit spins at more than 300 revolutions per second. Even when you keep the bit moving evenly, the nub can burn its profile into the wood. If you pause for a second or two, there's an even greater chance of gouging and burning. This is a huge problem with soft woods like pine. You can spend a lot of time and sandpaper getting rid of those burn marks. The spinning nub can even work its way under the grain and bite off long splinters of wood. And since the diameter of most nubs is a tiny 3/16 in., they're more likely to follow small dips or imperfections along the edge of a board.

Roller bearing pilots don't spin with the bit, but at the speed you move the router. They won't burn the wood and, since most are 1/2 in. in diameter, they do a better job of evening out edge imperfections. Bite the bullet and invest in the good bits.

DO I NEED BOTH SIX-POINT AND 12-POINT SOCKETS?

I saw a great bargain on one of those 124-piece socket wrench sets with both six- and 12-point sockets of the same size. Do you really need both types?

Unless you're an avid mechanic, a set of six-point sockets will handle 99 percent of the jobs you throw at them—and they'll do it with less knuckle-busting.

A 12-point socket is fine for basic household repairs, assembly jobs and auto repairs that don't involve serious rust. This type of socket is also easier to slip over nuts and bolts in confined or hard-to-see places; you don't need to rotate it as far as a six-point socket in order for it to "seat." And, though square-headed fasteners are rare these days, 12-point sockets can accommodate them. But a 12-point socket contacts a fastener only on its corners. It also (usually) has thinner walls. Even though a socket is made from hardened steel, the socket wall can flex, slip and round over the edges of a nut or bolt—especially when you're really cranking.

A six-point socket is designed so the six flat sides of the socket wall pry against the six flat sides of the fastener, instead of against the weak corners. This allows you to increase the pressure and reduces the likelihood of the socket slipping off the fastener and rounding the points. Also, the sides of a socket are angled back a few degrees to allow the socket to slide more easily over a fastener. This angle on a six-point socket is less than the angle on its 12-point counterpart, again providing more contact area inside the socket.

6-POINT SOCKET

12-POINT SOCKET

WHAT IS THE BEST SANDER FOR FINISHING CABINETS?

I'm building cabinets for my kitchen. This seems like a good excuse to buy a sander that has a little more finesse than my belt sander. What finishing sander should I buy?

We posed the question to four woodworking and four home improvement editors in the office and got a unanimous response: "Buy a random orbital sander."

All in all, there's really nothing "wrong" with square-based, orbital finishing sanders. They "vibrate" the sandpaper in thousands of little orbits. They're easy to control and they're inexpensive to operate, since they use standard sandpaper in one-sixth, one-quarter, one-third or half sheets. Orbital finishing sanders can leave small spiral swirls on wood if you're not meticulous, but by sanding down through 180-grit, you can avoid this. However, random orbital sanders take things a whole step further.

Random orbital sanders work far more aggressively and quickly. The circular bases spin at about 10,000 rpm while wiggling about 1/8 in. off center at the same time. This creates a truly random sanding pattern, which removes wood quickly and minimizes swirl marks. This speedy randomness also allows you to smooth joints where the rails and stiles of your cabinets meet at right angles.

Many woodworkers find they only need to go down to 100- to 120-grit paper with their random orbital sander for surfaces that will be painted or receive a clear finish. (For surfaces that are to be stained, consider a light hand-sanding with the grain to remove any and all remaining swirl marks.) But beware, the aggressiveness of a random orbital sander can cut through a veneer or damage the edge of a board in a flash. It takes a few tries to learn how to control them. Also, at a buck a sheet, the adhesive or Velcro-backed sandpaper discs are spendy, but you'll work faster and wind up with better-looking cabinets.

RANDOM ORBITAL SANDER

FINISHING SANDER

The **random orbital sander** (left) works fast and can smooth joints like the one on this cabinet door without leaving cross-grain scratches. The **finishing sander** (right) is easier to control but not as effective at smoothing joints.

DO I REALLY NEED A ROUTER TABLE?

Whenever I use my router on small projects and pieces the clamps get in the way; I get tired of moving them. Will a router table solve this problem?

With a router table you don't have to hassle with clamping the workpiece. Just guide it over the table and past the bit. You can build your own router table and fence using plans included in many basic router books. Or for less than $200, you can choose from dozens of commercially made tables. Buy the biggest tabletop you can afford (or fit in your workshop); you'll get more accurate cuts on long pieces. Fences with two adjustable, replaceable wood or particle board sections mounted to a solid one-piece metal fence are

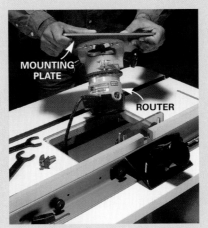

MOUNTING PLATE

ROUTER

the best. You can shim out one side to plane board edges or slide the sections tight to the router bit to eliminate extra space around the bit. Make sure the table has an easily adjustable bit guard and slots in the table to mount featherboards or other accessories. Removable base plates (see photo) make it easier to mount your router and take it out to change bits and make height adjustments. Since router tables leave the spinning bit exposed, always use the bit guard and use push sticks when necessary.

FAST, EASY AND ELEGANT
HARVEST TABLE

Simple off-the-shelf materials and basic tools make this the easiest table you'll ever build! And you can complete it in an afternoon.

by **David Radtke**

The top of this table is as tough as a hardwood floor—literally. It's made of hardwood veneer flooring that's glued and screwed to a 3/4-in. plywood base. The hardwood legs are not usual table fare either; they're made from standard stairway newel posts. The rest of the wood parts are used in a unique way to complete the look of the table. The legs are fastened with special steel brackets and hanger bolts that are easily removed for storing the table in a small space or for easy disassembly on moving day.

Almost everything you need is available at home centers or full-service lumberyards and will easily fit into your trunk (if you have the lumberyard cut your plywood to size). The only parts I couldn't find at a local home center were the heavy-duty steel apron brackets and hanger bolts for strong leg connections. We'll give you a mail-order source at the end of the article.

Harvest table details

PROJECT DIMENSIONS:
30" H X 30-1/2" W X 64-7/8" L

Project Facts

- TIME: 4 HOURS TO CUT AND ASSEMBLE (EXTRA TIME FOR FINISHING)
- COST AND SKILL LEVEL: $225; BEGINNER AND UP
- TOOLS: COMBINATION SQUARE, MITER SAW, SCREW GUN AND TAPE MEASURE

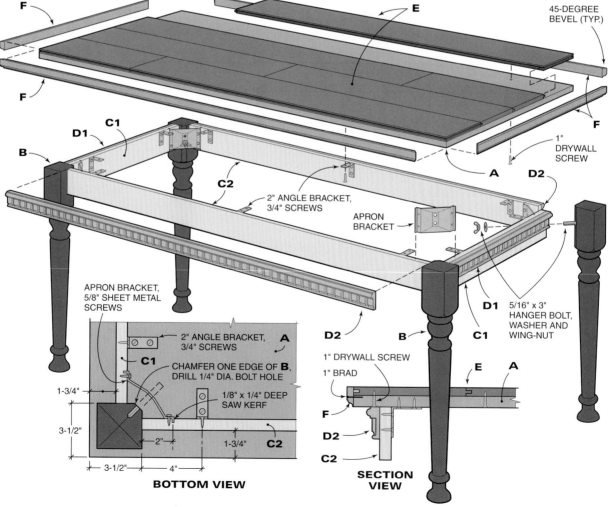

45-DEGREE BEVEL (TYP.)

1" DRYWALL SCREW

2" ANGLE BRACKET, 3/4" SCREWS

APRON BRACKET

5/16" x 3" HANGER BOLT, WASHER AND WING-NUT

APRON BRACKET, 5/8" SHEET METAL SCREWS

2" ANGLE BRACKET, 3/4" SCREWS

CHAMFER ONE EDGE OF **B**, DRILL 1/4" DIA. BOLT HOLE

1/8" x 1/4" DEEP SAW KERF

1-3/4"

3-1/2"

2"

1-3/4"

3-1/2"

4"

BOTTOM VIEW

1" DRYWALL SCREW

1" BRAD

SECTION VIEW

The length of the table is designed to accommodate two chairs comfortably side by side. The width is designed to fit four widths of tongue-and-groove veneer flooring laid side by side. If you decide to use a different brand of flooring from ours (see Buyer's Guide, p. 112), adjust the width and size of your table accordingly. This table used a single package of flooring; a larger table would require a second package.

Getting the right materials makes the assembly go like clockwork

If you can't find the exact materials listed in our Buyer's Guide, select substitutes. The 48-in. colonial-style newel posts were a staple in the stair parts section at a local home center. If newel posts aren't the right shape or length for your table design (you may decide to build a coffee table), you can also buy table legs (see Buyer's Guide, p. 112, for details). If you plan to paint the legs, choose poplar or maple because their smooth surfaces paint up beautifully. Oak is porous and looks best stained and varnished.

Hauling a big piece of plywood home in a standard sedan can be a problem as well, so ask the store clerk to cut it to the dimensions you need. Lumberyards and home centers will usually charge a small fee for cutting the plywood for you, but here's a place where the benefit is well worth the extra buck.

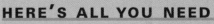

HERE'S ALL YOU NEED

ITEM
- Hardwood veneer flooring
- 3/4" plywood base
- Stairway newel posts
- Wood trim
- Hardware

CUTTING LIST

KEY	PCS.	SIZE & DESCRIPTION
A	1	3/4" x 29-5/8" x 64" plywood subtop (base)
B	4	3" x 3" x 28-1/2" factory-turned newel posts (cut as shown)
C1	2	3/4" x 3-1/2" x 22-5/8" oak aprons
C2	2	3/4" x 3-1/2" x 57" oak aprons
D1	2	3/4" x 2-1/4" x 22-5/8" dentil molding
D2	2	3/4" x 2-1/4" x 57" dentil molding
E	1 pkg.	Harris Tarkett Vanguard flooring (Wheat Oak)
F	1	3/8" x 1-5/16" x 16' oak edge trim (Princeton doorstop) cut to fit

The prefinished flooring top we used has a plywood substrate with about a 1/8-in. thick solid wood surface. This style flooring is meant to be installed as a floating floor, not glued to flooring underlayment. However, for a small area like this table, gluing and screwing the flooring to the plywood below is just fine. Large areas such as floors need to move independently from the plywood or subfloor below.

You can use a power mitersaw with a sharp blade for cutting the parts, but I found the simple, inexpensive handsaw miter box worked really well for getting straight 90-degree cuts as well as the 45-degree miters for the edging around the tabletop.

To get the flooring edges to align perfectly with the plywood subtop, you'll find that a sanding block or a belt sander along the edge will straighten the edges for the final trim piece around the perimeter.

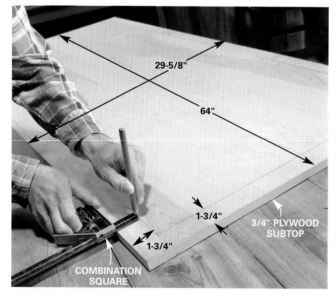

1 CUT your newel post perfectly square using a simple miter box as a guide. Cut the top first, then flip it end-for-end and trim the other end.

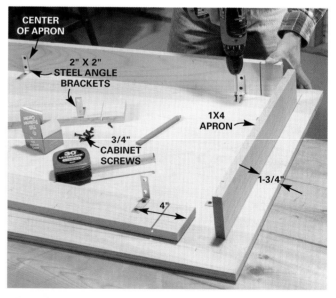

2 CUT the aprons to length, then cut a 1/8-in. wide by 1/4-in. deep saw kerf 2 in. from the end. To make the kerf wide enough with the slender handsaw shown, make individual cuts on each side of your mark, then knock out the center section with a knife. A little too wide is still OK.

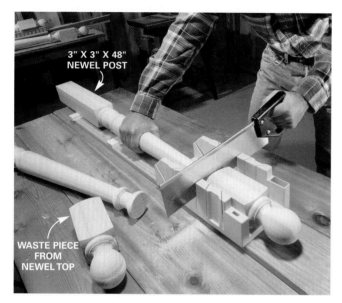

3 DRAW guidelines on the underside of the plywood to later align the aprons. Place a mark 3-1/2 in. in from each edge to mark the end points of the apron pieces and the edges of the legs. The size of our plywood subtop accommodates the dimensions of the flooring with a bit left over.

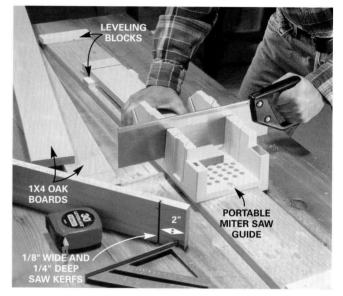

4 POSITION the aprons along the lines drawn in the previous step. Screw the aprons to the underside of the top using steel angle brackets. Use three brackets for the two longer aprons. Slightly bend the angle brackets if they're not holding the aprons square to the plywood subtop.

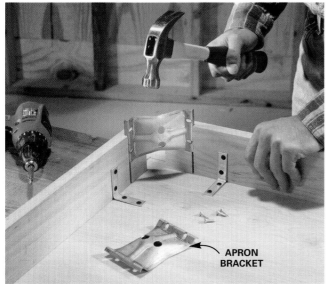

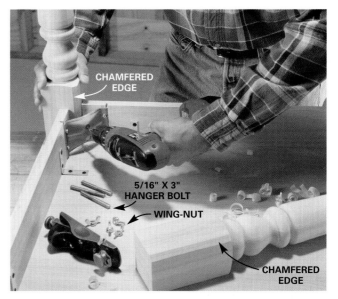

5 TAP the apron brackets into the saw kerf cuts you made earlier. With the bracket centered on the apron, screw it to the aprons with 5/8-in. sheet metal screws (purchased separately).

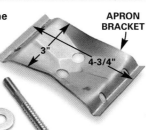

APRON
BRACKET

3"

4-3/4"

6 SHAVE OFF one upper edge of each leg (chamfer) with a hand plane to create a flat spot for drilling. Cradle the leg tightly between the aprons and against the subtop, then drill a 1/4-in. pilot hole into each leg.

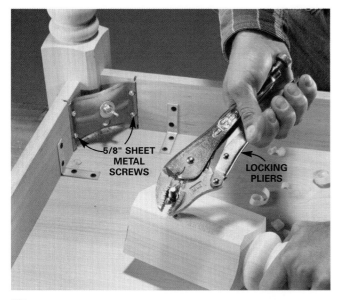

5/8" SHEET METAL SCREWS

LOCKING PLIERS

7 TURN the hanger bolt into the pilot hole with a locking pliers clamped around the Wing-Nut (to protect the threads). Leave about 1-1/4 in. of the bolt exposed, then remove the Wing-Nut. Slip the leg and bolt into place and tighten the Wing-Nut to the bracket.

HAPPY CLAMPER

SPRING CLAMPS

DENTIL MOLDING

8 GLUE the dentil molding to the aprons and clamp them in place. If you don't have enough clamps, let the freshly glued and clamped section set for 45 minutes, then move to the next apron. Use a clamp every 8 in.

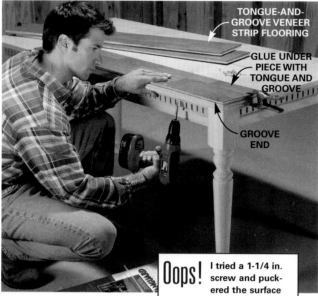

TONGUE-AND-GROOVE VENEER STRIP FLOORING

GLUE UNDER PIECE WITH TONGUE AND GROOVE

GROOVE END

Oops! I tried a 1-1/4 in. screw and puckered the surface of the flooring in a couple of spots when I drove the screw in a half turn too tight!

9 POSITION the first piece of flooring with the grooved side and end perfectly aligned with the corner of the plywood subtop. Apply a couple of dots of construction adhesive to the underside of each piece of flooring and then screw through the bottom of the plywood subtop into the flooring. Use 1-in. drywall screws (two on each end).

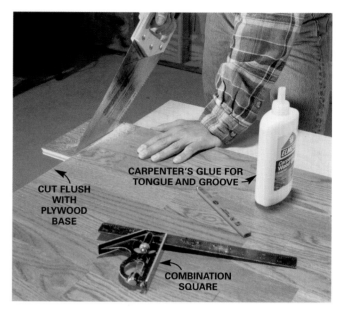

CUT FLUSH WITH PLYWOOD BASE

CARPENTER'S GLUE FOR TONGUE AND GROOVE

COMBINATION SQUARE

10 TRIM the ends of the flooring flush with the edge of the plywood subtop. Stroke the saw gently, cutting on the downstroke, and be sure the piece you're cutting has been glued and screwed first to hold it steady. Glue and nail the 1-5/16 in. edge trim to cover the edge of the flooring and the plywood underneath. It's much easier to prefinish these pieces—you'll save yourself the trouble of carefully staining and varnishing them right alongside the finished flooring.

Choose a tough finish for your table parts

We chose an oil stain (see Buyer's Guide) that matched our prefinished flooring. Be sure to sand all the parts with 150-grit sandpaper before staining. Let the stain dry and apply two coats of a waterborne polyurethane varnish. We used a semigloss poly acrylic finish by Minwax. To minimize tedious cutting in with a brush, be sure to prefinish the wood edge trim before you glue it to the sides of the tabletop. Protect the back of the trim with masking tape as you stain and varnish it so the wood glue will bond to the trim.

Prime the legs with a brush-on primer. When that's thoroughly dry, sand it with 120-grit sandpaper and then apply two coats of spray enamel for a really smooth finish. 🏠

Buyer's Guide

- Many brands of engineered wood flooring are sold at home centers. We designed the size of the table for Vanguard Wheat Oak (9/16 in. thick) by Harris Tarkett. To locate a dealer near you, call Harris Tarkett at (800) 842-7816 or visit its Web site at www.harristarkett.com.
- Order your set of four apron brackets (part No. 34303) for $3.49 plus shipping from Rockler at (800) 279-4441 or visit its Web site at www.rockler.com.
- We used Ace Hardware brand cherry oil stain.
- Check out the variety of table legs at Osborne Wood Products (800-849-8876, www.osbornewood.com) and Woodturner's Inc. (877-603-9663, www.queenannelegs.com).

Top, leg, apron and molding options

You can build this simple project exactly as we've done or put your own spin on it. Feel free to choose from a variety of wood species for your aprons, legs and edge moldings. Look through the molding bins at your lumberyard and home center. Color can also change the overall look of the project.

Keep in mind that you can choose from a variety of materials for your tabletop as well, from ceramic tile to plastic laminate flooring, so pick the material that suits your sense of style. Whatever you choose, follow the step-by-step photos and clear drawings to guide you through the basic process.

You can fix it™

RENEW A WORN SCREWDRIVER

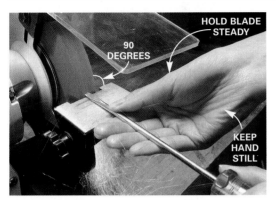

90 DEGREES
HOLD BLADE STEADY
KEEP HAND STILL

1 SET the tool rest at a right angle to the grinding wheel. Push the screwdriver tip straight into the grinding wheel until the damaged portion is removed and the tip is flat.

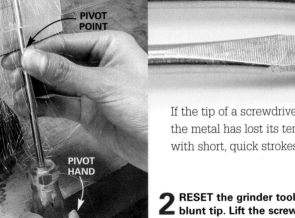

PIVOT POINT
PIVOT HAND

2 RESET the grinder tool rest to thin the blunt tip. Lift the screwdriver on and off the grinding wheel by pivoting it against the tool rest edge. Grind both sides equally until the tip is thinned to the desired thickness.

Rescue those chipped and bent flat-blade screwdrivers from the trash! With a bench grinder and a little time, you can regrind a damaged flat-blade screwdriver tip to the original shape or thin it to fit eyeglass and other small screwheads.

In all grinding procedures, safety is the most important factor. Grinding without safety glasses is just plain foolish. Grinding wheels throw a steady stream of sparks when they're in contact with metal. Do not wear loose long sleeves and keep your fingers and hair away from the spinning wheels.

Set the grinder tool rest so it's as close as possible to the grinding wheel without touching. Butt an index finger into the tool rest and steady the screwdriver blade with your thumb. Use your other hand to push the screwdriver into the grinding wheel (this keeps both hands as far from the spinning wheel as possible).

Photos 1 and 2 show how to repair or modify a damaged flat-blade screwdriver tip. Grinding will generate heat, so after a few seconds of grinding, pull the tool away from the grinding wheel and let it cool or quench it with water. If the tip of a screwdriver overheats during grinding and turns blue, the metal has lost its temper and weakened. Remove any bluing with short, quick strokes against the grinder.

AWL RIGHT PHILLIPS SCREWDRIVER

Can awl of us find our awl when we need it? Grab an old, battered Phillips screwdriver and grind the tip into a sharp cone shape on a bench grinder. (Wear eye protection.) Now you have a heavy-duty awl for starting screws and finish nails right on the mark, and chipping dried glue from project corners.

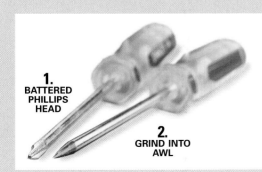

1. BATTERED PHILLIPS HEAD

2. GRIND INTO AWL

Ask™ Handyman

HOW CAN I MAKE BASIC HOMEMADE MOLDINGS?

The cherry and walnut moldings I need for my small projects are either expensive or unavailable. Got any ideas?

Here's a safe and easy way to make custom moldings for your furniture projects and picture frames. Choose a wide, knot-free board and rout the profile along its length (top). Set the table saw fence to the width you need and saw off the first length of molding (see below), being sure to use a push stick as you end the cut.

That's it—repeat the process on the just-sawn board. This simple technique eliminates the danger and vibration of routing profiles on narrow strips of wood.

1. Rout first WIDE, CLEAR BOARD

2. Then cut HOMEMADE MOLDING

SHOULD I REPLACE MY CORDLESS DRILL BATTERIES?

My old cordless drill has a rechargeable battery that's shot. I can't find a replacement battery. Can you tell me where to get a replacement?

First, find a factory-authorized service dealer (check the Yellow Pages under "Tools, Electric") and ask about the replacement price. Brace yourself; it might shock you. A new 12-volt battery for an old drill of mine costs $45. Next I called a battery dealer, Batteries Plus (800-MR-START; www.batteriesplus.com). They quoted me a price of $33 to rebuild the battery, which includes a six-month warranty. Rebuilding consists of opening the battery pack and replacing the ten 1.2-volt cells (10 times 1.2 volts equals 12 volts) with new ones.

Find rebuilders in the Yellow Pages under "Batteries." They'll tell you if they can do the job. If the drill is still working, rebuild the battery pack.

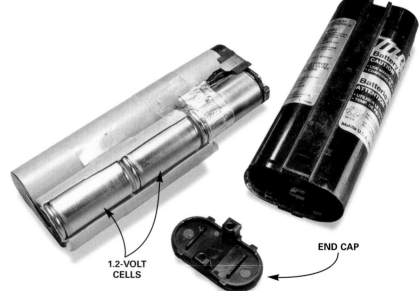

1.2-VOLT CELLS

END CAP

DON'T KNOW WHERE TO RECYCLE YOUR RECHARGEABLE BATTERIES?

Call 1-800-8BATTERY or go on-line at www.rbrc.org to find the closest drop-off location for rechargeable batteries, with the exception of car batteries. Rechargeable batteries are the type found in nearly any gadget that you plug in to recharge—like cell phones, power tools, laptops and camcorders.

WHAT ABOUT THE LETTER 'D'?

You guys are always specifying "d" sizes for nails such as 16d, 8d, etc. What in the world does "d" mean? How about giving us the nail lengths along with the "d" designation?

The "d" stands for penny, so 8d refers to an 8-penny nail, 16d to a 16-penny nail and so on. It's a way to indicate nail length, as you can see in the table at right.

Now for the obvious question: Where does the sizing system come from and why does "d" stand for penny? The "d" goes way back to the time when the Romans occupied what is now England. The "d" is associated with a Roman coin called the denarius, which was also the name for an English penny.

So what's that got to do with nails? It was associated with nails when they were hand-forged, one at a time. Some say a hundred 3-1/2 inch nails would have cost 16 pennies and thus became known as 16-penny nails. Others say that the number and the "d" indicate that one 16d (3-1/2 inch) hand-forged nail cost 16 pennies.

Who knows which version is true or why the "d" designation persists even in the building codes today, but fortunately, retail boxes of nails are marked with the penny size as well as the length in inches. As you can see in the photo, length is only one factor of many in choosing a nail.

NAILS FOR LIGHT CONSTRUCTION

SIZE	LENGTH (IN INCHES)
4d	1-1/2
6d	2
8d	2-1/2
10d	3
12d	3-1/4
16d	3-1/2
20d	4
30d	4-1/2

CASING   COMMON   SINKER   DUPLEX   SIDING

3-1/2" (16d)

COMMON   SINKER   DUPLEX

2-1/2" (8d)

HOW DO I CUT A PERFECT CIRCLE?

I'm building a table with a round plywood top. Got a better way than a jigsaw and a steady hand to make the top?

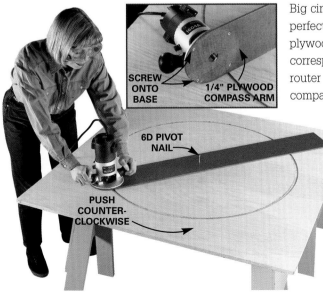

SCREW ONTO BASE

1/4" PLYWOOD COMPASS ARM

6D PIVOT NAIL

PUSH COUNTER-CLOCKWISE

Big circles are tough to cut, especially when they need to be perfectly round. Make a compass arm for your router from 1/4-in. plywood or hardboard. Remove your router's plastic base and drill corresponding holes in your compass arm. Attach the arm to your router and install a straight-cutting 1/2-in. carbide bit. Pin the compass arm to the plywood with a 6d nail. The top of your finished circle will face down.

Start the cut with the bit depth set at 1/4 in. and increase the depth of cut about 5/16 in. for each pass. When you start, gently ease the router down into the workpiece and push counterclockwise. Reset the depth for each cut and be sure to support the cutout on each side with your sawhorses as you make the final "through" cut. A firm grip is necessary to keep the router steady on the last cut.

CRAFTING POSTS WITH
YOUR CIRCULAR SAW

Create stronger, more attractive decks and fences using these simple tricks of the trade.

by **Jeff Gorton**

Honing your circular saw skills will pay big dividends when you're building decks and fences. Good techniques will speed up your work, create stronger joints and show off your craft, since all the cuts and joints are highly visible. In this story, we'll show you how to get a perfectly square cut on the end of a 6x6 post, cut notches and shape deck posts with your circular saw.

You'll need a circular saw with a sharp 7-1/4 in. blade to make the deep cuts we'll be showing. A 24-tooth carbide blade (less than $10 at hardware stores and home centers) is a good deck-building blade.

SQUARE-CUT
A 6X6 POST

Here's an easy method for making a smooth, clean cut on a 6x6 when you cut it to length. By rotating the post a quarter turn after each cut, you can use the previous cut to guide the blade for the next cut. Since a 7-1/4 in. blade cuts a little less than halfway through, you'll have to finish the cut with a handsaw. To prevent kickback, position both sawhorses on the keeper side of the line and allow the cutoff piece to fall.

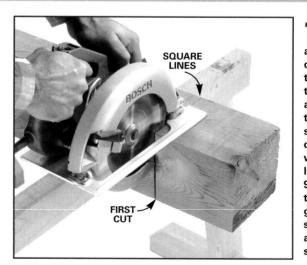

SQUARE LINES

FIRST CUT

1 MARK the post for length and use a Speed square or combination square to draw a line around the post. Make sure all the lines meet at the corners. Set the saw for maximum depth and saw to the waste side of the first line. Rotate the post 90 degrees and using the first cut as a guide, cut the second side. Cut the third and fourth sides the same way.

2 CUT the wood remaining in the center with a sharp handsaw.

116

1 CUT the 6x6 to length and mark the notches. Set the saw to the depth of the notch as shown and make both cross-cuts. Then reset the blade to maximum depth and make the four rip cuts. Cut to the waste side of all lines and stop at the crosscuts.

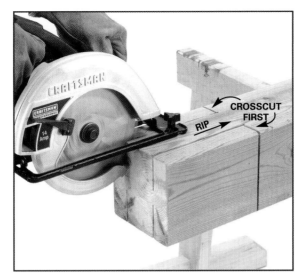

CROSSCUT FIRST

RIP

NOTCH A 6X6 POST

Create a sturdy connection by notching a 6x6 post to accept a beam. You could

make these notches using the technique shown in Photos 2 and 3, p. 118, but the ripping method shown at right is a little faster, especially for long

notches. If you're using treated posts, brush a wood preservative onto the freshly exposed wood.

2 COMPLETE the rip cuts with a handsaw. Clean up uneven edges with a sharp chisel.

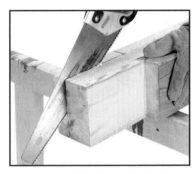

CRAFT A **BEVELED** POST CAP

Placing a cap over your rail posts not only looks good but also protects the vulnerable end grain of the post from the weather. Caps for 6x6s usually must be special-ordered, but you can make your own from 2x10 material and save the wait and money. This jig is made from 16-in. pieces of 2x8 framing and 1/2-in. plywood (see illustration). Setting the plywood guide on the jig to your circular saw requires some trial and error. Adjust it so the blade leaves a slight reveal on the top of the cap. Secure the cap to the posts with construction adhesive and 3-in. galvanized finish nails.

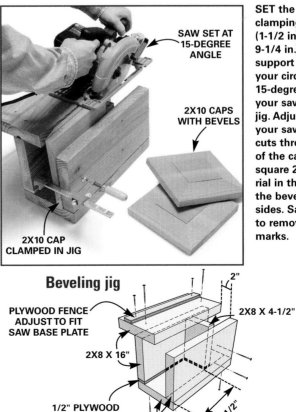

SAW SET AT 15-DEGREE ANGLE

2X10 CAPS WITH BEVELS

2X10 CAP CLAMPED IN JIG

SET the jig fence by clamping a scrap 2x10 (1-1/2 in. x 9-1/4 in. x 9-1/4 in.) to the outer support of the jig. Set your circular saw to a 15-degree angle. Run your saw through the jig. Adjust the fence so your saw blade just cuts through the top of the cap. Set the square 2x10 cap material in the jig and cut the bevel on all four sides. Sand the caps to remove any saw marks.

Beveling jig

PLYWOOD FENCE ADJUST TO FIT SAW BASE PLATE

2X8 X 4-1/2"

2X8 X 16"

1/2" PLYWOOD SPACER

2X8 X 16"

2"

9-1/2"

NOTCH THE **MIDDLE** OF A POST

Rail posts often require notching to fit around a deck joist (**Photos 2 and 3**). Enclosed notches like these are easy to make with a series of saw kerfs. After the chunks are broken out, you'll have a little cleanup to do with a sharp wood chisel.

SQUARE YOUR SAW BLADE

You can't make clean cuts unless the blade is square to the saw's bed. Most saws have an adjustment screw near the angle gauge for this purpose. With the saw unplugged and the blade set to maximum depth, retract the blade guard and hold a square against the bed and blade to make sure they're exactly 90 degrees to each other. Adjust the screw if necessary.

Next check to make sure the blade is parallel to the saw bed. With the saw unplugged and blade fully extended, hook a combination square or Speed square on the back of the bed and slide it tight to the blade. They should line up. Most saws don't have adjusting screws for this. Make adjustments by carefully bending the bed sideways until the blade and bed are parallel.

1-1/2"

7-1/4"

BED TIGHT TO 4X4

1 **MARK the** notch on both sides and the top of the post. Unplug the saw and loosen the depth adjuster. Hold the bed of the saw tight to the post and move the blade until the teeth just touch the line. Tighten the depth adjuster.

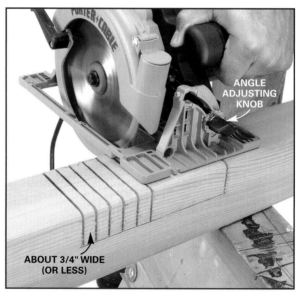

ANGLE ADJUSTING KNOB

ABOUT 3/4" WIDE (OR LESS)

2 **SAW to the** inside of the lines on both ends of the notch. Then cut saw kerfs every 3/4 in. across the notch. Just eyeball these cuts—they don't have to be perfect.

SMOOTH WITH CHISEL

BREAK OUT CHUNKS

3 **PRY OUT the** chunks. Then use a chisel to smooth the bottom of the notch.

1 SCREW lengths of 1x6 together as shown to make a tight-fitting collar for your post. Rough-cut your post about 4 in. longer than its finished length. Screw the collar to the post about 7 in. from the end. Set the saw to cut a 45-degree angle and adjust the blade to cut about 1-1/2 in. deep. Keep the saw bed tight to the collar as you saw all four sides of the post.

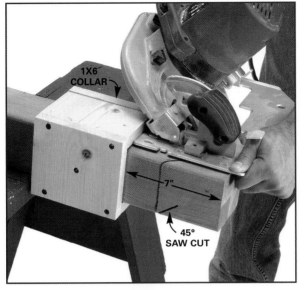

1X6 COLLAR

7"

45° SAW CUT

2 SET the saw to cut 90 degrees and the blade depth to 2 in. Remove the screw and adjust the position of the collar to cut 1-1/2 in. beyond your first cut. Saw around the post, using the collar as a guide.

2"

1-1/2"

3 SET the saw to cut 3/8 in. deep. Readjust the position of the collar and cut a decorative groove around the post. Move the collar another 1/8 in. and saw again to make a wider groove.

3/8" DEEP X 1/4" WIDE NOTCH

CUT A
DECORATIVE
POST TOP

Photos 1 – 3 show one way to cut a decorative post top using a simple

wood collar as a guide for the saw. Make the collar by cutting two pieces of 1x6 about 1/32 in. longer than the post width and two more pieces 1-1/2 in. longer than this. Screw the pieces together to form a snug-fitting collar. Slide the collar over the 4x4 and secure it with two screws on opposite sides to hold it in place. The holes left from the screws will swell shut and become nearly invisible with time. Practice various patterns on a scrap 4x4 and keep track of all the collar locations by marking the post before you reposition the collar. When you have a design you like, simply transfer these marks to each post to duplicate the cuts.

In **Photo 1**, we show cutting the 45-degree angles on the post top before cutting the post to length. The extra post length supports the bed of the saw, making it easier to cut accurate angles.

You can cut any size groove with a circular saw if you're patient enough to make multiple passes (**Photo 3**). But you'll save time and get better results using the same collar to guide a router fitted with a straight-cutting router bit. ⌂

Gallery
of Ideas

FROM OCTOBER 2001, P. 84

STACKABLE SHELVES

If you need shelving, storage, a desk or "all of the above," check out this modular system. It's got lots of storage space for your electronic gear and books, plus a nifty recess to accommodate a stool. Best of all you can easily customize this system to suit your storage needs and wall space.

Project Facts:
Cost: $250
Skill level: Intermediate
Time: 15-20 hours

Special tools: Circular saw, jigsaw, clothes iron, laminate edge trimmer

TRADITIONAL PORCH SWING

The smooth, gentle glide of this porch swing will keep you daydreaming for hours. In fact, you may lose your ambition for good! Simple cuts and no-hassle glue and screw assembly techniques make it a great first-time woodworking project.

Project Facts:
Cost: $150
Skill level: Ambitious beginner

Time: 8-10 hours (plus painting time)
Special tools: Jigsaw, circular saw, tablesaw

FROM MARCH 2002, P. 53

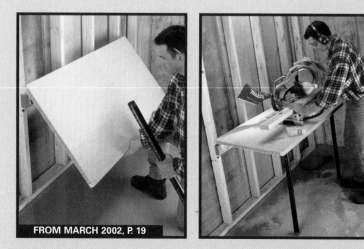

FROM MARCH 2002, P. 19

FOLD-DOWN WORKBENCH

Here's an easy-to-build, inexpensive and sturdy workbench that tucks away in seconds. Perfect for garages, laundryrooms, or rooms where you're short on space and long on projects. The main ingredients? A solid core door, pipe and pipe flanges, and gate hinges.

Project Facts:
Cost: Under $50
Skill level: Beginner

Time: 2-3 hours
Special tools: Circular saw

To order photocopies of complete plans for the projects shown above, call 715-246-4344 or write to:
Copies, The Family Handyman, 511 Wisconsin Dr., New Richmond, WI 54017.
Many public libraries also carry back issues of The Family Handyman magazine.

Wordless™
Workshop

by **Roy Doty**

THREE GARAGE
STORAGE PROJECTS

These projects organize odds and ends, clear clutter and clean up the workbench and garage floor. You can build each in less than a day using only basic tools.

by **Jeff Timm**

ONE: **ROTATING CORNER SHELVES**

Set aside a Saturday to build this handy bin and you'll clean up all those loose boxes of screws, bolts and other small stuff that clutter your garage or workshop. This bin rotates on a pair of lazy Susan rings to maximize corner space and provide quick, easy access. A stationary upper shelf secured to the wall steadies the bin so it'll spin easily and won't tip over. You can add as many shelves as you need. We left one bay open top to bottom for storing tall things like levels and straightedges. You won't need special joints or fasteners to construct it; simple butt joints and screws hold it all together. You need only basic carpentry tools to cut and fasten the pieces.

Materials and cost

This project costs about $100. We constructed it from one and a half 4x8 sheets of birch plywood ($40 per sheet, about $25 per half sheet). Birch plywood is easy to work with because it's smooth and flat, but you can cut your costs by about half if you use 3/4-in. CDX-grade plywood ($15 per sheet). Buy two lazy Susan rings, 12-in. round ($6) and 3-in. square ($1) diameters from a woodworkers' store if your home center doesn't carry them. (One mail order source for lazy Susans is Rockler, 800-279-4441; www.rockler.com. The 12-in. part No. is 28985; the 3-in. part No. is 28951.) You can find all of the other materials at most home centers, including the 3-in. vinyl base we used for the shelf edging ($2 per 4-ft. length). See the complete Materials List opposite.

Careful cutting and layout make assembly a snap

Cut all the pieces to size from the cutting diagram. Accurate cuts will result in tight, clean joints. Clamp a straightedge to the plywood to guide your circular saw when making the straight cuts. Use a carbide blade with at least 36 teeth to minimize splintering.

Photo 1 shows you how to mark the circle for the plywood bottom. Substitute a narrow strip of 1/4-in. thick wood for the compass arm if you don't have Peg-Board.

Tip

Mark the centerline of each shelf on the opposite side of the dividers to help position the screws (Photo 3).

Use the bottom as a template to mark the arcs on the quarter-circle shelves (**Fig. B**). Use a bucket to mark the arcs on the tops of the dividers.

Electrical

Tapes

Auto

Stains

Spray Paint

Fig. A: Bin details

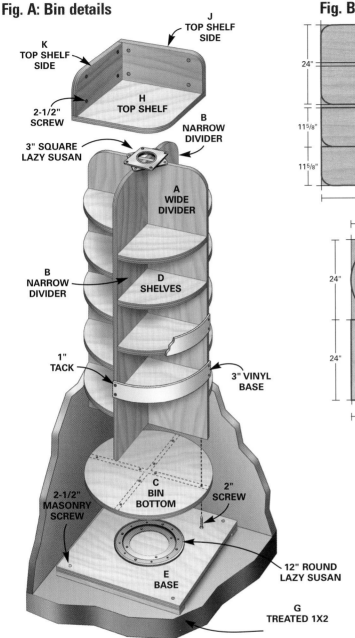

J TOP SHELF SIDE

K TOP SHELF SIDE

2-1/2" SCREW

H TOP SHELF

3" SQUARE LAZY SUSAN

B NARROW DIVIDER

A WIDE DIVIDER

B NARROW DIVIDER

D SHELVES

1" TACK

3" VINYL BASE

2-1/2" MASONRY SCREW

C BIN BOTTOM

2" SCREW

E BASE

12" ROUND LAZY SUSAN

G TREATED 1X2

Fig. B: Cutting layout

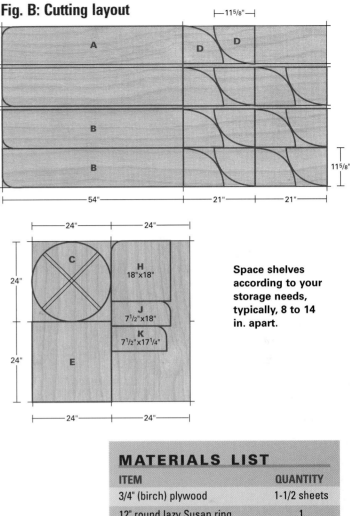

Space shelves according to your storage needs, typically, 8 to 14 in. apart.

MATERIALS LIST

ITEM	QUANTITY
3/4" (birch) plywood	1-1/2 sheets
12" round lazy Susan ring	1
3" square lazy Susan ring	1
2" No. 8 screws	1 lb.
3/4-in. No. 6 flat head screws	16
4' strips of 3" vinyl base	10
1" tacks	1 lb.
Tube of vinyl base adhesive	1
2' treated 1x2s	2
2-1/2" x 3/16" masonry screws	3
2-1/2" screws	8

CUTTING LIST

KEY	SIZE & DESCRIPTION
A	Wide divider, 3/4" x 24" x 54"
B	Two narrow dividers, 3/4" x 11-5/8" x 54"
C	Bin bottom, 3/4" x 24" diameter
D	Up to 16 shelves, 3/4" x 11-5/8" x 11-5/8"
E	Base, 3/4" x 24" x 24"
G	Two treated 1x2s, 1 x 2 x 24"
H	Top shelf, 3/4" x 18" x 18"
J	Shelf side, 3/4" x 7-1/2" x 18"
K	Shelf side, 3/4" x 7-1/2" x 17-1/4"

Before assembling the pieces, lay out the shelf locations on the dividers. Make the shelves any height you want, but making them different heights in adjacent sections simplifies the screwing process.

Fasten the shelves to the two narrow dividers first (**Photo 2**), then set them upright and attach them to the wide center divider (**Photo 3**).

Drilling an access hole is the trick to mounting the lazy Susan

At first glance, attaching the 12-in. lazy Susan is a bit mysterious. The lazy Susan rotates on ball bearings with the top ring secured to the bin bottom and the bottom ring secured to the base. Securing it to the base is straight-forward—you center it and screw it down. Once it's fastened, you have to drive screws upward to fasten the top ring to the bin bottom. The bottom ring of the lazy Susan has a special 3/4-in. access hole to help here. Drill a 3/4-in. hole in the plywood base at the access hole point (**Photo 4**). Then poke your screws through the access hole to fasten the top ring to the bin base (**Photo 5**).

The 3-in. lazy Susan rotates on square plates. You won't need an access hole to fasten them. Just screw through the holes in the corners (**Photo 6**).

Putting the unit in place

If you're placing the base on a concrete floor, rest it on treated 1x2s to avoid rot. Level it with shims, if needed, for smooth rotation. Fasten the support shelf to the walls with 2-1/2 inch screws (**Photo 7**).

Anchor the base of the bin to the floor with masonry screws set in the exposed corners. Predrill the holes into the concrete with a 5/32-in. masonry bit or the size the screw package recommends.

The vinyl base provides an edge for the shelves. Buy the type that's not preglued. The 4-in. wide type is most common, but buy the 3-in. wide type if you can. Otherwise, use a sharp utility knife to trim an inch off the 4-in. one. Secure it to the shelf edges with adhesive and 1-in. tacks.

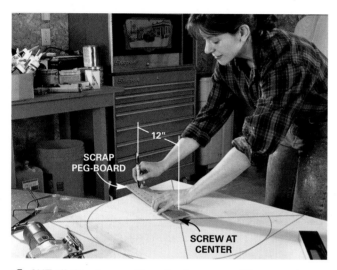

1 CUT all the pieces with a circular saw and jigsaw, using the dimensions in Fig. A and our Cutting List. Mark the circle cut for the bottom with a 12-in. compass made from a scrap of Peg-Board. Cut it out with a jigsaw. Then trace the arcs of the shelves using the bottom as a template. (Note: The shelf sides are 11-5/8 in.)

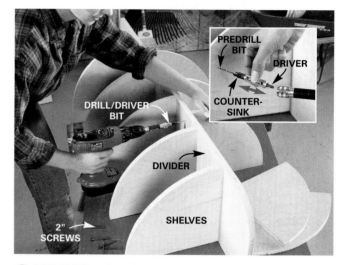

2 MEASURE and mark the shelf locations on the dividers, spacing them anywhere from 10 to 14 in. apart. Align the shelves with these marks, then predrill and screw the shelves to the two narrow dividers with 2-in. drywall screws. A drill/driver bit speeds this process ($10 at home centers).

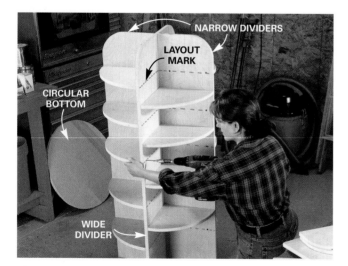

3 CONNECT the two shelf assemblies to the wide center divider with 2-in. drywall screws. Center and screw the circular bottom to the dividers.

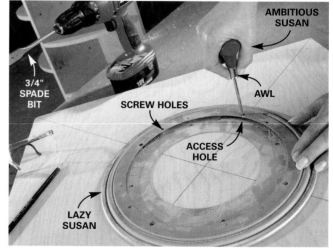

4 CENTER the 12-in. lazy Susan on the base. Align the screw holes on the top and bottom rings. Locate the access hole in the lazy Susan and mark its location on the plywood with an awl or nail. Remove the lazy Susan and drill a 3/4-in. hole at the mark. Center the lazy Susan again, aligning the access hole to the hole drilled in the plywood, and fasten the bottom ring to the base with 3/4-in. No. 6 flat head screws.

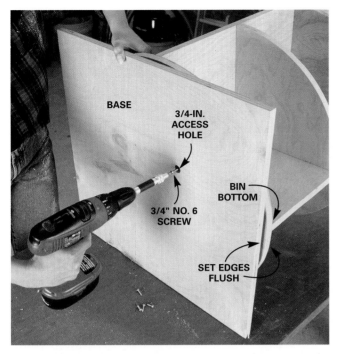

5 CENTER the base on the bin bottom and align a screw hole in the top ring of the lazy Susan with the access hole. Fasten the top ring of the lazy Susan to the bin bottom with a 3/4-in. No. 6 flat head screw driven through the access hole. Turn the bin bottom to align the remaining screw holes in the top ring with the access hole, and fasten with additional screws.

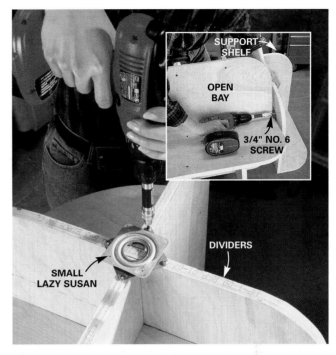

6 SCREW the bottom ring of the 3-in. lazy Susan to the dividers on top of the bin with 3/4-in. screws. Assemble the support shelf (Fig. A). Mark the bin rotation center on its bottom (about 13 in. from each wall) so the bin will clear the wall by about an inch when it rotates. INSET: Center the 3-in. lazy Susan at the rotation center on the support shelf. Screw the top ring of the lazy Susan to the support shelf with the 3/4-in. screws.

7 SET the bin on treated 1x2s with the base about 1 in. from the walls. Shim to level if needed. Level the support shelf and screw it to the wall studs with 2-1/2-in. screws. Spin the bin to test for smooth operation. If it runs rough, shim the base or slide it side to side slightly until it spins smoothly. Predrill and fasten the base to the floor with 2-1/2 in. masonry screws.

8 SQUEEZE a 3/8-in. bead of cove base adhesive along the shelf edges. Position the vinyl base with the lip to the top, curling out. Secure the ends with 1 in. tacks. Trim the ends flush with a utility knife.

TWO: **EASY-REACH BENCHTOP TOOLS**

Workbench cluttered with bench-top power tools? Here's the solution:

Screw each tool to a 3/4-in. plywood base with lag screws and flat washers. Plane or saw a 40-degree angle on one edge of a 3-in. x 3/4-in. board and cut it into cleats. Screw two cleats to each base with the angled edge facing inward. Now, with 1/4-in. x 3-in. lag screws, screw another 3/4-in. board or long piece of plywood with a 40-degree edge to the wall, being sure the screws go into wall studs. That's it—tool clutter ended.

Hang the tools from either end of the base, but be sure to hang only the lighter-weight bench-top tools. For larger tools like table saws and planers, we recommend horizontal storage, not wall-hung.

BENCH-TOP TOOLS

LAG SCREW

40-DEGREE BEVEL

TOOL CAN HANG FROM EITHER END

THREE: **JUMBO FASTENER TOTE**

A plastic carton for 2-liter soda bottles makes a great organizer and carryall for screws and nails. Buy a carton of soda at a grocery store and replace the bottles with 12-oz. coffee cans. Fill the cans with hardware and screw on a wood handle for easy carrying. Screwdrivers, nail pullers, pliers and other small tools fit so neatly in the small recesses that you'll think this carton was designed as a caddy. ⌂

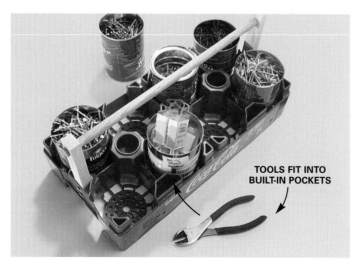

TOOLS FIT INTO BUILT-IN POCKETS

ADD HANDLE

EIGHT-PACK CARRIER

Great Goofs™ True tales by real readers!

Doggone it

I was building a doghouse for my son-in-law's dog in my compact 8 x 12-ft. workshop. Everything went fine till it was time to take it outside and paint it. I tried to get it out the door front-to-back, then side-to-side, then flipped it top-to-bottom, but it was still a couple of inches too wide. After all this work, I wasn't about to dismantle this fabulous project. Two hours later, I finally got it outside—after I removed the trim, the door and the door frame!

Window chopping

While remodeling our kitchen and dining room, I set my power miter saw onto sawhorses placed in the dining room. The only available spot was right in front of the brand-new thermal pane window. I thought nothing of this until the saw grabbed a chunk of trim I was cutting and sent it hurling out the back of the saw, right through the window behind.

Higher learning

A few years ago, I needed a bookcase for all the books we were accumulating. I decided that I'd make it floor-to-ceiling so we wouldn't run out of room anytime soon. After I built the bookcase, I brought it into the room to tip it into place. No matter how I angled the bookcase, the ceiling was too low for it. The only way to salvage this nice woodworking project was to cut off the bottom. I did save the pieces and luckily was able to use them in our new home (with higher ceilings) three years later.

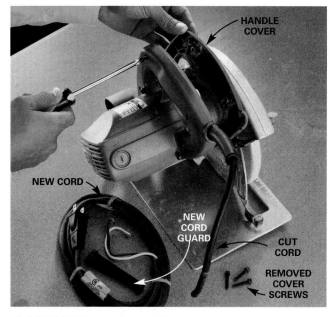

1 LOOK OVER your saw and locate the screws that secure the handle cover or casing. Unscrew the cover or casing and pull it off to expose the internal wiring.

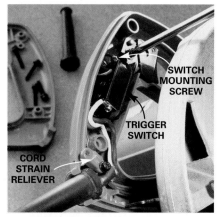

2 REMOVE one of the cord strain reliever screws, loosen the second screw and twist the strain reliever free from the cord. Remove the switch mounting screw and pull out the switch.

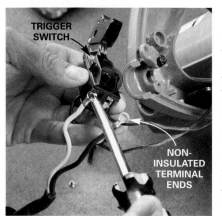

3 UNHOOK the old cord from the switch by unscrewing the terminal ends from the switch body. Crimp non-insulated terminal ends on the new cord (if necessary) and attach the new wires to the switch just like the old one.

REPLACE A SEVERED CIRCULAR SAW CORD

Whether you set the moving saw blade down on the cord or absentmindedly cut through it, the story's always the same. You're stuck with half-cut wood and a dead saw. Resist the temptation to grab some tape and splice the cord back together. The cord won't be able to take the abuse it was designed for, and the National Electrical Code forbids this repair. If the cord's cut near the plug, just add a new plug, but if it's too short to work with, pick up a new cord ($8) at an authorized service center. If the cord guard ($2) is cracked or damaged, replace it as well.

Photo 1 shows how to access the internal wiring by removing the handle cover. Screw locations vary and the entire casing may need to come apart, but don't dismantle more than necessary (keep the disassembled parts together so nothing gets lost). After the cover is removed and the wiring is exposed, pull out the trigger switch as shown in Photo 2. Remove the damaged cord and hook up the new one as shown in Photos 3 and 4. Fold the new wires into the same recesses as the old wires. Make sure all the wires are fully tucked inside the tool casing and that the cover will fully seat before screwing it down.

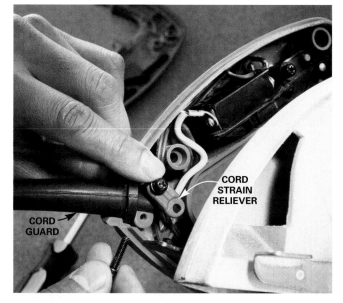

4 REMOUNT the switch and seat the new cord guard. Flip the cord strain reliever over the new cord, insert the loose screw and tighten both screws to hold the cord in place. Replace the handle cover or casing and saw away.

REPLACE A SLEDGEHAMMER HANDLE

When you're swinging a big-impact tool like an ax, maul or sledgehammer, every miss takes its toll on the handle. Eventually the handle will break or the tool head will loosen. Replacement wooden handles secured with wedges ($8) are OK, but for a few dollars more you can buy a replacement fiberglass handle that could still be swinging in 100 years. The kit contains a fiberglass handle and an epoxy packet. The epoxy and hardener are in one packet with a divider rod in the middle. When you remove the rod, you can mix the contents without mess or smell.

Photos 1 and 2 show how to remove the most stubborn old handle. Next, clean the inside of the eyehole. Epoxy won't bond to rusty or greasy surfaces. Insert the new handle (Photo 3) and bounce the bottom of the handle on concrete if you have trouble getting the top of the handle core flush with the top of the tool head. If they're still not flush, file or carve the new handle to fit.

The epoxy mix (Photo 4) will seal all the gaps between the handle core and the sledgehammer head, but it must be thoroughly blended or it won't set up. The temperature needs to be between 75 and 115 degrees F for proper curing. Pour the epoxy between the handle core and the hammerhead as shown in Photo 4. Wipe off any excess and let it cure for a week before using the tool.

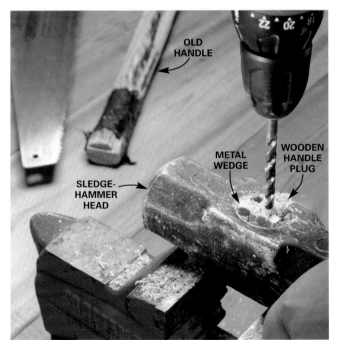

OLD HANDLE

METAL WEDGE

WOODEN HANDLE PLUG

SLEDGE-HAMMER HEAD

1 CUT OFF the old handle just above the tool head. Open the jaws of a vise wider than the remaining wooden handle plug and rest the ends of the tool head on the vise jaws. Drill 1/4-in. holes in the wooden handle plug until it looks like Swiss cheese (drill around the metal wedge in the center of the plug).

2 KNOCK OUT the wooden handle plug from the top of the tool head with a hammer and the biggest bolt you can find in your shop or garage. It takes a couple of good whacks with a hammer to get the plug started (so take a big swing), but once you get it going it'll push right out.

CAULKING CORD SEALER

3 CLEAN the inside of the eyehole with sand-paper. The scuffed surface helps the epoxy bond. Insert the handle into the tool eyehole until the top is flush (Photo 4). Seal the gap between the handle and head with the supplied caulking cord sealer to keep the epoxy from leaking out.

MIXED EPOXY

HANDLE CORE (FLUSH WITH HAMMERHEAD)

4 MIX UP the epoxy packet (inset) for at least two minutes until the color is completely uniform. Cut a corner off the bag and pour the epoxy around the top of the new handle. If epoxy leaks out around the caulking cord sealer, press the sealer into the seam until the leaking stops.

BUILD-THEM-ANY-SIZE
PATIO PLANTERS

This clever design lets you build them big or small, painted or stained, for indoor or outdoor use.

by David Radtke

This planter is designed to make your patio or deck gardening much easier. Instead of filling it with dirt and planting each flower or plant individually, you simply set prepotted plants right into the planter. You can conveniently switch plants as the season changes or unload the planter and move it to a new location.

We designed this project to fit any pot with an 11-in. diameter or less and a maximum height of 10-1/2 in. To create the illusion of a fully planted box, you just fill in around the pots with wood chips, bark or other mulch covering. The base or bottom of the planter has 7/8-in. holes drilled every 6 in. to drain away any excess water. The side boards have a 1/4-in. space between them to ventilate the mulch and keep it from getting soggy.

We've shown you two planters of different lengths,

but you can adapt them to fit your unique space. You can even change the width by nailing a treated 2x2 to the side of the 2x12 base piece to accommodate a slightly wider pot. To build either the small or large planter shown, follow our clear step-by-step photos and refer to the Cutting List for lumber lengths.

Buying the right lumber

You'll notice the legs are treated pine and not cedar like the sides and top apron. Treated pine is less likely to split along the grain (a nasty problem with cedar). Pick treated 2x12 material for the legs with as few large knots as possible. You'll be able to cut around knots on a single board, so bring a tape measure when you select the lumber. Choose straight cedar for the sides and remember that some knots here can add to the overall beauty.

Feel free to use other species of wood such as redwood, cypress or even a plantation-grown tropical wood like ipe (available at some lumberyards).

Project Facts:
Cost: $75
Time: 6 to 8 hours
Skill Level: Beginner/intermediate
Tools:
- Jigsaw
- Circular saw
- 12-in. Speed square (as cutting guide)
- Drill with pilot/countersink bit
- Power screwdriver
- Clamps
- Hammer
- Tape measure

CUTTING LIST

KEY	QTY.	DESCRIPTION	FOR LARGE PLANTER	FOR SMALL PLANTER
A	4	Treated pine legs	1-1/2" x 11-1/4" x 13"	1-1/2" x 11-1/4" x 13"
B	1	Treated pine base	1-1/2" x 11-1/4" x 48"	1-1/2" x 11-1/4" x 36"
C	4	Cedar side panels	1-1/2" x 5-1/2" x 48"	1-1/2" x 5-1/2" x 36"
D	4	Cedar end panels*	1-1/2" x 5-1/2" x 14-1/4"	1-1/2" x 5-1/2" x 14-1/4"
E	2	Cedar side aprons	1-1/16" x 4-1/2" x 57"	1-1/16" x 4-1/2" x 45"
F	2	Cedar side aprons*	1-1/16" x 4-1/2" x 20-1/4"	1-1/16" x 4-1/2" x 20-1/4"

*Cut to fit

Fig. A
Leg template (enlarge approximately 400%)

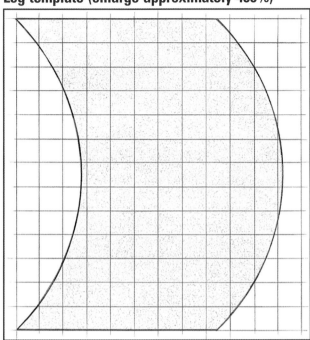

ONE SQUARE = 1 INCH

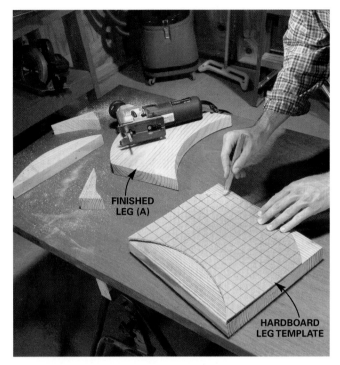

FINISHED LEG (A)

HARDBOARD LEG TEMPLATE

1 USING a full-size template made from Fig. A, trace the outline of the planter legs onto pressure-treated 2x12 pine boards. Sand the edges with a finish or belt sander followed by 100-grit hand-sanding to gently ease the edges.

C

12" SPEED SQUARE

D

SUPPORT BLOCK

2 MAKE straight cuts using a 12-in. Speed square held firmly against the back of the 2x6.

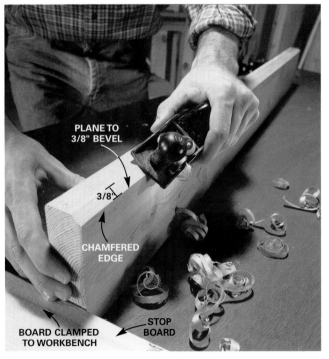

PLANE TO 3/8" BEVEL

3/8"

CHAMFERED EDGE

BOARD CLAMPED TO WORKBENCH

STOP BOARD

3 PLANE only the edges where the side boards C and D meet. This chamfered edge should be about 3/8 in. wide when completed. Clamp a board to the edge of your workbench to stop the workpiece from drifting while you stroke the edge of the board with the plane.

Use paint, stain or a combination of both

We chose an exterior enamel paint for the legs and apron pieces to accent the deck oil stain/sealer on the base and sides. Stain is a better choice than paint for the base and sides because they'll be exposed to more mois-

ture than the legs and top. The photo below shows the excellent results you can get by staining the entire project with a transparent exterior oil deck stain. Pre-painting and pre-staining all of the parts prior to assembly will provide even more protection and help your planters last longer.

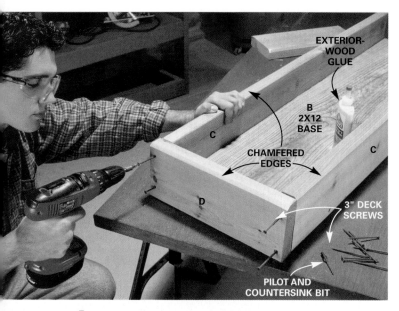

EXTERIOR-WOOD GLUE

B 2X12 BASE

CHAMFERED EDGES

C

C

D

3" DECK SCREWS

PILOT AND COUNTERSINK BIT

4 CUT your 2x12 base to length, then screw the lower sides (C) to the base. Align the base and sides so they're flush on the bottom sides. Predrill for each screw using a pilot/countersink combination bit. Then screw the ends to the sides.

CLAMP

C

A

2-1/2" DECK SCREWS

LEAVE 3/16" TO EDGE

D

SHIMS

5 SHIM the base up 1-3/4 in. on each side using scrap pieces of wood, then clamp the legs one at a time to the sides (C). Screw the sides to the legs with 2-1/2 in. deck screws. Use three screws per leg.

B

C

C

A

DRILL 7/8" DRAIN HOLES EVERY 6"

D

6 CLAMP the upper sides flush to the tops of the legs. Align the upper and lower side ends before securing this piece in place. Use three 2-1/2 in. deck screws per leg. Next, screw the upper end panels (D) to the upper sides. Make sure the chamfers face each other on each side.

5/4 X 6 CEDAR DECK BOARD

7 RIP the 5/4 x 6 deck boards to 4-1/2 in. to make the top apron frame. Use a rip guide on your circular saw or a table saw if you have one. Plane and sand the cut edge to match the factory-machined edge of the deck board.

6d GALVANIZED CASING NAILS

F

E

E

C

D

F

8 GLUE and nail the side apron pieces (E) flush with parts C below. Next, nail the apron end pieces to the end panels (D). You'll notice the inside edge of F will be about 1/4 in. out from the inside of the planter to adequately cover the tops of the legs.

4

Plumbing, electrical and appliance repairs can be intimidating. But you can successfully tackle them with the information in this chapter!

House Systems

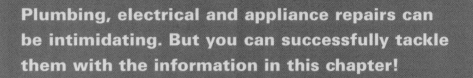

You can fix it™

REMOVE LINT FROM A CLOTHES DRYER

Every year, nearly 25,000 dryer fires cause millions of dollars in damage and hundreds of injuries, some fatal. Dryer fires start when built-up lint near the motor, gas burners or heating elements catches on fire. This fire can then spread to ignite lint in the vent pipe. The best precautions are to empty the lint trap after every load, vacuum behind the machine regularly, keep flammables away from the dryer, and annually clean lint from inside the dryer cabinet and vent duct.

We show how to "de-lint" a gas dryer with a front access panel. Electric dryers have a heating element instead of a gas burner. If you have an electric dryer, or your dryer differs from the one shown, consult your manual for instructions on accessing the heating element or cabinet interior.

The most important step in cleaning the dryer is to remove any lint buildup around the motor and gas burner or heating element. Then clean out the vent duct with a 4-in. dryer vent cleaning brush ($20 to $40 at an appliance repair store, or via the Internet at www.repairclinic.com).

If your dryer has a plastic vent ducting, replace it with a metal one. The plastic ducting itself can catch dust or lint in the vicinity on fire and set the house ablaze. Rigid or flexible metal ductwork is much safer.

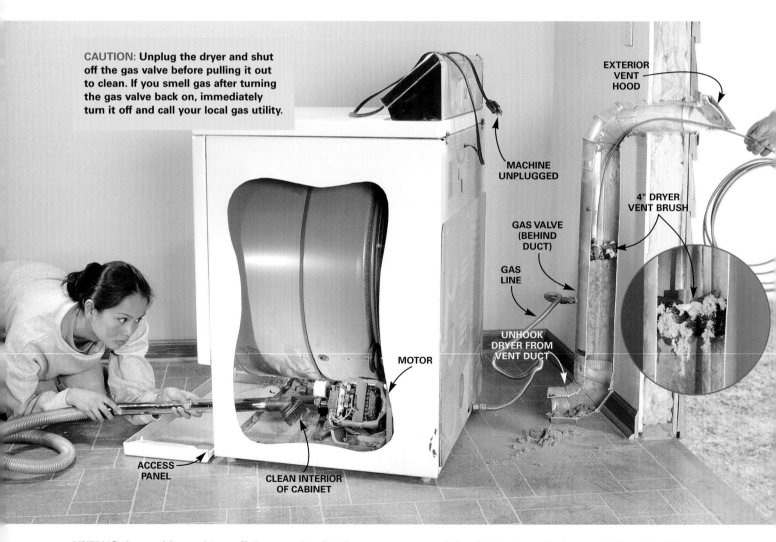

CAUTION: Unplug the dryer and shut off the gas valve before pulling it out to clean. If you smell gas after turning the gas valve back on, immediately turn it off and call your local gas utility.

EXTERIOR VENT HOOD

MACHINE UNPLUGGED

4" DRYER VENT BRUSH

GAS VALVE (BEHIND DUCT)

GAS LINE

UNHOOK DRYER FROM VENT DUCT

MOTOR

ACCESS PANEL

CLEAN INTERIOR OF CABINET

UNPLUG the machine and turn off the gas valve. Pry the access panel loose with a big flat-blade screwdriver. Vacuum inside the cabinet, especially around the gas burner and motor. Use your vacuum's brush attachment to loosen built-up lint. Disconnect the vent from dryer and push a vent cleaning brush through the exterior vent hood. Or disassemble vent and clean it by hand.

ADJUST A WASH BASIN POP-UP DRAIN

When the stopper in your lavatory wash basin doesn't pop up, you may be tempted to remove it and just use a rubber plug. But try these simple tricks first, and your drain will snap closed and pop open like new again.

When you lift the control rod behind the faucet, a pivot rod pushes the stopper closed so the sink holds water. The most frequent problem with pop-up drains is that the setscrew connecting the control rod and lift rod slips and throws everything out of alignment. Realign the pop-up mechanism and tighten the setscrew as shown.

If the stopper has been removed from the sink, reinsert it before realigning the pop-up mechanism. Some stoppers simply twist onto the pivot rod, but others require removal of the retaining nut. Pull the control rod down so the stopper pops up (that way you'll be able to grab it when it's loose). Completely unscrew the retaining nut and slide it onto the pivot rod. Now hold on to the stopper with one hand and reach under the sink and pull the pivot rod out of the pop-up body until the stopper comes free. Be careful not to lose the pivot bushings on each side of the pivot ball. Drop the stopper into the sink and slide the pivot rod into the bottom hole of the stopper. Retighten the retaining nut, then adjust the pop-up mechanism as shown. Mark the location of the setscrew on the control rod with a permanent marker to simplify future adjustments.

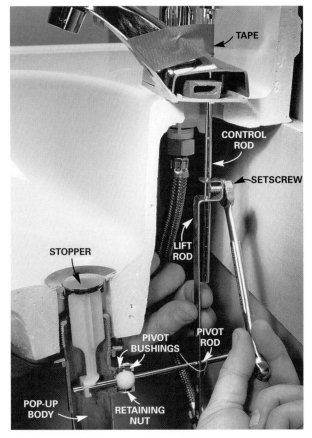

PUSH the control rod all the way in, then lift it up 3/4 in. and tape it to the faucet. Loosen the setscrew so the control rod slides freely through the lift rod linkage. Push up on the lift rod until the stopper is all the way down, then torque the setscrew down with an open-end wrench or a small pliers.

CLEAN A CLOGGED SHOWERHEAD

Here's a quick fix for a clogged showerhead. Pour white vinegar into a plastic sandwich bag until it's half full. Pull the bag over the showerhead until its spray channels are submerged. Tape the bag to the showerhead pipe with electrical tape and leave on overnight. Scrub away any remaining buildup with an old toothbrush. Your showerhead will be as good as new. **Note: Vinegar may damage old, worn finishes.**

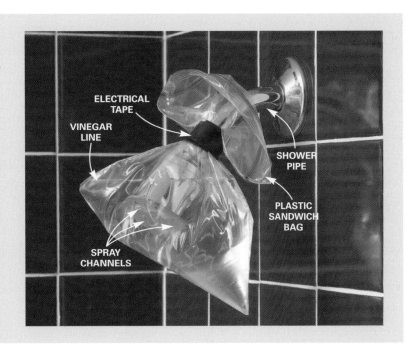

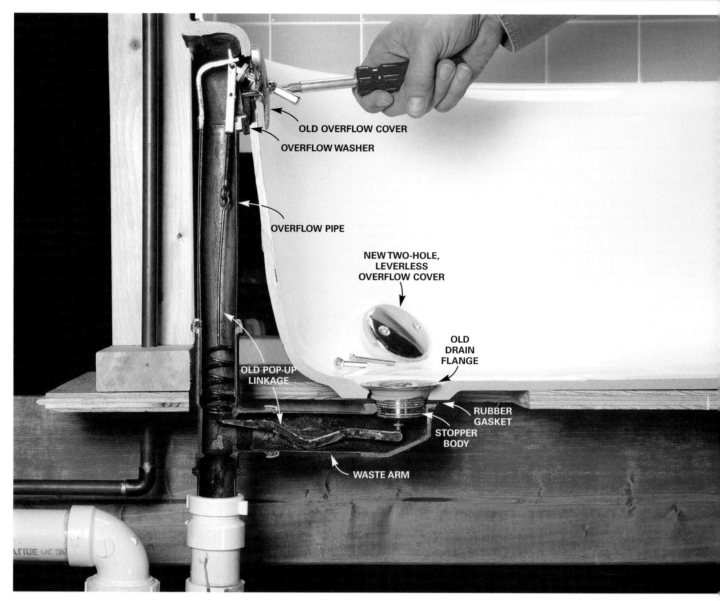

OLD OVERFLOW COVER

OVERFLOW WASHER

OVERFLOW PIPE

NEW TWO-HOLE, LEVERLESS OVERFLOW COVER

OLD DRAIN FLANGE

OLD POP-UP LINKAGE

RUBBER GASKET

STOPPER BODY

WASTE ARM

NEW LIFT-AND-TURN STOPPER

STOPPER THREADS INTO STOPPER BODY

When the stopper in your lever-style bathtub drain won't pop up anymore because the linkage is damaged or clogged, replace it with a much simpler lift-and-turn style drain. The linkage in a lever-style drain attracts dirt and hair like a magnet, and must be cleaned regularly in order to keep the drain working properly. The lift-and-turn drain has no complicated linkage to dig out and clean—almost everything catches in the drain grate. Buy the replacement kit at hardware stores and home centers for about $15 to $40.

Photo 1 (facing page) shows how to remove the overflow plate and linkage. The linkage may stick and be stubborn to remove. Grab hold of it and tug hard until it pops out. Screw on the new overflow plate once the linkage has been removed.

The toughest part of the job is removing the old stopper body, but it's all downhill after that. Remove the old stopper body as shown in **Photo 2**. If you're having trouble unscrewing it, try heating it with a hair dryer set on "high." The heat may help loosen the old plumber's putty. The old stopper body can also be cut out with a reciprocating saw and metal blade, but be very careful because it's easy to cut into and damage the bathtub.

All that's left is to install the new stopper body and stopper. Slide the new rubber gasket on top of the drainpipe under the tub and insert the new drain flange with plumber's putty on it as shown in **Photo 3**. Use the supplied bushing if the new threads are different from the old. Screw the stopper into the stopper body and congratulate yourself on a job well done.

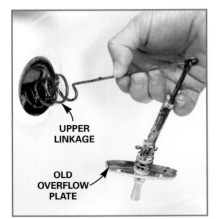

UPPER
LINKAGE

OLD
OVERFLOW
PLATE

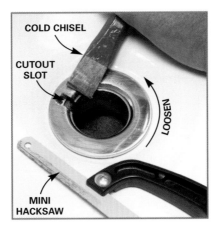

COLD CHISEL

CUTOUT
SLOT

LOOSEN

MINI
HACKSAW

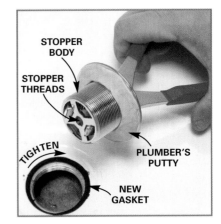

STOPPER
BODY

STOPPER
THREADS

TIGHTEN

PLUMBER'S
PUTTY

NEW
GASKET

1 UNSCREW the overflow plate and pull the upper linkage out of the overflow pipe. Pop out the drain stopper and remove the lower linkage as well. Tug firmly when extracting both parts of the linkage because they may bind inside the overflow pipe.

2 CUT a notch 1/4 in. wide and deep in the old stopper body with a mini hacksaw. Check progress frequently to ensure you don't cut into the tub. Wedge a 3/4-in. cold chisel into the cutout slot and pound counterclockwise with a hammer to free the stopper body (use caution when hammering so you don't scratch the enameled tub). Completely unscrew and remove the stopper body.

3 SLIDE in a new gasket. Then roll a pencil-sized bead of plumber's putty and press it around the underside of the new stopper body rim. Stick the jaws of an 8-in. pliers into the stopper body grate and thread it into the drainpipe.

LAMP REPAIR TIP

Fix a flickering lamp light bulb in several easy steps. First, try tightening the bulb in the socket and plugging the lamp into a different outlet. If the lamp still flickers, unplug it and check the cord for fraying where it enters the plug. Replace it if necessary. If the cord's in good shape, chances are the bulb isn't fully contacting the metal contact tab located at the bottom of the lamp socket. Make sure the lamp is unplugged, and adjust the contact tab as shown in the photo below.

Replace the bulb and turn on the lamp. If the problem persists, the lamp switch, socket or cord is worn out.

CAUTION: Unplug lamp first

CONTACT
TAB

LAMP
SOCKET

UNPLUG the lamp, unscrew the bulb and gently pry the metal contact tab 1/8 in. up off the bottom of the lamp socket with a screwdriver. Scrape off rust or corrosion with the screwdriver and blow any grit out of the socket.

You can fix it™

REPLACE A
KITCHEN FAUCET

The instructions always make it look soooooo … easy. But here's the REAL nitty-gritty on pulling out the old and putting in the new.

by **Travis Larson**

Installing a new kitchen faucet isn't tough at all. Actually, the directions that come with your new faucet are probably all you'll need to do that part of the job. Barring unforeseen problems, you could be washing up under the new faucet in an hour or so.

But what the directions *don't* mention are the bugaboos

Tip

Before disconnecting the drain lines, take a Polaroid snapshot or make a sketch of the layout to help you put it all back together.

that can pop up while you're trying to get the old one out. You may be faced with bushwhacking your way through a dark, dank jungle of drainpipes, water lines, a garbage disposer and maybe more, just to access the faucet. Then, you'll be called on to perform pretzel-like contortions inside the sink cabinet to pull an old faucet with connections that may be so badly corroded you'll swear they're welded together. Here's what you need to know to get through the tough parts.

The right stuff

Chances are, you'll need to make more than one trip to the hardware store for parts, but to give yourself a fighting shot at completing the job with one-stop shopping, consult this list.

■ **Shutoff valves:** Before you shop for your new faucet (see "Selecting a Faucet," p. 139), take a look under the sink and make sure that there are shutoff valves feeding the faucet. If you don't have shutoff valves, add them. If you have them, confirm that they're in working order by turning on the hot and cold water at the faucet and shutting off the valves. If the faucet still drips, install new ones. Most likely you have 1/2-in. copper supply pipes. If so, add easy-to-install solderless "compression fitting" valves (**Photos 9 and 10**, p. 142) to your shopping list. But if not, buy whichever valve type is compatible with your pipes.

■ **Supply tubes:** Next, measure the existing supply tubes and buy new stainless steel–sleeved supply tubes (**Photo 9**). They're designed to give rupture-free service for years and can be routed around obstacles without kinking.

DISHWASHER DISCHARGE HOSE

P-TRAP

WATER SUPPLY LINES

SHUTOFF VALVES MISSING

1 DISCONNECT the drain lines and P-traps if they block your access to the faucet and water supply pipes. (Place a bucket or coffee can under the P-trap to dump residual water after you pull it free.)

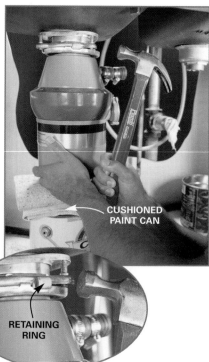

2 UNPLUG the garbage disposer, or shut off the circuit breaker in the main service panel if the disposer is directly wired. Disconnect the dishwasher discharge line and place a 1-gal. paint can under the garbage disposer with some rags on top to cushion the disposer when it drops free. Release the disposer by tapping the retaining ring with a hammer in a counterclockwise direction.

CUSHIONED PAINT CAN

RETAINING RING

We'll show you the unexpected problems that crop up—and how to solve them

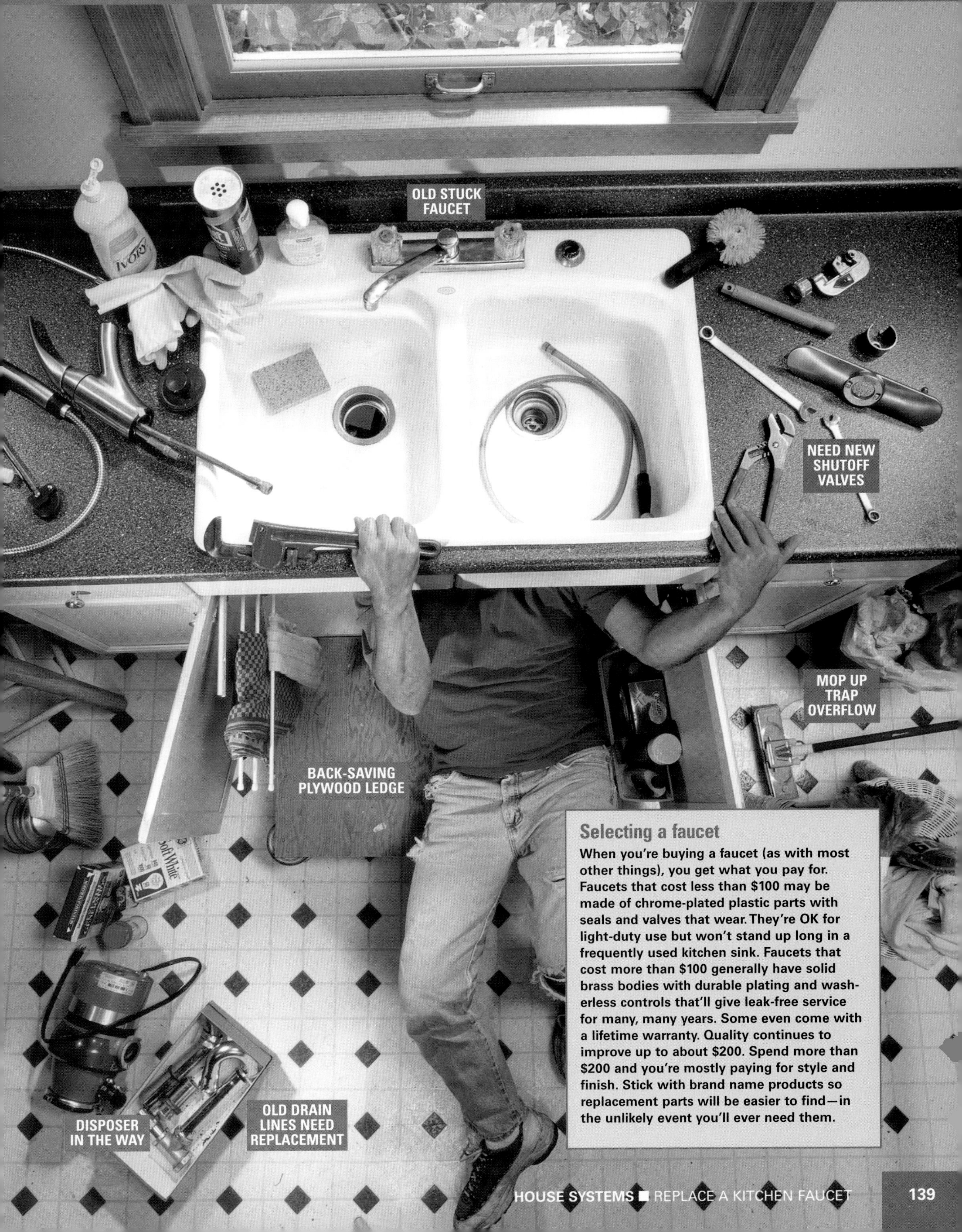

OLD STUCK FAUCET
NEED NEW SHUTOFF VALVES
MOP UP TRAP OVERFLOW
BACK-SAVING PLYWOOD LEDGE
DISPOSER IN THE WAY
OLD DRAIN LINES NEED REPLACEMENT

Selecting a faucet

When you're buying a faucet (as with most other things), you get what you pay for. Faucets that cost less than $100 may be made of chrome-plated plastic parts with seals and valves that wear. They're OK for light-duty use but won't stand up long in a frequently used kitchen sink. Faucets that cost more than $100 generally have solid brass bodies with durable plating and washerless controls that'll give leak-free service for many, many years. Some even come with a lifetime warranty. Quality continues to improve up to about $200. Spend more than $200 and you're mostly paying for style and finish. Stick with brand name products so replacement parts will be easier to find—in the unlikely event you'll ever need them.

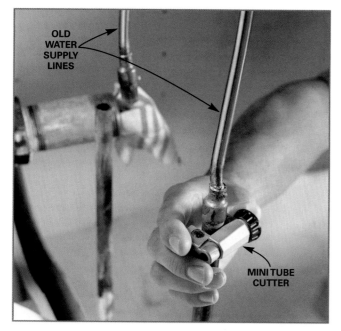

OLD WATER SUPPLY LINES

MINI TUBE CUTTER

3 SHUT OFF the water below the sink if you have valves, or shut off the main water supply valve if your old faucet is plumbed directly without valves. Open the kitchen faucet and another lower faucet to bleed off any pressure and to drain the water. If you're installing or replacing valves, cut the water lines directly below the fittings with a tube cutter or hacksaw.

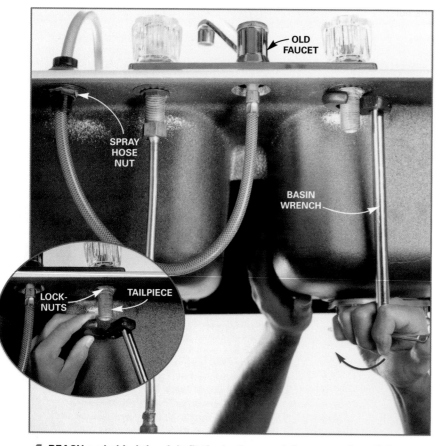

OLD FAUCET

SPRAY HOSE NUT

BASIN WRENCH

LOCK-NUTS   TAILPIECE

4 REACH up behind the sink, fit the basin wrench jaws onto the tailpiece nuts and turn counterclockwise to loosen. Then disconnect the spray nozzle hose, remove the faucet and clean the sink area under the old faucet flange using a putty knife.

■ **Basin wrench:** Also buy a basin wrench ($15; **Photo 4**). This weird little wrench is made specifically for removing and installing those hard-to-reach fasteners that clamp older faucet assemblies to the sink. (Newer faucets have plastic Wing-Nuts that

Tip Prop up a scrap of plywood on some 1-qt. paint cans in front of the cabinet. You'll be much more comfortable lying under the sink. Otherwise, the edge of the cabinet would be digging into your back (see p. 139 photo).

can usually be loosened and tightened by hand.) A basin wrench's spring-loaded jaws pivot so you can either loosen or tighten nuts in tight spaces. If you need to remove drain lines to access the faucet, get a pipe wrench or a slip-joint pliers (**Photo 1**). For cutting copper tubes, buy a conventional tubing cutter. But if your copper supply lines are within a few inches of the back of the cabinet, buy a special mini tube cutter (**Photo 3**). You'll also need a set of open-end wrenches for disconnecting and hooking up the water lines.

Getting at it

After you pull out all of the cleansers, buckets and old vases from under the sink, go ahead and lie under there and see if you can easily access the faucet. If so, go right to **Photo 3**. If not, it's time to start dismantling the things blocking your path.

Most likely, the main obstacles will be the pipes and P-traps that drain the sinks. Don't be afraid to pull them out, but more important, don't be afraid to replace them with new ones. If you have older, chrome-plated drain lines, the pipe walls may be so corroded that they'll crush in the jaws of a pipe wrench or slip-joint pliers. After you remove them, throw all the parts in a box for matching them exactly at the store later. If you have plastic drain parts, be very careful during removal—you may be able to reuse them.

Sometimes a garbage disposer can be a 20-lb. roadblock. Don't be discouraged—it's easier than you think to remove it and then reinstall it after the faucet is in (**Photo 2**). Unplug it and pull it out of the cabinet to get it out of the way. If it's hard-wired, shut off the circuit breaker that controls the disposer, disconnect the disposer from the sink and set it aside inside the cabinet with the electrical cable still attached.

5 FOLLOW any manufacturer's preassembly instructions and place the optional flange (see Photo 8) over the faucet opening. Finger-tighten the flange nuts underneath the sink and check the alignment of the flange, faucet and sink hole from above.

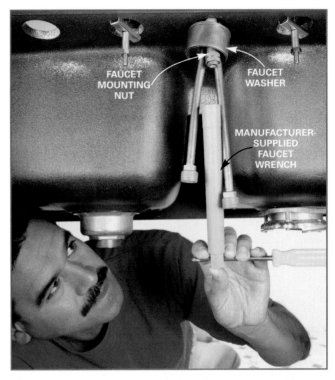

6 CHECK the operation of the faucet and handle to confirm you're not putting it in backward, and thread the feeder lines through the flange and sink holes. Then slip on the faucet washer and tighten the faucet-mounting nut from below. Spread the faucet supply tubes if necessary to gain tool clearance (some manufacturers provide a tool for this).

7 HAND-TIGHTEN, then snug up the flange nuts with an open-end wrench. You can only turn the wrench about a one-sixth revolution at a time.

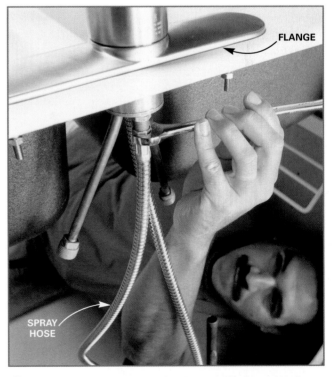

8 THREAD the spray nozzle line through the faucet body, then thread the spray hose fitting onto the faucet supply tube and tighten it. Pull the nozzle out of the faucet to make sure the hose under the sink operates freely, then attach the counterweight following the manufacturer's instructions.

Disconnecting the old faucet

The first step in removing the old faucet is to disconnect the water supply lines (Photo 3). If there are no shutoff valves and the water pipes are hooked up directly to the faucet sup-

Tip

With most faucets, only three of the four holes are covered, so you'll either need to get a blank insert or use the extra hole for a liquid soap or instant hot water dispenser. Plan to do the installation while you're under the sink with everything torn apart.

ply lines, or if you're replacing defective valves, turn off the main water supply valve to the house and cut off the pipes (Photo 3) below the connections with a hacksaw or tube cutter. Make sure new valves are closed before turning the water back on to the house. Once the water lines are disconnected, use the basin wrench to loosen the old faucet and remove it (Photo 4).

When all else fails...

Sometimes, in spite of all your best efforts, it's simply impossible to loosen the old faucet nuts. *Calm down!* Try soaking the threads with penetrating oil and try again. If that doesn't do it, it's time to pull out all the stops and pull the sink so you can get at the nuts. It's not that tough to do. Loosen the screws on the bottom of the sink rim for a clamp-down sink, or cut the caulk between a drop-in sink and countertop with a utility knife and lift out the sink. Then you'll be able to go after those nuts with a locking pliers or a pipe wrench to free the old faucet.

Follow the manufacturer's directions to mount the new faucet, then remount the sink (with the new faucet) and hook up the water lines as we show. 🏠

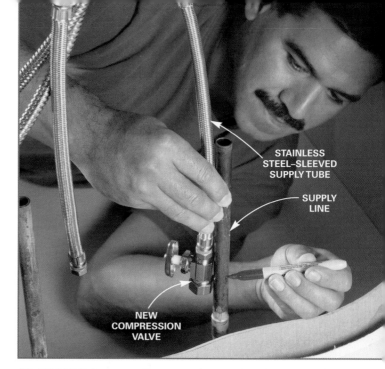

STAINLESS STEEL–SLEEVED SUPPLY TUBE

SUPPLY LINE

NEW COMPRESSION VALVE

9 TIGHTEN the new valves onto the supply tubes and mark the feeder lines just above the compression nuts on the valves for cut-off.

10 CLEAN the copper tubing with fine sandpaper, then slip the nut, compression ring and valve body over the supply line pipe and tighten. Close the valve, turn on the main water valve and check for leaks. Place a bucket under the faucet and turn the faucet on to check for leaks. Reassemble the garbage disposer, P-traps and other drain lines.

Look, ma — no handle

Electronic faucets, used for years in restaurants, public restrooms and other commercial settings, are working their way into the home bathroom. Delta e-Flow faucets offer the same benefits as their more experienced counterparts:

- SAFETY Since you set the faucet to a specific temperature, water can't be accidentally turned on to scalding levels.
- CONVENIENCE If you have kids, older folks or people with limited use of their hands in your household, the automatic on-off is a great feature.
- WATER CONSERVATION The automatic shutoff saves water. When you're brushing your teeth or shaving, the faucet turns on only when you rinse your razor or toothbrush. It also prevents overflows.
- CLEANLINESS Hands-free operation minimizes the spread of germs on the handle.
- STYLE The e-flow faucets are available in chrome and nickel finishes. The handles are available in blue, green, red and three other colors.

The unit can be either battery operated or hard-wired into your home's electrical system. Installation is standard, except for one extra wire and a flexible hose connection. The "brains" of the faucet sit in a small box you install under the vanity. The faucets cost $370 to $510 at home centers, hardware stores, and specialty kitchen and bath stores. Delta Faucet Co., 55 E. 111th St., Indianapolis, IN 46280; (800) 345-3358. www.deltafaucet.com.

REPLACE A KITCHEN
SINK-BASKET STRAINER

If you discover a puddle of water in the cabinet under your sink, it may be caused by a leaky basket strainer. Old plumbing fittings can be tricky to loosen, but we'll show you how to tear them apart and put them back together without any strain. You can pick up all the necessary supplies at a hardware store or home center.

To be sure the leak is coming from the basket strainer instead of a pipe joint, test the basket for leaks as shown in **Photo 1**. Once you confirm that the basket strainer is leaking, begin the removal process (**Photo 2**). **Photo 3** shows how to remove the strainer locknut, which holds the basket tight to the sink. Completely remove the locknut, friction ring

and gasket, and lift the old basket out of the sink.

Scrape off the old putty with a plastic putty knife so you don't scratch the sink. Seal the new basket ($6 to $12) in the sink with plumber's putty ($1) as shown in **Photo 4**. Plumber's putty cannot be used on certain new sinks, but these will be labeled to that effect. If you can't use plumber's putty, use a non-water-based silicone. Excess putty will squeeze out between the new basket strainer and the sink when you tighten the locknut in place. Wipe it off with a rag or paper towel. Make sure to insert the cardboard friction ring between the rubber gasket and the locknut so the locknut spins freely, without catching on the gasket.

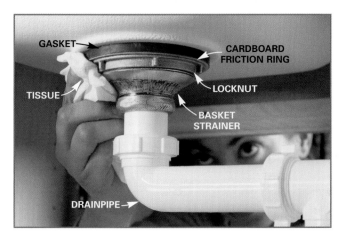

1 FILL UP the sink with water and touch a tissue between the bottom of the basket strainer and the sink. If the tissue picks up any water, you've got a leaky basket strainer.

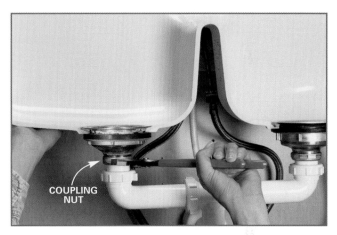

2 LOOSEN the coupling nut at the base of the strainer basket with a slip-joint pliers and slide the nut completely off the threads. If the basket spins, hold it tight as in Photo 3.

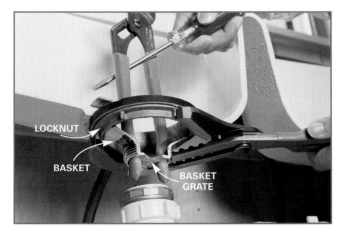

3 USE a 16-in. slip-joint pliers ($18) or spud wrench ($15) to unscrew the strainer locknut. If the entire basket spins, insert the handles of a pliers into the strainer grate and stick a screwdriver between the handles to hold it still. If you can move the drainpipe out of the way, you can insert the pliers handles up into the strainer grate from the bottom to get a better handle on it yourself.

4 ROLL plumber's putty between your hands into a rope the size of a pencil and wrap it around the lip of the drain opening. Press the strainer firmly down into the putty, add the rubber gasket, friction ring and locknut under the sink, and retighten the locknut.

Handy hints® from our readers...

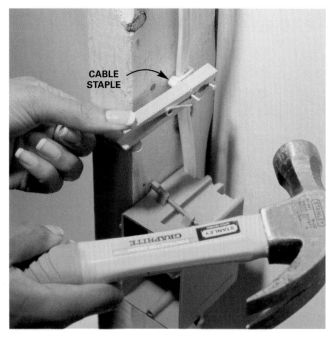

CLOTHESPIN STAPLE HOLDER

Grabbing and nailing electrical cable staples can be hard on your fingers. Make the job easier by using a clothespin to grab the nails for the staple. Hold the pin in position and hammer the staple until it's set. Remove the pin and drive the staple home.

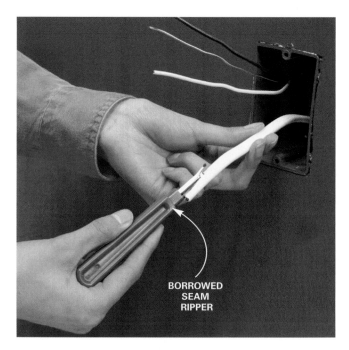

SHEATHING STRIPPER

Strip electrical cable sheathing with a sewing seam ripper! Slide the ripper up the cable to slice through the sheathing and expose the internal wires.

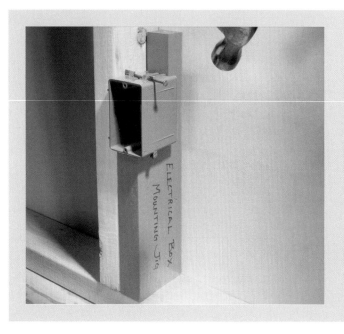

NIFTY ELECTRICAL-BOX MOUNTING JIG

Mount a roomful of electrical boxes at the same height by creating a box-mounting jig. Cut a notch (sized to the depth of the electrical boxes you're using) in a 2x4, 8-1/2 in. from the bottom of the board. To position electrical boxes, place the jig on the baseplate of the wall with the notch facing forward. Set the electrical box in the notch and nail it in place. (This jig only works for uniformly sized boxes.)

BAR CLAMPS ARE QUICK AND VERSATILE

The clamps shown here are ideal for working alone because they tighten with one hand, leaving the other hand free to hold up the board. They're available at home centers and hardware stores and cost about $15 to $25, depending on the length.

When you're soldering pipes, tighten a clamp across two floor joists for temporary support (above photo). Use the same trick to support drainpipes, ducting or framing members while you work on them.

CLEARING WATER LINES WITH A SHOP VACUUM

If you have trouble sweating plumbing lines because of residual water in the line, shut off the water main and open some faucets to drain most of the water. Then attach a wet/dry vacuum hose to the end of the pipe with duct tape and suck out the remaining water. The dry pipes make soldering a breeze.

ROUGH-DUTY LIGHT BULBS

After replacing the 20th burned-out light bulb in my garage door opener, another kind of light bulb finally came on in my head. I realized the reason they burned out so often was the vibration from the motor and garage door mechanism. Why not use a "rough service" bulb (about $3) like the ones mechanics use in their trouble lights? Can't find rough-service bulbs? Use vibration-resistant ones designed for use in ceiling fans.

THIRD-HAND SCREW HOLDER

Inserting a screw into a tight opening is a tricky task. Hold the screw on the end of your screwdriver by sticking it through the center of a piece of plastic wrap. Put the screw on the end of the screwdriver and pull the plastic back over the handle. Once the screw is set, simply pull off the plastic.

SIMPLE KITCHEN
LIGHTING IMPROVEMENTS

*You don't need to spend a lot of time or money
for a brighter kitchen!*

by **Spike Carlsen**

The kitchen in the house where I grew up was lit by a single fluorescent ring bulb smack dab in the middle of the ceiling. It was too bright when you clicked it on for a midnight snack and too dim when it came to reading the fine print on the Nestlè chocolate chip package. But like most kitchen lighting back then, it "worked."

These days, "workable" just doesn't cut it. Most kitchens now serve as dining room, office and family room. Lights are on in the kitchen more than in any other room in the home. And since we cook, work, play and pay bills there, we need a wide range of lighting to create a pleasant environment for all our activities and to prevent eyestrain and accidents.

In the course of totally remodeling a kitchen or building a new home, you might be able to afford the luxury of working with an architect or designer to get your lighting and wiring just right. But until then (which for some of us is never), there are simple ways to improve kitchen lighting without a lot of hassle, dust and expense. Here are a few of the easiest, least painful improvements.

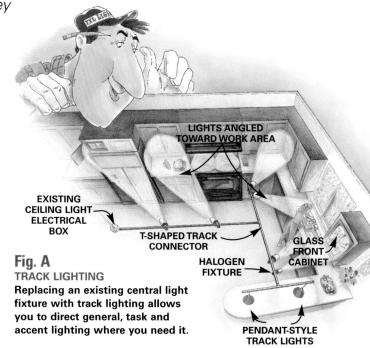

Fig. A
TRACK LIGHTING
Replacing an existing central light fixture with track lighting allows you to direct general, task and accent lighting where you need it.

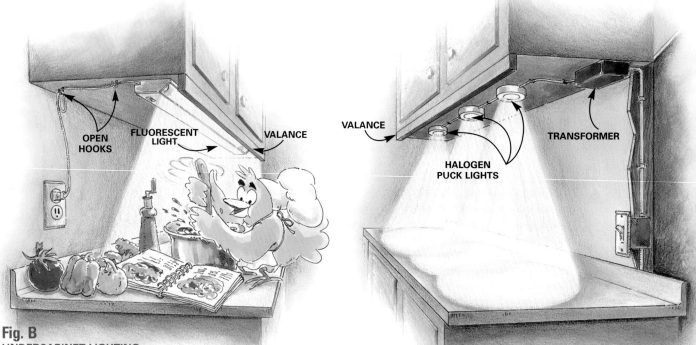

Fig. B
UNDERCABINET LIGHTING
Fixtures installed beneath cabinets cast bright, unobstructed light directly onto the work surface. Install them toward the front of the cabinets with a small valance, if necessary, so lights don't shine in your eyes. Halogen lights (right) burn hot to create a pure, bright light. Fluorescents (left) are long-lived, inexpensive to operate and easy to install.

Track lighting lets you direct light anywhere you want

A single overhead fixture provides good light for general cleaning and navigation but does a lousy job of casting light inside cabinets—especially in deep and corner units. One solution is to use the existing light fixture electrical box as a starting point for a new track lighting system (**Fig. A**).

Track lighting—available in incandescent, fluorescent, and high- and low-voltage halogen versions—has multiple fixtures that allow you to direct and focus light where you need it. T-, L- and X-shaped connectors let you install tracks and lights in hundreds of configurations. A wide variety of specialized fixtures allow you to customize and rearrange your lighting as needed. There are highly focused units with reflector bulbs for task lighting and others for general or mood light. Many systems have adapters for pendant lighting too.

Once you've selected your fixtures, position them so they don't shine directly in your eyes. Don't install fixtures directly in line with sinks and other work areas; your head will block the light. Install them to the sides instead, then angle them toward the target spot. Install them where they won't interfere with the swing of upper cabinet doors. And since track lighting fixtures are so prominent, select a system that complements the look and feel of your kitchen.

Undercabinet lighting puts light where you need it most

Your body and the upper cabinets often block the light from centrally located ceiling fixtures, keeping it from reaching the countertops where you need it most. To avoid working in dim shadows, install lights beneath the upper cabinets (**Fig. B**) to illuminate those cutting boards and cookbooks.

Undercabinet lighting is available in three varieties:

Fluorescent lights are reasonably priced and long-lived, and they cast an even, "cool" light. Designers warn that fluorescent lights used in proximity to certain strong wall or countertop colors can create an "unappetizing" glow. T-5 fluorescent bulbs—about half the diameter of standard fluorescent bulbs—provide good illumination without being obtrusive.

Halogen lights, most commonly in the form of small discs or pucks, cast a white, highly focused light that's easy to work by. Halogen light closely resembles sunlight. Surface-mount and recessed fixtures are available.

Incandescent lights come in a variety of wattages and configurations. Strips of incandescent mini-bulbs tend to be of lower wattage and work better for ambient light than for true "working" light.

Whichever type of lighting you select, install it toward the front edge of the cabinets so it illuminates the entire countertop rather than the wall. Install a 1- to 2-in. valance along the lower edge of the cabinet to keep light from shining directly in your eyes. Where possible, install continuous lighting so countertops are evenly lit. If you have shiny countertops, use frosted bulbs or frosted lenses over the bulbs to minimize harsh reflections.

According to electrical code, the cord of a plug-in-type fixture can't be permanently secured to the cabinet or wall with staples or other fasteners (although it can be draped over an open-ended hook). A more permanent, but more involved, solution is to install lights that can be "hard wired" directly into the home's electrical system and controlled with a wall switch, like the fixture shown on the right in **Fig. B**.

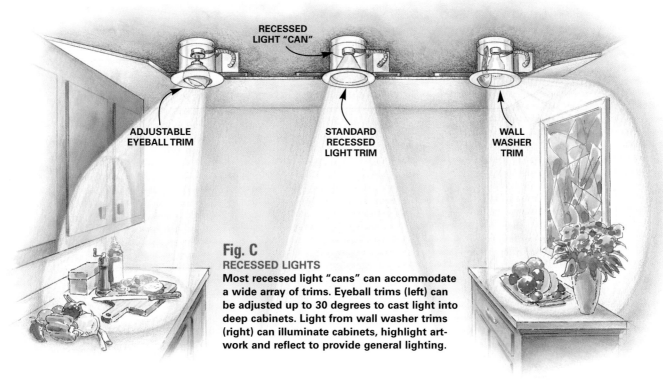

RECESSED LIGHT "CAN"

ADJUSTABLE EYEBALL TRIM

STANDARD RECESSED LIGHT TRIM

WALL WASHER TRIM

Fig. C
RECESSED LIGHTS
Most recessed light "cans" can accommodate a wide array of trims. Eyeball trims (left) can be adjusted up to 30 degrees to cast light into deep cabinets. Light from wall washer trims (right) can illuminate cabinets, highlight artwork and reflect to provide general lighting.

Special recessed light trims focus light where you need it most

Standard recessed lights, especially those installed in soffits or around the perimeter of a room, tend to light up walls, floors, cabinet fronts and the top of your head—places where light isn't really needed. Most recessed light manufacturers produce a basic "can" fixture (**Fig. C**) that can be fitted with a variety of trims ranging from the basic baffled cylinder to adjustable eyeballs and wall washers. These last two versions in particular allow you to direct light where it's needed. The cost to swap out a trim is usually less than $20 per fixture and the job takes only a few minutes.

Make sure your new trims are produced by the same company that manufactured the recessed can housing and that the trim is compatible with that specific "can." Look inside the can for the name and the model number.

Add a dimmer switch for flexibility

Improving kitchen lighting doesn't simply mean adding more lighting; it also means adding flexible lighting. Many designers divide kitchen lighting into three categories: general lighting (for overall illumination), task lighting (for detailed tasks) and accent lighting (for setting a mood or illuminating glass-front cabinets). A dimmer switch allows an existing light to serve all three functions. Install the highest wattage bulbs your fixtures are rated for, then use them full blast for chopping carrots, slightly dimmed for putting away groceries, and greatly dimmed for enjoying romantic dinners. Replacing a standard switch with a dimmer takes less than an hour and costs as little as $8.

Fluorescent and low-voltage lights need special, more expensive dimmer switches.

Simply switching bulbs can make a huge difference

Improving your kitchen lighting can be as simple as switching to different light bulbs (**Fig. D**), and there is a wide range to choose from. A standard reflector-type floodlight casts a beam of light (beam spread) of about 70 degrees, which is good for general lighting. A spotlight confines the beam spread to about 20 degrees—much better for task lighting. A narrow spotlight bulb (NSP) can narrow the beam spread to 12 degrees for bright, highly focused light. A standard A-type light bulb casts its light very broadly. So check your bulbs. A standard light bulb mistakenly placed in a recessed or track light fixture will provide only a fraction of the light that the recommended spot or reflector bulb would provide.

A bulb's capacity to light a particular surface is dramatically affected by distance. If 100 percent of the light from a bulb reaches a surface 1 ft. below it, only one-fourth of that light hits the surface if the bulb is raised to 2 ft. above the surface, one-ninth at 3 ft. and a mere one-sixteenth at 4 ft. You math whizzes get the equation, right? So when you need bright task lighting, keep the light as close to the work surface as you can, use a bulb that focuses more light and/or use a higher wattage bulb if the fixture is rated for it. 🏠

70-DEGREE BEAM SPREAD FLOODLIGHT

20-DEGREE BEAM SPREAD SPOTLIGHT

360-DEGREE BEAM SPREAD A-TYPE BULB

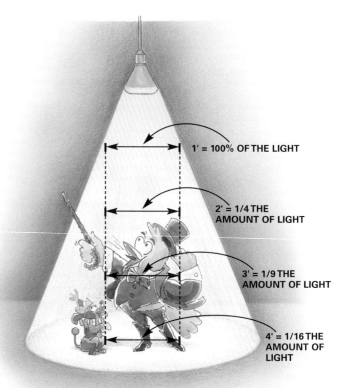

1' = 100% OF THE LIGHT

2' = 1/4 THE AMOUNT OF LIGHT

3' = 1/9 THE AMOUNT OF LIGHT

4' = 1/16 THE AMOUNT OF LIGHT

Fig. D
BULB HEIGHT AND TYPE GREATLY AFFECT BRIGHTNESS
As distance increases between bulb and surface, light levels fall off dramatically. For optimum lighting, keep fixtures close to the surface you're illuminating—and use the correct bulb.

Ask™ Handyman

NO POWER FOR THE SUMP PUMP?

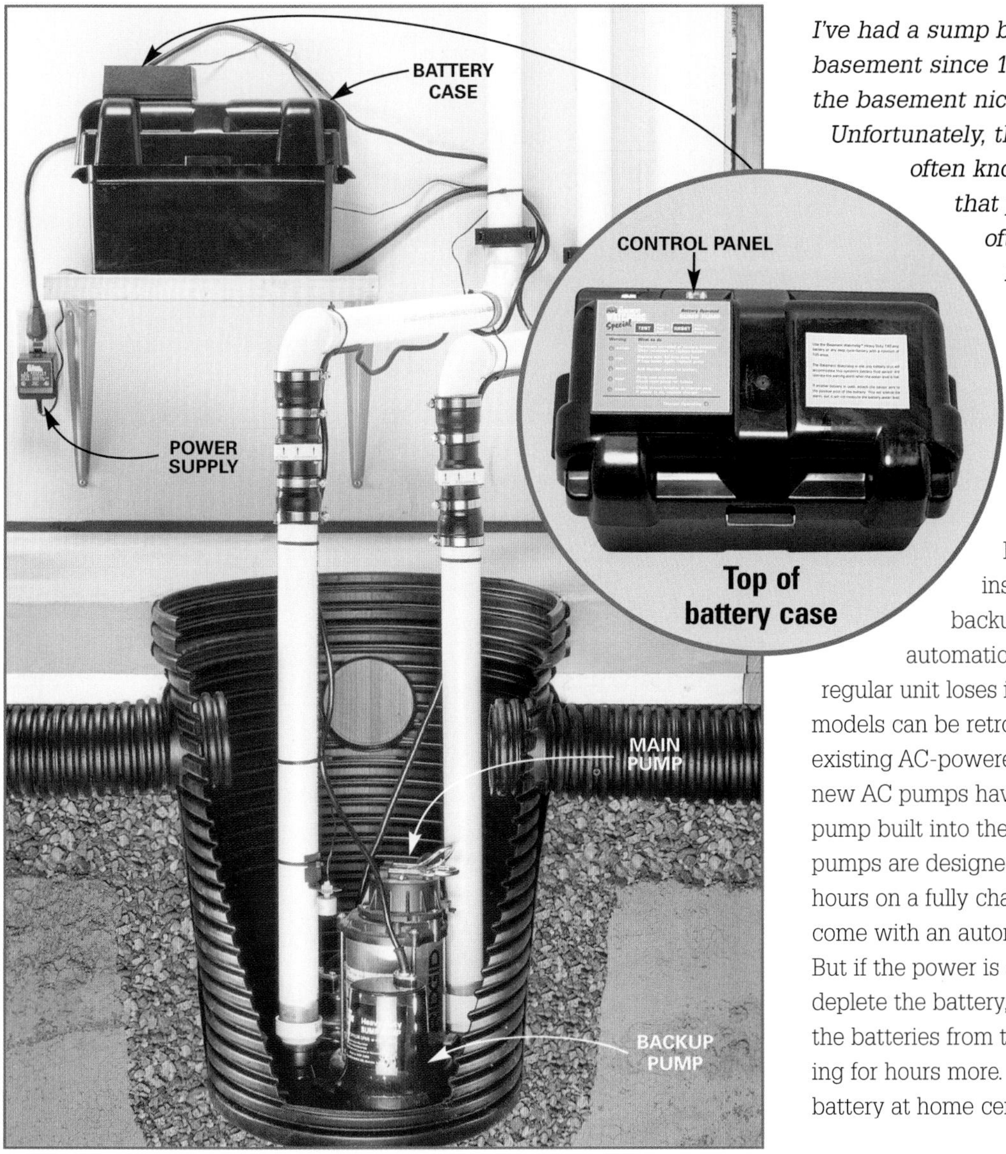

BATTERY CASE

CONTROL PANEL

POWER SUPPLY

Top of battery case

MAIN PUMP

BACKUP PUMP

I've had a sump basket and pump in my basement since 1968. It usually keeps the basement nice and dry.

Unfortunately, the really bad storms often knock out the electricity that powers the pump. I've often had to bail out the basket by hand with a bucket to keep the water at bay—sometimes for hours at a time. I'd appreciate any suggestions or solutions.

Home centers sell easily installed, battery-powered backup sump pumps that automatically start pumping if the regular unit loses its power source. Some models can be retrofitted to supplement any existing AC-powered sump pump, and most new AC pumps have the battery backup pump built into the unit. Most backup sump pumps are designed to run six to eight hours on a fully charged battery. (The units come with an automatic battery charger.) But if the power is off long enough to deplete the battery, you can always swipe the batteries from the cars to keep it pumping for hours more. The cost? $375 with a battery at home centers.

COOL NEW, NEVER-FAIL SUMP PUMP SYSTEM

The time you need your sump pump most is in a driving rain. That's also the time you're most likely to get hit by a pump-stopping power outage. The SmartPump keeps on pumping rain or shine.

This "intelligent" pump has an independent controller that automatically switches the pump over to battery-powered mode in the event of a power outage. Fully charged batteries can pump more than 10,000 gallons of water and are automatically recharged when power is restored. The pump will kick into "turbo mode" if the amount of water exceeds the pump's normal capacity. The controller also runs a daily self-diagnostics test, detects pump jams (and tries to clear them!) and sounds an alarm if problems persist.

The unit can be adapted to fit existing sump baskets and discharge pipes. At $994, peace of mind doesn't come cheap. And you supply the 12-volt batteries. A less expensive version is also available.
Wayne Water Systems, 100 Production Dr., Harrison, OH 45030; (800) 237-0987. www.waynepumps.com

BREAKER NUMBERS

GFCI LABEL

CIRCUIT BREAKER AEROBICS

I recently bought and moved into an older three-story home. The electrical system has been upgraded (there are 20 circuit breakers in the panel box). How can I find out which circuit breaker goes where without running up and down the steps?

Put on your track shoes, or find some helpers. It's a good idea to have a well-marked breaker panel, but it will take several hours to track down all the circuits.

First, draw floor plans of your house. Mark on the plans the location of all receptacles and lights. Go room by room and be thorough. Don't forget the garage and the exterior. Then, turn on all the lights. Look for receptacles that are controlled by switches (often floor or table lamps are plugged into them) and turn them on.

Next, go to the service panel. There's a stamped number next to each breaker (**see photo**). Turn off breaker No. 1.

Now the hunt begins. Go through the house and note which lights are off. Mark these lights and their switches on the floor plan with a number "1." Then plug a small lamp or radio into each receptacle; if it's dead, mark with a 1. As you go, put a Post-it note or a piece of tape on each device as it's marked off. Test both outlets of duplex receptacles (upper and lower) because they may be on separate circuits. Back at the panel, turn on breaker No. 1 and turn off breaker No. 2 and repeat the process. The process will speed up as you mark off devices. When you're all done, you can laminate these floor plans and post them by the electrical panel.

Now when problems arise or electrical work needs doing, you can confidently refer to your floor plan and turn off the correct circuits.

ARE YOU REALLY SAFE? GFCI PROTECTION

I'm not sure if my receptacles are the GFCI-protected kind. Can you explain how to find out?

A GFCI-protected receptacle can be one of two types: It can be the type with GFCI circuitry built into it, easily identified by a test and reset button on its face, or it could be a standard receptacle wired to a remote GFCI receptacle or a GFCI circuit breaker in the main panel. GFCI receptacles should be labeled (**see photo**) but aren't always.

The easiest way to check is by using a GFCI Receptacle Tester ($12 to $15). Plug it into the questionable receptacle and push the test button. The remote GFCI, if present, will trip and the tester's lights will go out. If this occurs, find the remote GFCI and reset it. Sometimes the remote GFCI you have to reset is a GFCI circuit breaker in the main panel. Then label the receptacle on the faceplate as GFCI protected.

IS A MICROWAVE WORTH FIXING?

My microwave oven still cooks stuff but not nearly as fast as it used to. A friend told me that the magnetron (whatever that is) is shot. I'm considering replacing the magnetron myself. Do you have any advice?

Yes — don't go anywhere near it! Microwave ovens have capacitors that store up to 4,000 volts for long periods of time after the oven has been used. In fact, this stored voltage electrocutes an average of four people every year. The only two "repairs" a homeowner should attempt are changing the light bulb and tripping the circuit breaker located on the back of most machines.

As far as having the oven repaired, a new magnetron would run anywhere from $80 to $130, plus $80 in labor to install it. You'd need to be very emotionally attached to your oven to justify that expense.

SHOULD I KEEP MY GAS METER FREE OF ICE AND SNOW?

My gas meter is under an eave and near the sidewalk, so it's often buried under snow from the snow blower or encased in ice from snow melting off the roof. My husband claims that meters are built to be outside and can handle anything nature dumps on them. Should I be concerned?

Tell your husband he's wrong—*again*. There's an air vent on the bottom of the regulator (that flying saucer–shaped thing) that has to be exposed to the atmosphere for the internal diaphragm to operate properly. If gas isn't running into the house when the regulator vent plugs up, the gas supply may be shut off, causing appliance pilot lights to go out. This means no cooking, heat or hot water until the hole is cleared or the ice melts on its own. If gas is running when the vent plugs up, the situation can be even more serious. Excessive gas pressure can form in the home's gas lines after the appliances shut down. If any appliances have defective valves, gas can build up inside the house and cause a catastrophic explosion.

Keep your meter free of snow, and ask your utility company if it provides and installs metal ice shields (usually for free) to its customers. The shield functions like a little roof to protect the regulator from water dripping down on it and freezing. If your utility company doesn't offer ice shields, you can build your own little lean-to roof for your meter from plywood or sheet metal.

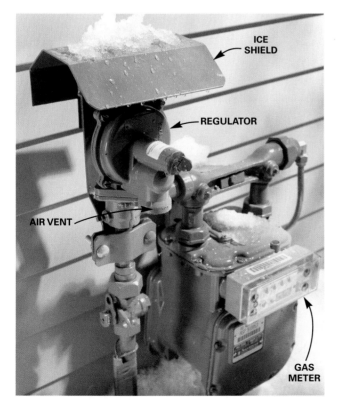

ICE SHIELD

REGULATOR

AIR VENT

GAS METER

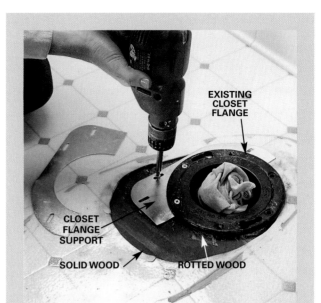

EXISTING CLOSET FLANGE

CLOSET FLANGE SUPPORT

SOLID WOOD

ROTTED WOOD

DO I HAVE TO REPLACE THE ROTTED FLOOR UNDER THE TOILET?

While replacing my toilet wax ring, I noticed that the floor directly under the toilet flange was rotted out. Do I need to rip out all the flooring and replace it, or is there a less painful solution? Help—we're down to one toilet!

If only the area directly below the flange is rotted, you can install a two-piece steel closet flange support. It goes under the flange and transfers the load of the flange and toilet (and you) out onto more solid surrounding wood. But if your floor is severely rotted, say more than an inch beyond the flange, you're stuck replacing the flooring around the toilet. Order a flange support for about $18 from Prairie Home Products Inc. (800-367-1568). The company offers one type for cast iron flanges and one for plastic or brass.

KEEP YOUR FRIDGE
HUMMING

Six maintenance steps will prevent most refrigerator breakdowns.

by **Jeff Timm**

It's hard to believe, but six simple maintenance steps will prevent almost 100 percent of refrigerator breakdowns and eliminate those service calls. Take these steps and you can forget spoiled food, lost time waiting for repair people and shelling out $70 an hour plus parts for the repair itself. In this story, we'll show you how to keep your fridge humming and trouble-free. And we'll also tell you what to check if a problem does occur.

CAUTION: Always unplug your fridge before working on it!

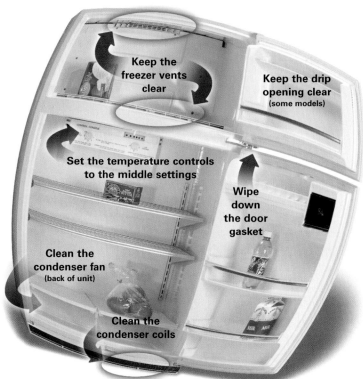

Keep the freezer vents clear

Keep the drip opening clear (some models)

Set the temperature controls to the middle settings

Wipe down the door gasket

Clean the condenser fan (back of unit)

Clean the condenser coils

ONE **CLEAN THE CONDENSER COILS** (5 minutes)

You can eliminate more than 70 percent of service calls with this simple cleaning step. Skip this chore and you'll be contributing to your appliance repairman's retirement fund. Not to mention handing over $5 to $10 a month extra to your utility company because the fridge isn't running efficiently. Do it twice a year or more often if you have shedding pets. Their fur clogs up the coils fast.

Condenser coils are located on the back of the fridge or across the bottom. These coils cool and condense the refrig-

erant. When the coils are clogged with dirt and dust, they can't efficiently release heat. The result is your compressor works harder and longer than it was designed to, using more energy and shortening the life of your fridge. Clean the coils with a coil cleaning brush ($6 at appliance parts stores) and vacuum. The brush is bendable to fit in tight areas and can be used for cleaning dehumidifier and air conditioner coils too.

GRILLE

VACUUM WITH NOZZLE ATTACHMENT

COIL CLEANING BRUSH

1 **UNSNAP the grille at the bottom of the refrigerator to access the coils. If your** coils are located on the back, you'll have to roll the fridge out to get at them.

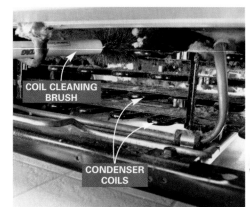

COIL CLEANING BRUSH

CONDENSER COILS

2 **CLEAN the coils with a special coil cleaning brush. Vacuum the coils as you** brush. Be careful not to bend the fan blades. A gentle brushing will do the job.

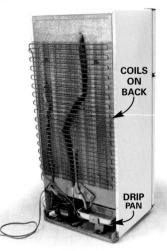

COILS ON BACK

DRIP PAN

NOTE: Some refrigerators have the coils on the back of the unit. Brush and vacuum these coils in the same manner as coils found under a refrigerator.

TWO CLEAN THE CONDENSER FAN (5 minutes)

If the coils are located on the bottom of the fridge like ours, clean the condenser fan and the area around it. (Fridges with coils on the back don't have a fan.) The fan circulates air across the coils to help cool them. At times, paper, dirt, dust and even mice can get sucked into the fan and bring it to a complete stop.

Below we show you how to clean the fan. Yours could be in a different area, but it's always next to the compressor. Most refrigerators will have a diagram on the back or folded up under the front grille showing the location of the major parts. While you're under there, wipe out the drip pan that collects water from the defrost cycle and allows it to evaporate.

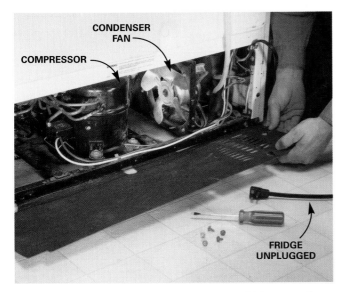

CONDENSER FAN

COMPRESSOR

FRIDGE UNPLUGGED

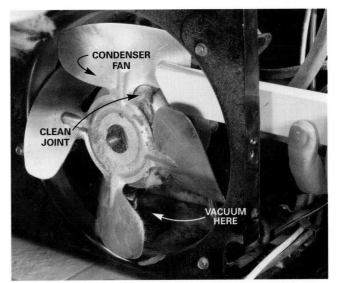

CONDENSER FAN

CLEAN JOINT

VACUUM HERE

1 ACCESS the condenser fan by rolling the fridge away from the wall and removing the lower back cover with a screwdriver. Replace the cover when you're finished. It's essential for good air circulation.

2 CLEAN the fan blades with the brush and vacuum so air can move freely across them. Also clean the shaft by vacuuming the crease where the blade meets the motor. Don't lubricate the shaft; oil will attract dirt and cause problems.

THREE WIPE THE DOOR GASKET (2 minutes)

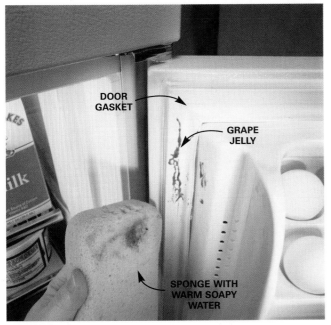

DOOR GASKET

GRAPE JELLY

SPONGE WITH WARM SOAPY WATER

WIPE the door gasket regularly with warm water and a sponge. Don't use detergent—it can damage the gasket.

Prevent an expensive gasket repair bill ($100 to $200) and cut down air leaks by keeping your door gasket clean. Syrup, jelly or any other sticky stuff dripping down the front sides of your refrigerator can dry and glue the gasket to the frame. The next time you open the door, your gasket can tear. Keep it clean and you'll get a nice, tight seal, keeping the cool air where it belongs, in the fridge.

Tip
To prevent wear, lubricate the door handle side of the gasket by sprinkling baby powder on a cloth and wiping it down once a month.

FOUR **CLEAR THE FREEZER VENTS** (5 minutes)

These little vents on frost-free fridges allow air to circulate in the freezer (see right). Don't block them or let crumbs or twist ties get sucked in around the evaporator fan or clog the drain tube. To help save energy, keep your freezer about three-quarters full to retain cold air. But don't pack it any fuller—the air needs to circulate.

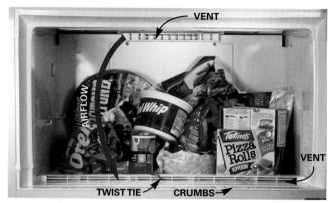

CLEAR food packages away from the vent openings and clean the air return so crumbs and twist ties don't clog them.

FIVE **SET THE TEMPERATURE CONTROLS TO THE MIDDLE SETTINGS** (1 minute)

This step won't necessarily prevent a repair, but it'll extend the life of your fridge by allowing it to run more efficiently, which reduces your electric bill. Your fridge has at least two temperature controls (except on manual defrost types, which have one). The one for the food compartment is a thermostat that turns the compressor on and off. The second, for the freezer, is just an air baffle. The baffle lets cold air from the freezer sink into the food compartment. Closing the baffle makes the freezer colder.

SET the temperature controls to the middle settings. Make any adjustments according to a refrigerator thermometer (photo below). The optimum setting for your fridge is between 38 and 42 degrees F; the freezer, between 0 and 10 degrees.

PROPER SETTING FOR FREEZER

PROPER SETTING FOR FRIDGE

SIX **CLEAR AND CLEAN DRIP OPENINGS** (2 minutes)

Drip openings allow water that has melted from the defrost cycle to flow down to a pan located by the compressor, where it evaporates. Check your owner's manual for the location on your fridge. On cycle defrost fridges, a channel directs the water to a tube in the food compartment (see photo at right). On frost-free types, look for a small cap under the crisper drawers that covers a hole, or an opening in the back of the freezer or refrigerator. If the drain opening clogs, water will build up under the crisper drawers and eventually pour out onto the floor. 🏠

FIND DRIP CUP HERE

CHANNEL COLLECTS WATER–WIPE IT OUT

OPENING TO DRIP TUBE

DRIP CUP–WIPE IT OUT

LOCATE the drip opening and wipe it out, being careful not to press any debris down into the hole. Suck out crumbs with a vacuum.

You can **fix** it™

REPLACE A PULL-CHAIN LIGHT FIXTURE

1 TURN OFF the power, remove the light bulb and unscrew the fixture from the electrical box. Pull the fixture down, but keep your hands away from the wires. Touch one voltage tester probe to the black wire, and the other to the white wire. If the voltage indicator doesn't light up, the power is off.

CAUTION: **Turn off power at the main service panel.**

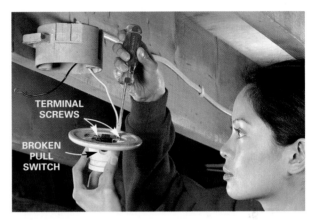

TERMINAL SCREWS

BROKEN PULL SWITCH

2 LOOSEN the terminal screws and unhook the wiring from the old fixture. If the wire ends are broken or corroded, strip off 3/4 in. of sheathing, and bend the bare wire end into a hook.

Pull-chain light fixtures are handy for basements and storage areas—until they quit working. The internal switch mechanism can wear out, or pulling too hard on the cord can snap the chain or completely pull it out of the fixture. Replacing the broken fixture is simple and inexpensive ($2 at any home center or hardware store). Pull-chain fixtures are made from either plastic or porcelain, but we recommend the porcelain because it withstands heat better and lasts longer.

Before starting, flip the circuit breaker or pull the fuse to disconnect the power to the light, then test to make sure the power is off (**Photo 1**). Replace the broken fixture as shown in **Photos 2 and 3**. There may be an unused bare ground wire inside the electrical box. If it falls down while you're replacing the fixture, wrap it in a circle and push it up as far into the electrical box as possible.

3 ATTACH the black wire to the gold terminal screw on the new fixture and the white wire to the silver terminal screw. Wrap the wires clockwise so they cover at least three-quarters of the terminal screws. Firmly tighten the screws so the copper wire compresses slightly. Twist the fixture to spiral the wires into the electrical box. Screw the new fixture to the box snugly, but don't overtighten it or the porcelain might crack.

CAUTION: **Aluminum wiring requires special handling. If you have aluminum wiring, call in a licensed pro who's certified to work with it. This wiring is dull gray, not the dull orange that's characteristic of copper.**

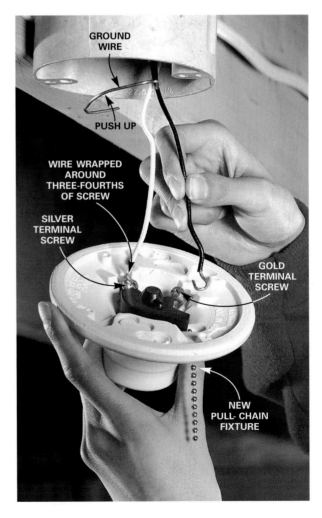

GROUND WIRE

PUSH UP

WIRE WRAPPED AROUND THREE-FOURTHS OF SCREW

SILVER TERMINAL SCREW

GOLD TERMINAL SCREW

NEW PULL-CHAIN FIXTURE

Which
Should I buy?

CHEAP VS. EXPENSIVE FURNACE FILTERS

The furnace filters at my hardware store range in price from 75¢ to $40. What am I really getting with a more expensive filter?

Basically, you're getting a filter that requires less changing and captures more, and smaller, particles. The 75¢ woven fiberglass filters do one thing—screen out dirt and debris that could damage your furnace blower motor, though they do take out some pollen and mold spores. If you can remember to swap them out every month and air quality isn't an issue, these will do the job.

But if you're the kind of person who forgets to change the oil in your car, buy $4 pleated filters, which require changing only every three months. If you stretched out the accordion-like material in these filters, you'd find two, three or four times the amount of surface area. This means they can capture smaller particles for longer periods of time without impeding the airflow of your furnace.

If members of your household smoke or have allergies or asthma, or if you have pets, look into the more

expensive, high-efficiency electrostatic filters—ones that both filter and magnetically attract contaminants. Some are effective for up to a year. They can filter out bacteria, dander, odors and smoke particles. But health experts warn that you may be wasting your money on these $20 to $40 filters unless you take the following steps: Use them in conjunction with a high-efficiency vacuum cleaner, install a dedicated air purifier, wash or vacuum the filter monthly and take other steps to clean up your air and house as well.

Many filters carry a MERV (minimum efficiency reporting value) rating, which indicates their effectiveness. The higher the MERV rating, the more effective. Most spun filters have a MERV rating of 4. Standard pleated filters average MERV 6. Electrostatic pleated versions start at MERV 8, with the highest quality ones hitting MERV 12.

Filters work harder in summer! Changing filters isn't only a heating season chore. Many blower motors work at a higher speed in air conditioning mode than in heating mode, meaning you should change filters *more often* in the summer. A clogged filter can make both your furnace and your air conditioner work harder and less efficiently.

WOVEN FIBERGLASS FILTERS

PLEATED FILTERS

HIGH-EFFICIENCY ELECTROSTATIC FILTER

You can buy a dozen 75¢ filters (left), four $5 filters or one $20 filter to get you through the year. Which you should buy depends on how good your memory and health are.

TYPE L VS. TYPE M COPPER PIPE

We're adding a bathroom and I'll be doing the plumbing. At my hardware store I can buy 10-ft. lengths of 3/4-in. Type M pipe for $4 or the same length and diameter Type L pipe for $6. What's the difference?

The difference is the wall thickness of the pipe and therefore the pressure it can handle. The exterior dimensions are identical, meaning you use the same copper fittings. You also use the same tools, materials and techniques to cut and sweat them. The beefier Type L is often used underground, in hot water heating systems, for gas line (where permitted), and for commercial plumbing. Most plumbers use the less-expensive Type M for residential projects: One told me, "Type L pipe will last 300 years and Type M only 250." But check with your building inspector; some areas require Type L.

Acidic water with a pH of 7 or less can be hard on copper pipe. If you have a well and find out from testing that the water is acidic, you may want to use the thicker-wall Type L pipe; better yet, use "plastic" CPVC pipe and fittings. Note that most "city water," even in areas of the country where the water is acidic, is balanced to eliminate this problem.

TYPE L COPPER PIPE

TYPE M COPPER PIPE

Type L copper pipe, about $6 per 10-ft. section, is recommended where you need strength and protection. But for normal "in the wall" household plumbing, Type M copper pipe, at $2 less per length, is just fine.

WHICH SIZE EXTENSION CORD?

My neighbor told me I should buy a heftier extension cord for my circular saw when I use it in the far corner of my backyard. Is it really worth the dough?

All UL-approved cords have an electrical current limit that's based on the size of the wire inside and the cord length. (**NOTE:** The bigger the gauge number, the thinner the cord.) A thin cord or a long cord that's feeding a power-hungry tool will heat up, especially if it's coiled, because the heat stays contained within the coils rather than dissipating in the air. The thinner the wire and the longer the cord, the bigger the electrical draw and the more heat generated.

Typical cord limits are shown in the chart. Cord sizes are imprinted on the surface of the cord sheathing (see photo below). The most common construction cord sizes are 12-3, 14-3 and 16-3. The first digits denote the gauge of the cord while the second number denotes the number of wires it contains. Two wires carry the current; the third wire is a ground wire. Sixteen-gauge cords are

CURRENT LIMITS ON EXTENSION CORDS (AMPS)

CORD SIZE	CORD LENGTH		
	25 ft.	50 ft.	100 ft.
18-gauge	7 amps	5 amps	2 amps
16-gauge	12 amps	7 amps	3.4 amps
14-gauge	16 amps	12 amps	5 amps
12-gauge	20 amps	16 amps	7 amps

only heavy enough for work lights and small power tools such as drills. If you work with portable table saws, circular saws or other larger tools that draw 10 to 15 amps, get to the hardware store and purchase a 50-ft., 12-3 extension cord. Almost every power tool has a nameplate attached to the motor housing that lists the amperage requirements of the tool (see photo, above right).

Just remember: Always uncoil extension cords before using them and always use an extension cord that's big enough for the job. A heavy cord not only is safer but also will add years to the life of your tools.

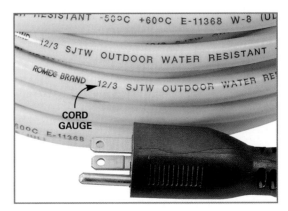

CORD GAUGE

ADD A NEW
ELECTRICAL OUTLET

You may not need to fish wires, drill holes and patch drywall to install a new outlet. Here's a simpler way.

by **Art Rooze**

Need to put in a new electrical outlet, but hate the idea of cutting holes in your walls to run the cable? Maybe you don't have to. If you can keep all your work within one "bay"—that is, the area between two studs—you can add an outlet quickly and easily, and without any cutting or patching mess.

The procedure we show here allowed us to center our TV against a wall in the family room that had no outlet. We could have run an ugly (and possibly dangerous) extension cord, but since there was already an outlet in the other side of that same wall (facing into an adjacent bedroom), we just added a new outlet in the family room, drawing power from the bedroom outlet.

Of course, this only works if you can use an outlet as a power source that's opposite, or nearly opposite, the place where you want your new outlet. To determine whether you can safely use an existing outlet, follow the list below.

NEW REMODELING BOX

How to find a power source

■ If a switch or outlet is on a circuit that often blows its breaker or fuse, don't make matters worse by adding yet another outlet to the circuit.

■ Electrical codes restrict the number of lights or outlets that can be connected to one circuit. Typically, you can have no more than eight lights or outlets on a 15-amp circuit. To determine the amp rating of a circuit, just look at the number on its breaker or fuse in your main electrical panel.

■ Most electrical codes now require outlets in kitchens and bathrooms to be on separate 20-amp GFCI circuits. So before using the method we show here to add an outlet in a kitchen or bathroom, check with an electrical inspector. If you add an outlet to a kitchen or bath, it must be GFCI protected. Don't power your new outlet from a kitchen or bathroom outlet.

At existing outlet

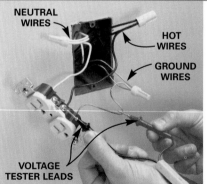

NEUTRAL WIRES
HOT WIRES
GROUND WIRES
VOLTAGE TESTER LEADS

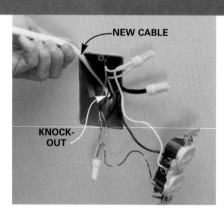

NEW CABLE
KNOCK-OUT

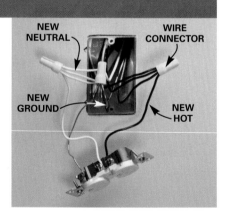

NEW NEUTRAL
WIRE CONNECTOR
NEW GROUND
NEW HOT

1 TURN OFF the power at the main panel, unscrew the outlet and use a voltage tester to double-check that the power is off. With either lead touching a ground wire (bare copper), touch the other lead first to the neutral terminals (silver colored), then to the hot terminals (gold colored). If the light glows with either contact, the circuit is live. Find the right breaker and turn it off.

2 FEED a length of new cable through one of the knock-out holes at the back of the existing box (punch out the hole with a screwdriver). Feed through enough cable to reach the new box (Photo 4), plus an extra foot. Use 14-gauge wire for a 15-amp circuit.

3 STRIP 10 in. of sheathing from the new cable to expose the wires. Run the new cable, with sheathing, at least 2 in. up inside the box. Strip 5/8 in. of insulation off the ends and connect the wires from the new cable to the existing bundles—white to white, black to black, ground to ground. Use new connectors of adequate size for the four wires in each bundle.

■ Codes also limit the number of wires that can enter an electrical box, depending on the inside volume of the box and the gauge of the wires. The outlet-addition methods we show here are based on the most common wiring (14-gauge wire on a 15-amp circuit) and an 18-cu.-in. box (typical inside dimensions are about 2 in. x 3-1/4 in. x 3 in. deep). If the circuit is 20-amp—which means thicker, 12-gauge wire—or if the existing box is smaller than 18 cu. in., you can't wire a new outlet as we show here unless you replace the existing box with a larger one. Plastic box sizes are stamped on the inside at the back. Always confirm the required box size with your local building inspector. In most regions, you have to obtain an electrical permit for this work from your local building department. This helps ensure a safe job.

Run the cable

Once you've determined the outlet that you'll use as a power source and have shut it off, use an electronic stud finder to locate the studs on both sides. You can put your new outlet anywhere between these two studs.

Hold the face of the new electrical box against the wall where you want it to go, and trace around it with a pencil. Cut out the hole with a drywall saw. Note: Be sure to buy a "remodeling" box (shown on p. 158) that can be secured to the drywall, not one that must be mounted on a stud.

Next, unscrew the existing outlet on the other side of the wall from its box (Photo 1) and punch out one of the knock-outs at the back of the box using a screwdriver. Then feed the new cable through the knock-out into the wall cavity (Photo 2). Feed in enough cable to reach the new outlet location—plus about 1 ft. Connect the wires of the new cable to the existing wires (Photo 3).

Pull the cable out through the new outlet hole in the wall (Photo 4) and feed it into the new box. Then mount the new box in the opening. Photos 3 and 5 show how the electrical connections are made. Finally, call the electrical inspector to check your work. ⌂

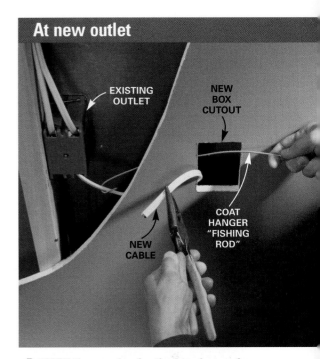

At new outlet

EXISTING OUTLET

NEW BOX CUTOUT

COAT HANGER "FISHING ROD"

NEW CABLE

4 MARK the opening for the new box and cut it out with a drywall saw. Fish for the new cable with a hook made from a wire coat hanger. Pull the cable through the opening cut in the wall. Then strip about 9 in. of sheathing off the end of the cable, insert the cable so the sheath extends about 1 in. into the box and mount the box in the wall as shown in Photo 5.

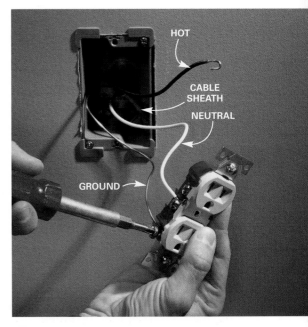

HOT

CABLE SHEATH

NEUTRAL

GROUND

5 CONNECT the new wires to the new outlet: white (neutral) wire to a silver-colored terminal screw; black (hot) wire to a gold-colored terminal screw; bare wire to the green grounding screw. Make sure the cable sheath remains secured inside the box.

Work safely
■ Before you tackle any part of this project, turn off the power to the circuit at the main electrical panel by switching off the breaker or removing the fuse.
■ Before touching any bare wires or terminals on a switch or outlet, use a voltage tester on all the wires to make sure the power is off (Photo 1).
■ If you have old, fabric-insulated wiring, call an electrician to recommend safe connections. With wiring like this, there's usually no ground wire and it's hard to tell the hot wire from the neutral, because both are coated with black insulation.

CAUTION: Aluminum wiring requires special handling. If you have aluminum wiring, call in a licensed pro who's certified to work with it. This wiring is dull gray, not the dull orange that's characteristic of copper.

SIMPLE REPAIRS FOR
GAS AND ELECTRIC RANGES

Before shelling out $50 for that service call, try these simple steps to get your range running right again.

by **Jeff Timm**

The gas burner on a gas range won't light

Standard gas range

1 **LIFT the hinged top. Most stove tops lift up (above). However, stoves with sealed burners don't have tops that lift (right).**

HINGED TOP

Sealed burner range

IGNITER

NO GAP AROUND BURNER

Step 1: Clean the pilot or igniter

A one-minute cleaning will solve 75 percent of burner problems. To get at the ignition system, lift the lid of your stove (**Photo 1, left**). Give it a rap with the heel of your hand if it's stuck. If your stove has sealed burners, identified by the igniter or little nub at the back of each burner (**Photo 1, left**), the lid won't lift. But you can clean the igniter the same way (**Photo 4, below**). If your burner still doesn't ignite, go to the next step on the next page.

Identify a standing pilot by a small gas tube running to a tip with a hole at the center of two burners (**Photo 2, below**). If the pilot (flame) is burning, skip to the next page.

Identify spark ignition by the ceramic nub either under the top (**Photo 3, below**) or beside the burner in a sealed burner range. It clicks when it's working.

Standing pilot

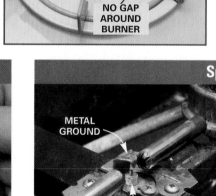

NEEDLE

PILOT ORIFICE

2 **POKE a needle into the pilot hole and clean out the soot or debris. Take care not to ream it wider. Brush the remaining soot and boiled-over food away from the tip with a toothbrush. Hold a lit match to the opening to relight the pilot, lower the lid and turn on your burners to test them.**

Spark ignition

METAL GROUND

IGNITER

WIRE

3 **IDENTIFY a spark ignition range by a little ceramic nub located between two burners. Look for wires running to it. The igniters on sealed burner ranges are alongside the burners (Photo 1, inset).**

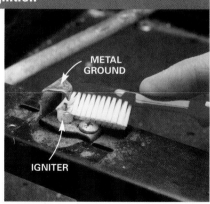

METAL GROUND

IGNITER

4 **BRUSH away gunk around and on the igniter with an old toothbrush. It's common for food that has boiled over to build up here. Clean the metal "ground" above the igniter wire, too. It must be clean to conduct a spark. Close the lid and turn the burner knob to "Light" to test the burner.**

If the burners on your stove don't light or heat up, read this article before you call the repair service. Chances are good you can solve the problem yourself with a five-minute cleaning or repair—and save $50 or more on a service call. We'll show you how, as well as how to troubleshoot the new-style electronic ignition burners and replace their key parts. We'll even show you how to test and replace the burner and socket on electric ranges.

All the repairs and cleaning that we show can be safely done without shutting off the gas to the stove. But don't leave a burner dial on. It'll emit gas into the room. If at any time you smell gas, turn off the gas at the shutoff behind the range or at the main supply near the meter and ventilate the room. Then call your local utility company or a service professional for assistance. (Look under "Appliances, Service and Repair" in your Yellow Pages.)

If the gas burner *still* won't light ...

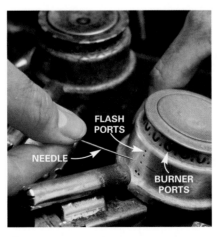

1 LIFT the burner assembly off the support arm as you slide it away from the burner valve port. It just rests there. Remove the shipping screws if they're still in place. (You don't have to reinstall them.) Your burner assembly may look a bit different from ours, but you can clean all the components the same way.

Step 2: Clean the burner assembly

This takes five minutes. Clean the burner assembly the same way for both spark ignition stoves and standing pilots. You'll need a small-diameter brush. We purchased a tube brush ($3) from a drugstore. Appliance parts stores have them too. If you have sealed burners, you're limited to cleaning only the burner ports (**Photo 3, below**). The other parts are sealed so they won't get clogged.

Set the assembly in place and try your burners. If they still won't ignite and you own a *spark ignition* stove, you may have a faulty switch, control module or igniter. You may want to call in a pro for these repairs. If you have a *standing pilot*, raise or lower the flame height slightly by turning a small setscrew located on the small gas line feeding the pilot. Consult your owner's manual or call a pro to help find this screw and to tell you the proper setting for your range.

2 SHOVE the brush into the flash tube to clear gunk and dust. Although some pros use water and degreasers to clean the burner assembly, we don't recommend them because they could cause rust.

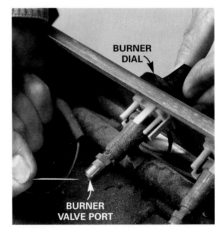

3 CLEAR all the flash ports with a needle, then do the same to the burner ports. Brush away any debris with a toothbrush.

4 STICK the needle in the burner valve port a few times to clear any debris.

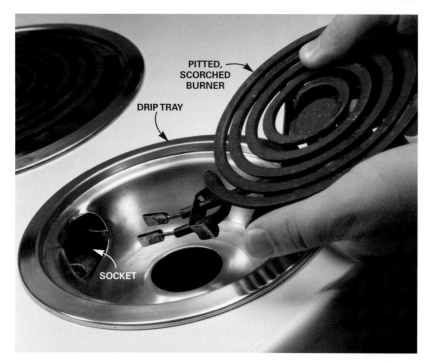

PITTED, SCORCHED BURNER

DRIP TRAY

SOCKET

1 COMPARE the nonfunctioning burner with the other burners. If it looks pitted and scorched, unplug the range, then slip the burner out of its socket and replace it. To remove a burner, simply lift it slightly and pull the prongs from the socket. You may have to wiggle it slightly to get the prongs to release. Some burners are held by a screw that you must remove.

TERMINALS

2 WIGGLE the burner in the socket. If it's loose in the socket, pull it out and spread the burner terminals slightly for a tighter connection. Do this gently—the metal is fragile and you don't want to crack the heating element! Then clean the socket with a wire brush. Reinstall the burner, plug the stove back in and test the results.

NEW SOCKET

OLD SOCKET

RELEASE CLIP

3 REPLACE a scorched socket by removing the screws that secure it to the range top. Then unscrew the range wires and screw them to the terminals on the new socket.

Diagnose the problem

If your range has a burner that's not working, chances are you can fix it without any special tools. To diagnose a burner problem, go through the steps in the order listed below. If the burners still don't work, call a service professional for help. Our list should take care of 95 percent of the problems that could occur with a burner. If you see burnt wires, have a pro look at the range. It could indicate a bigger problem.

> **CAUTION: Always unplug your electric range before removing a burner.**

1. Check the burner for wear. If it's pitted and scorched (**Photo 1**), replace it. New elements cost from $10 to $40.
2. Check the connections for a solid contact (**Photo 2**).
3. Remove a functioning burner of the same size and try it in the socket that's not working. If that burner works, replace the bad burner with a new one.
4. Inspect the burner socket. If it's charred or scorched, replace it (**Photo 3**). There are two main types of wire connections. Sockets have either screw connections (**Photo 3**) or wire leads that you attach to the range wiring with the supplied ceramic wire connectors. Sockets range in price from $9 to $25. 🏠

Tips for buying replacement parts

Before you go to purchase a part, write down the brand name, model number and serial number of the range. The range will have an engraved plate with this information usually located under the cooktop lid or on the back. Look in the Yellow Pages under "Appliances, Parts" for a supplier. Call first to be sure the part you need is in stock. Three Internet parts sources are listed below.

www.repairclinic.com
www.american-appliance.com
www3.sears.com

True tales by real readers!

A 'heated' conversation

The other day it was time for my annual changing of the smoke alarm battery. As I was changing the battery, the phone rang, so I dashed to answer it, putting the battery in my pocket. While enjoying a nice conversation, I felt a burning sensation on my leg and smelled a curious electrical odor. I started to jump around as the pain became worse. I reached into my pocket, grabbed the battery and the loose change in my pocket and threw them onto the floor. Evidently, the coins had shorted across the battery posts and heated up the battery, which then scorched my leg. Next time I'll let the answering machine get the call!

Fan-tastic!

We moved into our 1917 house in the middle of July. It was a hot summer and the first thing on our agenda was to install ceiling fans in a few rooms. I got the parts I needed and went at it. I had the typical problems you have in an old house, so I ended up working past midnight to get the job done. The next morning my wife was the first one out of bed. I heard her go into the kitchen. She knew I was awake and exclaimed, "Oh, what a great-looking ceiling fan." I yelled back, "Turn it on." A minute later, I heard a quick series of loud thuds. I ran into the kitchen and immediately saw the problem. My wife had opened the large pantry door right into the spinning fan blades. The fan now shakes a bit like Carmen Miranda, even after I relocated it and rebalanced the blades.

Can't stop the music

Last summer I decided to do some electrical work on my back porch. I wasn't sure which breaker controlled the current to the area and didn't feel like running back and forth each time to check the power, so I decided to use my son's portable radio as an aid. I plugged it in, turned up the volume and went downstairs to flip breakers. Well, I flipped every last breaker and I could still hear the radio blaring. Then I decided to flip the main breaker off. I could still hear it. I ran upstairs and unplugged the radio, only to have it keep playing! Then I read this on the back of the radio: "Two-way Power. 120v AC or 9v DC."

A big porcelain doorstop

A friend of mine decided to replace his toilet with a great-looking new one. We pulled out the old one with confidence and hooked up the new toilet in no time. After finishing, we decided to relax and watch the game on TV. About a half hour later, we heard laughter coming from the bathroom. We rushed over and found his wife unable to close the bathroom door. The new toilet protruded a few inches farther, blocking the door from closing.

INSTALL A
DIMMER SWITCH

There's more to changing a switch than connecting a few wires. You have to check grounding and box size for a safe, first-class job.

by **Jeff Gorton**

It doesn't take long to replace an ordinary light switch with a full-feature dimmer. But while you're at it, to make your home safer, you should upgrade the wiring to meet the latest requirements of the National Electrical Code. Our step-by-step instructions will show you how to install the dimmer, concentrating on details that will guarantee a safe installation.

The tools you'll need are inexpensive and will come in handy for all your electrical projects. You'll need a screwdriver, wire stripper, inexpensive voltage tester and needle-nose pliers to install a dimmer.

Double-check for hot wires in the box

Turn on the light and have a helper watch as you switch off the circuit breakers, or unscrew the fuses one at a time until the light goes out. Leave this circuit turned off while you work.

In **Photo 1**, we're using a non-contact voltage detector to double-check for voltage before removing the switch. These detectors are available at hardware stores and home centers for about $12. I prefer this type of tester because it'll detect voltage without direct contact with the metal conductor. That's huge—it means you can check potentially hot wires before you handle them. After you unscrew the switch and pull it away from the box, probe around inside the box with the detector to make sure there are no other hot wires from another circuit.

Make sure the box is large enough to accommodate the larger switch

Too many wires and devices stuffed into a box can cause dangerous overheating, short-circuiting and fires. The National Electrical Code specifies minimum box sizes to reduce this risk.

To figure the minimum box size required by the electrical code, add: 1 for each hot and neutral wire entering

> **CAUTION: If you have aluminum wiring, don't mess with it! Call in a licensed pro who's certified to work with it. This wiring is dull gray, not the dull orange that's characteristic of copper.**

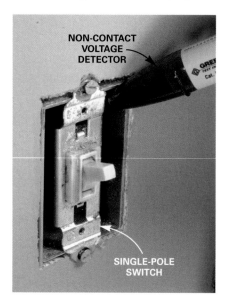

1 **TURN OFF** the power at the main circuit panel. Hold the tip of a non-contact voltage tester near each screw terminal to be sure the power is off. Then unscrew the switch and pull it from the box.

2 **MEASURE** the height, width and depth of metal boxes and refer to Fig. A (facing page) to determine the box volume. Plastic boxes have their volume stamped inside.

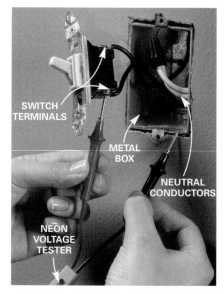

3 **TEST** for a ground. Turn the power back on. Then place the leads of a voltage tester between each screw terminal and the metal box. If the tester lights, the box is grounded. *Turn off the power again before proceeding.*

the box, 1 for all the ground wires combined, 1 for all the clamps combined, and 2 for each device (switch or receptacle) installed in the box. Multiply this figure by 2 for 14-gauge wire and 2.25 for 12-gauge wire to get the minimum box volume in cubic inches.

FIG. A: COMMON METAL BOX SIZES

HEIGHT/WIDTH/DEPTH (INCHES)	VOLUME (CUBIC INCHES)
3 x 2 x 2-1/4	10.5
3 x 2 x 2-1/2	12.5
3 x 2 x 2-3/4	14.0

To help determine the gauge of the wire in your switch box, look at the amperage of the circuit breaker or fuse in the main electrical panel. Fifteen-amp circuits are usually wired with 14-gauge wire and 20-amp circuits require 12-gauge or heavier wire.

Compare the figure you get with the volume of your

Tip

If the circuit breaker is labeled "15 amp," the wires are probably 14-gauge. For 20-amp circuit breakers, the wire will be 12-gauge.

existing box. Plastic boxes have the volume stamped inside, usually on the back. Steel box capacities are listed in the electrical code. We've listed the volume of the most common steel boxes in **Fig. A.** If you have a steel box, measure it (**Photo 2**) and consult the chart to see if it's large enough. If your box is too small, replace it with a larger one. It's possible to replace a box without cutting away the wall, but it's a tricky job. I'd recommend just removing about a 16-in. square of drywall or plaster and patching it after the new large box is installed.

Test your ground before you connect it

New dimmers have either a green grounding wire or screw that you'll have to connect to a grounding source if one is available. Houses wired with plastic-sheathed cable almost always have bare copper ground wires that you'll connect to the dimmer. But test first using the procedure shown in **Photo 3** to verify that the wire is connected to a ground.

Some wiring systems, like ours, rely on metal conduit for the ground. If you have one of these systems, **Photo 3** shows how to test the metal box to verify that it's grounded. If it is, attach a short ground wire to the metal box with either a metal grounding clip as shown in **Photos 4 and 5** or a green grounding screw screwed into the threaded hole in the back of the box. Then connect it to the dimmer.

If testing reveals your box isn't grounded, you can still install the dimmer, but you must use a plastic cover plate and make sure no bare metal parts are exposed.

The easy part is installing the dimmer

Some dimmers, like the one we're installing, have stranded wires attached. **Photos 7 and 8** show how to install this type of dimmer. Others have screw terminals instead. For these, strip 3/4 in. of the insulated covering from the wires in the box and bend a loop in each with a needle-nose pliers. Place the loop clockwise around the screw terminals and

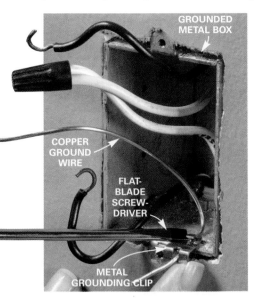

4 PRESS a grounding clip and 6-in. length of bare copper wire onto the metal box with a screwdriver. Cut away a little bit of drywall under the box to provide clearance for the clip.

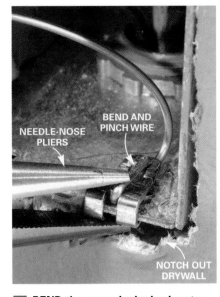

5 BEND the ground wire back onto the clip and squeeze it down tight so it won't interfere with the dimmer switch.

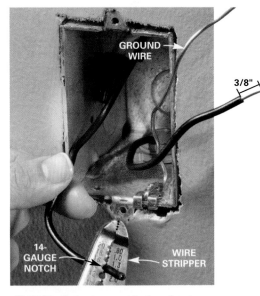

6 CLIP off the bent end of each wire with the wire cutter. Strip 3/8 in. of insulation from the end of the wires.

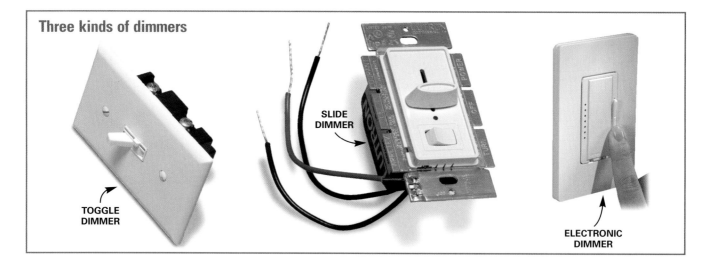

Three kinds of dimmers

TOGGLE DIMMER

SLIDE DIMMER

ELECTRONIC DIMMER

close the loop around the screws with the needle-nose pliers. Then tighten the screws.

It doesn't matter if you reverse the two switch wires to a single-pole dimmer. But if you're replacing a three-way switch with a three-way dimmer, label the "common" wire (it'll be labeled on the old switch) when you remove the old switch so you can connect it to the "common" terminal on the dimmer.

In most cases, the two switch wires will be some color other than green or white, usually black. But one of the wires may be white if your house is wired with plastic-sheathed cable (like Romex). Put a wrap of black tape around the white conductor to label it as a hot wire. ⌂

> **CAUTION: Call an electrician if the original switch is connected to two white wires. This may indicate a dangerous switched neutral.**

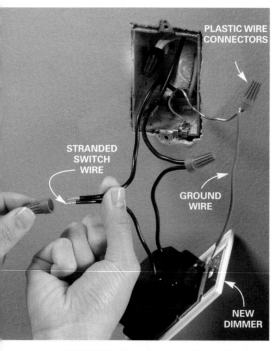

PLASTIC WIRE CONNECTORS

STRANDED SWITCH WIRE

GROUND WIRE

NEW DIMMER

7 HOLD the wires together with the stranded wire protruding about 1/8 in. beyond the solid wire. Match the size of the wire connector you're using to the size and number of wires being connected. Check the manufacturer's specifications on the package to be sure. Twist a plastic wire connector clockwise onto the wires to connect them. Stop twisting when the connector is snug.

NEW ELECTRONIC DIMMER SWITCH

SCREW TO BOX

8 FOLD the wires neatly into the box. Screw the dimmer to the box with the screws provided. Finish the job by installing the cover plate and turning on the power to test the new dimmer.

Buying dimmers

If the switch you're replacing is the only switch controlling the light, buy a standard single-pole dimmer ($5 to $30). If the light can be switched from two or more switches, buy a three-way dimmer switch. But you won't be able to dim the lights from every switch location unless you buy a set of special dimmers (about $70 per pair) with advanced electronics and install one at each switch location.

Most dimmers are designed to handle 600 watts. Add up the wattage of all the light bulbs you'll be dimming. Then read the dimmer package to make sure it can handle the load. Heavy-duty 1,000- and 1,500-watt dimmers are also readily available. Read the package if you'll be installing dimmers side by side in the same electrical box because the wattage rating is reduced to compensate for extra heat buildup.

Finally, you have to use a special device, not a dimmer, to control the speed of ceiling fans and motors. Most fluorescent lights can't be dimmed without altering the fixture.

5

Take a big deep breath of fresh air. This section shows you how to build a stone path, plant a garden, plus tackle dozens of other yard and garden projects.

Yard & Garden

PROJECTS & IMPROVEMENTS

MAKE A HOOP GREENHOUSE

This inexpensive greenhouse extends your growing season. Use it to protect seedlings and get an earlier start in the spring. And it'll keep your tender potted plants going longer in the fall.

To make a 4 x 8-ft. hoop house, buy a 10 x 25-ft. sheet of 4-mil plastic ($5) and nine 10-ft. lengths of 1/2-in. PVC pipe ($1 each; **inset photo**) from a home center. **Photos 1 – 3** show you how to build and use it. Choose a level spot with lots of sunlight and use the dimensions shown in **Photo 1**.

> **Tip**
> If the ground is hard or gravelly, wedge open the holes by driving a short length of PVC pipe into the ground with a mallet or hammer.

Once you use the third pipe in each group to clamp the plastic in place (**Photo 2**), your hoop house is ready to use. It dismantles in minutes for winter storage.

1/2" PVC PIPE

1 MARK the perimeter of your hoop house with twine and stakes. Following our pattern, push one end of each PVC pipe 6 to 8 in. into the ground, bend the pipe gently, and push the other end 6 to 8 in. into the ground as well. Place the pipes in pairs spaced about 6 in. apart.

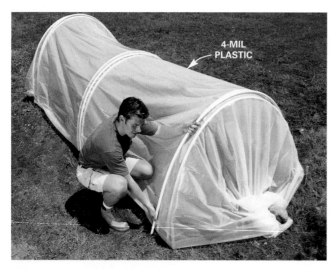

4-MIL PLASTIC

2 LAY the plastic sheet over the hoops. You can anchor extra material at the ends with heavy rocks. Then push a third pipe into the ground halfway between each pair.

3 SET your seedlings inside the house. Simply slide the plastic up or down for access and to control airflow and heat.

EARTH-FRIENDLY WEED CONTROL

Get rid of weeds in sidewalk and driveway cracks without chemicals by pouring boiling water on the weeds. The hot water removes the waxy coating many weeds use to retain moisture. Without the coating, it dries up and dies.

LATE SPRING PRUNING

When spring comes, resist the temptation to get out the pruners on the first warm sunny day and cut every withered old branch and stalk to the ground. With certain plants you have to wait

FIRST NEW GROWTH FROM OLD WOOD

a few weeks, even into June. "Dead" branches and vines may surprise you and spring back to life.

Subshrub late arrivals

Russian sage (Petrovskia), butterfly bush (Buddleia), wild indigo (Baptisia australis) and lavender belong to a class of plants that botanists call subshrubs. They grow like perennials, putting out new growth every year. But they have woody stems, and when spring comes, their new growth emerges from that old wood. This takes awhile. So don't prune these plants all the way to the ground in the fall. And when spring arrives, be patient. Wait until the green sprouts have appeared before you snip the dead branches.

Winter-burn healing

Too little water in fall may leave your evergreens vulnerable to drying winter winds, turning branches brown and brittle. Sun scald, low temperatures and salt can also cause winter burn. Hold back on the pruner, turn on the hose and give your evergreens lots of water in the spring. Burned branches may produce new growth and even green up on their own. Just as with subshrubs, wait until mid-June to prune. Hint: Wait until a healthy evergreen's early summer growth spurt is over to prune it for shape.

DEAD WOOD

WAIT to prune subshrubs until new growth has emerged from the old wood.

WINTER BURN

NEW GROWTH WELL BEGUN

PRUNE winter burn in late spring well after new growth has emerged.

A SAFER WAY TO LIFT

PUSH

BIG, HEAVY ROCK

LIFT

We all know how easy it is to move heavy stuff in a wheelbarrow, but what if you can't load it alone? Use the technique shown here to avoid having to lift heavy stones, bags of potting soil or shrubs up into a wheelbarrow. Just tip the wheelbarrow on its side and roll the stone into it. Then push on the top edge while you lift on the bottom to right the wheelbarrow. Be careful when you reach the top not to tip the wheelbarrow over in the opposite direction. Balance the load in the wheelbarrow and you're ready to roll.

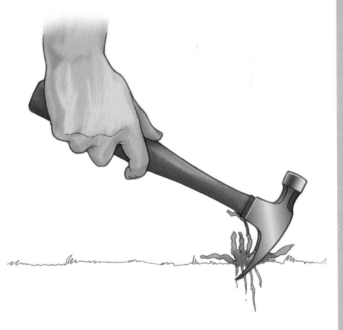

OLD-FASHIONED WEED WHACKER

Get rid of dandelions and other weeds—roots and all—by whacking and grabbing the weed with the straight claw of an old hammer and pulling. The lower you can grab the root, the better.

LOW-MAINTENANCE PERENNIAL GARDEN

Looking for a way to reduce the weed-pulling chore for your plants that come back every year? When you start a new perennial border, spread a nonwoven polypropylene black landscape fabric over the soil. The fabric keeps weeds under control, holds heat in cool spring weather (giving your plants a faster start), and lets water soak through to the roots. At a local garden center, buy a nonbiodegradable fabric that weighs about 3.4 ozs. per square yard (about $10 for a 3 x 25-ft. piece). U-shaped metal stakes (**Photo 2**), which are ideal to hold down the fabric, come in packs of 10 for about $2.

While this system works best for plants already started, you can also start your perennials from seed. Rather than cutting out the circles (**Photo 3**), cut the fabric into pie-shaped wedges with your utility knife. Then simply prep the soil and plant the seed.

SPACE plants according to sizes listed on the labels when you buy them. The hardy, drought-resistant plants we've selected will fill in and cover the mulch completely in two years. Then they will need annual pruning or even dividing.

1 **DIG AND BREAK UP** compacted soil with a sharp spade or U-bar and remove the weeds. Mix peat moss and/or composted manure into the soil if necessary.

2 **LAY DOWN** the landscape fabric, securing it at the corners with U-shaped metal stakes.

3 **DRAW** the garden pattern, including paths, onto the fabric with a light-colored chalk. Cut the plant holes with a utility knife and set the plants.

SEEDLINGS ON THE HALF SHELL

You don't have to buy seedling pots this spring. Instead, make your own from eggshells, using the egg carton as a tray. Next time you use eggs, carefully crack them in half, rinse out the egg residue, then poke a drainage hole in the bottom of each half shell with a sharp scissors or ice pick. Fill the shells with a lightweight, sterile potting mix formulated for seed starting, and sow the seeds. When the seedlings are ready for transplanting, gently crush the eggshell with your fingers and plant them, eggshell and all. The shell will improve your soil as it decomposes.

Gallery
of Ideas

GARDEN ARBOR

If you're looking for a straightforward weekend project to beautify your yard or garden, this project is for you. This graceful arbor doubles as a shade trellis to grow flowering vines and a garden retreat to melt away the hubbub of our busy lives.

This project may appear complex, but it's designed with foolproof methods for building the arches, measuring and cutting the lintel ends and getting the posts positioned. And the project is made from ordinary cedar lumber and pressure-treated pine.

FROM APRIL 2002, P. 36

Project Facts:
Cost: $350
Skill level: Intermediate
Time: 20-30 hours

Special tools: Doweling jig, pipe clamps, jigsaw, belt sander

RETAINING WALL

The curves in this wall may make the project look complex, but it's actually easier to build than walls with square corners. Once you level and position the base row of concrete blocks, you build the rest of the wall by simply stacking more blocks on top with staggered seams. It's like building with Legos; really heavy Legos!

It's a great way to terrace hilly land or carve out a space for a patio or garden. And once you're done, you'll have an attractive wall that will stand for generations.

FROM MAY 2002, P. 44

Project Facts:
Cost: $1200 (about $15 per square foot)
Skill level: Ambitious beginner
Time: 15 to 20 hours

Special tools: Plate compactor, hand compactor, 2- and 4-ft. levels

FROM APRIL 2002, P. 50

BAMBOO WATERFALL

If it seems like your storybook garden is still lacking something, the soothing sound of running water could be it. The answer may be your own version of this Japanese sluice made from real bamboo.

The project doesn't require much in the way of time, skills or tools. The complete article lists mail order sources for bamboo and provides complete instructions for the uphill spout, the downhill pond and recirculating pump, and the waterfall sluices in-between.

Project Facts:
Cost: $200-400
Skill level: Novice
Time: 8 to 16 hours

Special tools: Hacksaw, jigsaw, 3-lb. maul, 4-ft. level, drill

To order photocopies of complete plans for the projects shown above, call 715-246-4344 or write to:
Copies, The Family Handyman, 511 Wisconsin Dr., New Richmond, WI 54017.
Many public libraries also carry back issues of The Family Handyman magazine.

GARDEN PATH

This easy-to-build natural stone path will last a lifetime.

by **Jeff Gorton**

Stonework doesn't have to be complex or require special masonry skills. In most regions, you can buy flat flagstones that you can easily lay for paths and stack for solid stairs. We'll show you how to plan, lay out and build a set of natural stone steps using flat flagstones for the treads and solid blocks of stone, called wallstone, for the risers.

Our steps are built on a gradual slope, but by changing the riser and tread sizes you can build them on slopes as

steep as about 40 degrees. Rustic steps like these are well suited for informal garden paths like ours, but we wouldn't recommend them for entry or other steps that get heavy daily use.

In addition to the basic gardening tools, leather gloves and carpenter's level, you'll need a few special tools for breaking and moving stone. Buy a 4-lb. maul (**Photo 7**) for about $8 to chip and break stone. If you have to cut a few stones, buy a dry-cut diamond blade, available at home centers for $40. To move the stone, rent ($12 per day) or buy ($40 to $100) a two-wheeled dolly with large wheels.

Stone steps don't have to be exact

Make a rough sketch of the plans for your steps, including the approximate number of risers and any retaining walls you might have to build.

Begin by measuring the total horizontal distance the stair will travel along a *level* line (**Photo 1**). This is called the "run" of the stair. Then measure down from this level line to determine the total vertical distance, or "rise." Your goal is to arrive at a set of comfortable steps with rises of 6 to 8 in. and treads at least 12 in. deep.

First figure out how many step risers you'll need. Gentle slopes like ours require short risers and long treads, while steep slopes require taller risers (up to a maximum of 8 in. and short treads). If your hill has both steep and gentle slopes, break it up into sections and calculate the step layout separately for each area (**Fig. A**). Divide the total rise by about 6 in. for shallow slopes, up to a maximum of 8 in. for

FEATURES:

- Dry-laid stone (no mortar)
- No complex step calculations
- Basic tools
- Easy to adapt to your own y

steep slopes, to arrive at the approximate number of risers. In our case, the total rise was 29 in. Dividing by 6 yielded 4.83, which we rounded up to 5 risers.

Subtract 1 from the number of risers to determine the number of treads. Then divide the total run by this number to arrive at the depth of each tread. We divided the total run of 145 in. by 4 treads to arrive at a tread depth of a little more than 36 in. Using this information, mark the location of each stair riser on the ground with spray paint.

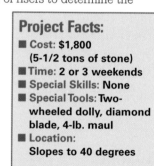

Project Facts:
- **Cost: $1,800** (5-1/2 tons of stone)
- **Time:** 2 or 3 weekends
- **Special Skills:** None
- **Special Tools:** Two-wheeled dolly, diamond blade, 4-lb. maul
- **Location:** Slopes to 40 degrees

Fig. A: Stone stair anatomy

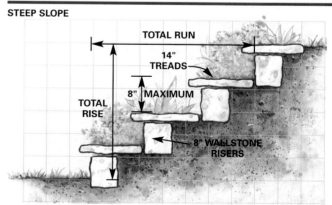

STEEP SLOPE

TOTAL RUN

14" TREADS

8" MAXIMUM

TOTAL RISE

8" WALLSTONE RISERS

1 OUTLINE the steps with spray paint and drive stakes at the top and bottom. Tie a level string line to the stakes. Measure the total run between the stakes and the total rise from the ground to the level line. Calculate the length of each tread (see Fig. A below) and mark them with spray paint.

2 DIG a trench for the first stone riser. Plan to leave enough of the riser stone exposed so the step will be at the correct height when you set the stone tread on top.

3 LEVEL the riser stones by removing soil or adding gravel as needed. Set the distance from the ground (or future path) to the top of the first riser stone equal to the riser dimension less the thickness of the tread.

4 DIG straight back, level with the top of the first riser stone to 10 in. beyond the mark for the second riser. Set the next riser stone so the distance from the dug-out ground to the top of the stone is equal to your riser height. Adjust the height of the riser by adding or removing gravel.

GENTLE SLOPE

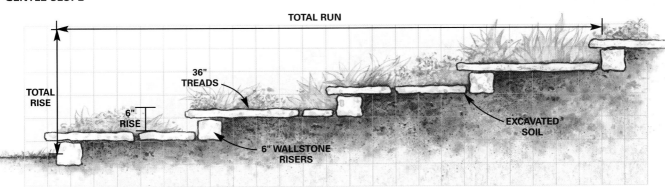

There's no margin for error when you're building wood steps, but luckily you can cheat a little on these rustic stone steps. You'll still have to calculate the height of each riser and the depth of the treads, but if you're off by an inch when you reach the top, it's not difficult to adjust the level or slope of the landing to make up for it.

 **Tip** If your route includes a space where the grade levels out, make this spot a small seating area (photo, p. 172).

Buying stone

A visit to your local stone supplier is the quickest way to find out what types, sizes and shapes of stone are available in your area. Look for flat stones called flagstones that range in thickness from 2 to 3 in. to use for your treads. Ours are limestone, but you may find that another type of stone is more readily available. You'll need some 6- to 8-in. thick blocks of stone, called wallstone, for the risers (**Photo 2**). Follow our instructions for figuring your riser height (**Photo 1**). Then pick out wallstones of this height to use for your risers. Try to

TWO-WHEELED DOLLY
FLAGSTONE

5 MOVE heavy flagstones by tipping them up on end and rocking them onto a two-wheeled dolly. Keep your back straight and lift with your legs.

SMALL STONE IN BACK
2X4 BLOCK FOR TAMPING
LARGE STONE OVERHANGS

6 ARRANGE large flagstones to overhang the lower riser about 2 in. Remove soil or tamp gravel into low areas to level the tops of the stones. Leave gaps between stones up to 2 in. wide.

3- TO 4-LB. MAUL
CHIP OFF POINT
SECOND RISER
GRAVEL TO LEVEL RISER

7 TRIM stones for a better fit by chipping away at protruding pieces with a heavy maul. Wear safety glasses.

POLYURETHANE CONSTRUCTION ADHESIVE
STONE CHIP SHIM
RISER STONE

8 SHIM unstable flagstone treads with stone chips. Tip the tread stone out of the way and glue the stone shims to the risers with polyurethane construction adhesive.

find flagstones of consistent thickness. It will make it easier to keep the stone steps all the same height.

Since stone is usually sold by the ton, and the number of square feet a ton will cover depends on the thickness of the stone, figuring quantities is best left to someone with experience selling natural stone. Note the dimensions on the sketch and take it with you to order the stone. Order about 15 percent extra to provide more shapes to choose from and avoid having to pay for a second delivery. You'll have no trouble finding uses for the extra stone.

Our project required about 3 tons of stone for the treads and landing and another 2-1/2 tons for the risers and wall. In our area, stone costs about $250 to $450 per ton plus $100 for delivery. In addition to the stone, order 1 ton of crushed gravel with aggregate 3/4 in. and smaller for leveling the treads and risers (**Photos 3 and 4**).

Start with level risers

With the tricky planning out of the way, you're ready to dig in and start building steps. Spread out some of the stone so you'll have many shapes to choose from. Then build one step at a time, starting at the bottom and working your way up. **Photos 2 – 11** show you how.

The first step is the trickiest to build. After that you just repeat the process until you reach the top. Set the first riser in place (**Photos 2 and 3**). Remember to bury it a few inches so the first riser won't be too tall. Now use the top surface of this riser stone to guide your shovel as you dig straight back into the hill to make a level spot for the first tread and the second riser. Be sure to dig out all of the sod. When the first two risers are in place, you're ready to set stones for the first tread. Pick larger stones to overhang the riser (**Photo 9**). The extra weight will keep them from tipping. Then fill in behind them with smaller stones.

For a safe set of steps, it's important to keep all the risers the same height. Compensate for variations in flagstone thickness by adjusting the height of the riser. If the stone you pick

Tip

To avoid moving stones more than necessary, arrange the stones into the shape of the treads near the stone pile, and then move the pieces to their permanent location on the steps.

for the tread is extra thick—say, 3 in. rather than 2 in.—bury the riser an extra inch so the total rise will be consistent. The same goes for keeping the top surface of the treads even. Put a little gravel under thin stones to raise them, or excavate under stones that are too thick. If a stone tips or rocks when you step on it, shim it with stone chips (**Photo 8**). Take your time adding gravel and removing soil until your step is just right. Then move on to the next one.

SMALL STONES AT BACK

16" SQUARE OF SOD

CUT AND SLICE SOD

DIRT LEDGE TO REMOVE

LARGER STONE AT FRONT

9 CUT 16-in. squares of sod from alongside the steps with a flat-blade shovel and lift them out. Remove enough soil to slope and blend the surrounding yard into the new steps. Replace the sod and water it.

10 BUILD a small retaining wall by stacking smaller stones and filling behind them with dirt. Stagger the joints at least 4 in. and step each layer back a couple of inches from the one below.

PRESS INTO CRACKS

50/50 SOIL AND COMPOST

11 FILL cracks with a 50/50 mix of soil and compost, and plant a hardy creeping groundcover such as thyme in the larger spaces.

Blend the steps into the landscape

Notching into the hill will leave bare ledges of soil along the edge of each tread. You can either remove soil to slope the surrounding landscape down to the steps or add stones along the edge to retain the soil. **Photo 9** shows how to cut out the sod and regrade the soil along the lower steps. On the three steps leading from the landing to the top of the hill, we buried wallstone along the edge to hold back the dirt (**Photo 10 and lead photo**).

Filling the cracks between stones is the final step in the project. Experts we talked to had varying opinions on the best material to use. Sand is easy but it will wash out. Pea gravel looks good but tends to fall out and get under your feet, and it's like walking on ball bearings. We settled on a 50/50 mix of compost and soil. It packs easily into the cracks and looks natural. And if you want, you can plant a durable creeping groundcover, like creeping thyme, in the large spaces. Besides looking great, it will fill in the spaces to keep out weeds and hold the soil in place. ⌂

GFCI-PROTECTED PLUG

LUMBER CRAYON

DIAMOND BLADE

CAUTION: Plug the saw into a GFCI-protected outlet or into a special portable GFCI plug.

MARK the stone with a crayon. Set the abrasive blade to cut about 1/2 in. deep and saw along the line. Increase the depth in 1/2-in. increments and make repeated cuts until you've sawed at least halfway through the stone. Direct a stream of water from a garden sprayer onto the blade as you saw to reduce dust and cool the blade.

SAW KERF

TURN OVER the stone and gently tap along the cutting line with a heavy hammer until it breaks.

Cutting stone

You'll probably get through the project without having to cut any stone. But if you need an exact fit or just can't find the right shape, cutting is an option. Buy a diamond blade (about $40 at home centers) to fit your circular saw.

DELUXE COMPOSTING

Turn lawn clippings, leaves and garden waste into beautiful (yes, beautiful!) compost.

by **Bonnie Blodgett**

This three-bin composter is designed to make composting tidy and effortless. It's big enough to hold most of your grass clippings, fallen leaves, pruning leftovers and the like so you don't have to haul them away. And the three-bin system speeds up the decomposition so you can return that organic fertilizer to your gardens where it'll improve the soil.

Garden waste goes into the far-left bin first. After a few weeks, you move it to the middle bin (turning and aerating it in the process), where it continues to decompose. After a few more weeks, you move it to the third bin (it's ready for another turn anyway), where it's well on its way to becoming finished compost. It takes four to six weeks to make compost from start to finish, assuming you've kept the piles moist and shredded any leaves or tough stalks before adding them to the bin. Meanwhile, you've been filling the bin at the far left with fresh debris to keep the cycle going.

Stuff to avoid: Meat and bones, oils and fats, feces, seed heads, diseased plants and weed roots. In addition, if your compost turns slimy and stinks, discard it and start over. Don't use it on your plants.

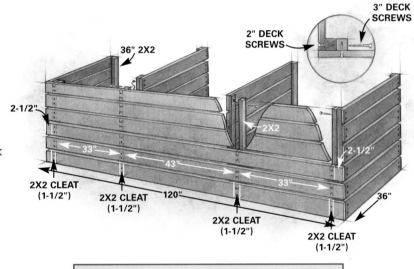

Materials
- Six 5/4 x 6 x 10-ft. cedar deck boards (back)
- Twelve 5/4 x 6 x 6-ft. cedar deck boards (sides)
- Twelve 2x2 x 3-ft. cedar (cleats)

1 CUT the 6-ft. boards into twenty-four 3-ft. lengths. Predrill screw holes and attach two of the 3-ft. boards to a pair of cleats with 2-in. deck screws. Square the frame by moving it until the two diagonal measurements are equal. Spread the remaining boards between the top and bottom boards so they're spaced evenly and screw them in. Repeat this procedure for the other three side panels and the back. To divide the bin into three sections, complete the back panel by screwing on two additional 2x2 cleats.

2 ASSEMBLE the bin by driving 2-in. deck screws through back boards into the side panels, one screw for each board. Then drive 3-in. deck screws through the 2x2 cleats on the back panel into the 2x2 cleats on each side panel. If uneven ground makes it difficult to align the sections, ask a friend for help.

You can fix it™

INSTALL A SIMPLER WEED TRIMMER HEAD

If you've ever struggled to replace or pull out a string trimmer line, you'll love this fix! The frustrating old trimmer head can be replaced with an easy-loading version for about $25 (adapter required for some models). Echo Inc. (800-432-3246) produces a universal trimmer head with a string-loading system so simple your kindergartner could figure it out. Short pieces of string line are pushed into the trimmer head, and a locking system catches the line like a fish on a hook. To change the line, simply pull it through the cutter head and push in a new piece.

Remove the old trimmer head as shown in **Photo 1**. Mounting procedures vary slightly, depending on the manufacturer and model number of the trimmer you own, so consult the manual before attaching the new head. **Photos 2 and 3** show how to mount the replacement head on machines with threaded shafts. Before mounting the new head, determine which triangular adapter piece and retaining nut fit the threaded shaft.

1 REMOVE the spool of line from the trimmer housing. The most common method is to push in, twist and pull off the spool. If your trimmer head differs, follow the manufacturer's instructions to remove the old head. The head is attached to the trimmer with a retaining nut or bolt. Ratchet it free and pull it off (some nuts and bolts will be reverse-threaded).

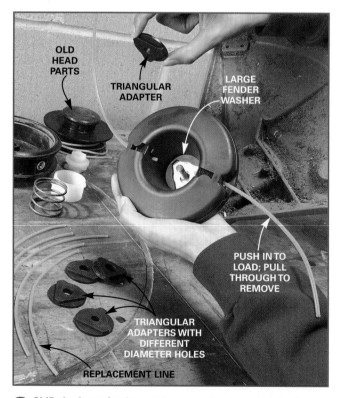

2 SLIP the large fender washer over the threaded shaft and the new trimmer head over the washer. Slide the triangular adapter piece onto the shaft and align with the triangular recess in the trimmer head.

3 SLIDE the small fender washer over the triangular adapter piece, attach the retaining nut and tighten it securely.

TUNE UP A LAWN MOWER

A lawnmower tune-up can increase fuel economy by a third, extend the life of the engine, reduce repair costs and decrease emissions by up to 50 percent.

The three main components involved in a mower tune-up are the air filter ($8), spark plug ($2) and oil ($2 for 20 ozs.), all of which must be changed. The needed parts and supplies can be found at home centers and hardware stores.

Start by changing the oil. Run the engine for a few minutes to warm up the oil so it'll drain better. Stop the engine, remove the drain plug and empty the old oil (tilt the mower back to get it all out, if necessary). Replace the

drain plug and fill the mower with oil until it's visible through the oil fill hole, or check the level on the dipstick.

A clean air filter helps maintain the proper fuel/air ratio, allowing the mower to burn less gas. Swap out the old air filter (**Photo 1**), and then remove and replace the spark plug (**Photo 2**). If the plug's rusted tight, spray it with a penetrating lubricant like Liquid Wrench or JB80. Let it soak in for 10 minutes before trying to loosen the plug again.

The spark plug will be factory gapped, but make sure there is a gap between the electrode and overhanging arm.

1 LOOSEN the air filter cover screw and drop the cover down. Pull out the old air filter and press in the new one (make sure the paper pleats are facing out). Replace the cover and firmly tighten the cover screw.

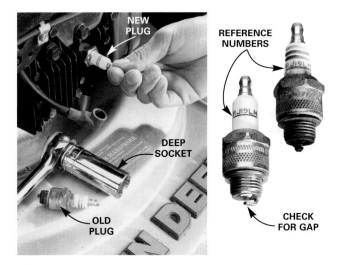

2 REMOVE the old plug with a spark plug wrench or deep socket. Hand-turn the new plug until the threads catch. Ratchet the plug down until it stops, then turn it another quarter turn (cranking down too hard can break the plug or render it nearly impossible to remove).

WINTERIZE YOUR LAWN MOWER

With a little post-season preparation, you can ensure that your mower will start like an Olympic sprinter when you roll it out in spring. Fill the fuel tank and add fuel stabilizer (for example, Briggs & Stratton or Gold Eagle Sta-Bil) to the gasoline to prevent fuel deterioration and the formation of gum, varnish and rust in the fuel system. Run the mower to circulate the additive throughout the fuel system. Lubricate the rest of the engine as shown in the photo. Thoroughly clean the outside and bottom of the mower, and disconnect the spark plug wire and the negative cable from the battery (if you have one). Lubricate all moving parts and spray rust inhibitor on the blade and surrounding unpainted metal parts.

When spring rolls around, simply replace the spark plug wire and battery cable, and your mower will run like a champ.

1 ADD fuel stabilizer to the gasoline, run the engine for five minutes and then remove the spark plug and pour two capfuls of engine oil into the spark plug hole. Pull the cord a couple of times to turn over the motor and disperse the oil throughout the engine.

Which
Should I buy?

IS A LAWN SERVICE WORTH THE DOUGH?

Our lawn is chockfull of weeds. Can one of those chemical lawn services do a better job of bringing my lawn back to health than I can?

If you really love your yard and yard work, and if you're really committed to figuring out your grass problems, you can do a darn good job. But you need a plan and the time to do it. You also need to be truly interested—not just cheap! But since your lawn is full of weeds, you might not be the Lawn Ranger you need to be.

Here's the lowdown. Homeowners can control the type, amount and timing of herbicides, insecticides, fungicides and fertilizers they need to apply. Large lawn services mix batches of fertilizer and herbicide formulated for the "average lawn." They have to—the person spraying your yard will probably do 15 to 25 yards in a day. So, if you have an atypical yard, the stuff they're putting on and the frequency may not do everything you expect. For instance:

1. Some weeds, especially perennial grassy weeds, are best controlled by hand weeding or by hitting them with weed killer two or three times at 10- to 15-day intervals. Most lawn companies aren't on that kind of schedule.

2. Broadleaf herbicides are less effective when applied in temperatures above 85 degrees F or if it rains within 24 hours of their application. Lawn services have a schedule to keep! It may not be feasible for them to pay as close attention to these conditions as you can. On the other hand, in certain areas certain herbicides can only be used by licensed turf professionals. Generally these restricted chemicals are more powerful and do a better job of controlling weeds.

3. The nutritional requirements of lawns that are shaded, diseased or stressed from thatch or overuse differ from those of the "average" yard. To compensate, you can adjust the amount and type of nitrogen, potassium and phosphorus levels in the fertilizers. Most lawn services can only make crude adjustments. Some sophisticated lawn service operations will custom-apply dry fertilizer, but it costs more.

4. Insects can be a big problem. Most of the lawn insecticides are quite toxic to you, your kids and pets. Caution and care must be used when applying them. There are watered-down, less potent insecticides sold to homeowners. But licensed professionals can apply more powerful and effective insecticides and are trained to know when and how to use them.

In short, if yard work is a low priority for you, a lawn service will do a better job, simply because *they'll do it!* Increasingly, lawn service operations will deliver customized treatments. You'll pay for it, but it'll get done!

Most lawn services charge $50 to $75 per application for an average suburban yard. It takes about one hour for a homeowner to apply a dry product ($15 to $35) to an average lawn. Multiply this by five applications per year, then ask yourself what your time is really worth.

Which is safer?

Some folks consider lawn services dangerous because of the "Keep kids and pets off" warning signs they stick in your yard when they leave. The fact is, the liquid fertilizers, fungicides and herbicides they use are in many ways safer than the granular stuff you spread. Liquid absorbs quickly into a plant; within three or four hours the already low danger is well below government guidelines. Granular materials, even the weak ones sold to the homeowner, can stay active for days.

PLASTIC OR WOVEN WEED BARRIER?

We're planting junipers around the foundation of our house. I hate weeding. Should I use plastic or one of those woven weed barriers?

Most professional landscapers use fabric weed barriers these days. Fabric blocks sunlight from the weed seeds hiding in the soil so they have less chance of germinating, and its woven construction allows moisture and air to work their way to the soil and roots. Make sure to cover the barrier with 3 to 4 in. of mulch; otherwise, weed seeds can finagle their way down to the fabric and actually sink roots through it.

Plastic may be the way to go if you have damp basement problems. Slope the soil away from your foundation 1 or 2 in. per foot, then install black plastic. Slit the plastic near the plants so water can penetrate to the roots. Shredded bark and wood chips tend to slide around or get washed off plastic, especially sloped plastic. To counteract this, either use gravel for mulch, which will stay put, or use the big metal staples available at landscape centers to secure fabric over the plastic, then install wood chips.

WOVEN WEED BARRIER   **6-MIL BLACK PLASTIC**

SOD OR GRASS SEED?

Under the cottonwood tree in our back yard, we have a 10 x 10-ft. bare spot where we'd like grass. Here in the Midwest, will we have better results with sod or grass seed?

It will take more patience and tending on your part, but you'll get better results with seed. Sod is great when you want instant lawn. You get grass that's thick, weed-free and fertilized. You can be mowing the stuff in two to three weeks.

But most sods are grown in wide open fields, a condition that favors bluegrass and other sun-loving grasses. And sod that's primarily bluegrass won't grow as vigorously under your shade tree as fescue and other shade-loving grasses. Head to a landscape center and buy a grass seed mix that's formulated for shade. Some mixes get pretty specific in their formulation, so if you know what kind of soil you're working with, you may find the ideal mix. And you'll save money—grass seed for your 100-sq.-ft. area will cost under $2, while sod could cost $20 or more. Plus, it's a lot easier carrying home a sandwich bag of seed than hauling a dozen rolls of sod.

Your seed will require more soil preparation and pampering. You'll need to rototill or loosen up the soil before planting, keep the area watered and battle weeds as they try to take root before the grass fills in. And you won't be playing croquet for at least six months. But once it's established, seed has the best chance of survival.

ENOUGH GRASS SEED FOR 100 SQ. FT. ($1.65)

ENOUGH SOD FOR 100 SQ. FT. ($21)

More isn't always better. You'll probably get better results in highly shaded areas using 1/2 lb. of grass seed than laying 11 rolls of sod weighing 25 lbs. each.

WATER GARDEN
AND STREAM

Preformed shells and ready-to-go pumps make pond building simple. Moving 5 tons of stone — well, that's another matter!

by **Spike Carlsen**

Whether it's a stream in the middle of the woods or a fountain in the heart of downtown, few things rival the sight and sound of moving water. It's relaxing, mesmerizing, contemplative. Well, you don't have to pack up the family and drive for hours for that experience. You can create your own water garden, complete with babbling brook, in your own back yard.

We'll show you how to create a water garden—without spending a fortune or your entire summer doing it. Preformed shells, rubber liners and off-the-shelf pumps and filters put the project's costs and skill requirements within easy reach of any do-it-yourselfer. You'll put in your share of sweat equity busting sod and hauling stone. But when you're done, you'll have a landscape feature to enjoy for years. Here's how to build it.

Water gardens—no two are the same

Since every yard and home-owner is different, every water garden is unique. Yours can be large or small, simple or complex.

There are two basic ways to create a water garden. The first is to use a flexible rubber-like liner made of EPDM, the same material used for flat commercial roofs. Using this method, you dig the shape and size pond you want, then line the hole with a sheet of this heavy-duty material. Home-owners who want to "dive into" water gardening in a big way choose this flexible liner; they can create large, deep ponds that can hold many, and many varieties of, fish and plants. For information on building this type of pond, see "Do-it-Yourself Water Garden," June '00, p. 118. To order a copy, see p. 220.

We elected to go the other route by using preformed rigid shells or liners. (Actually, we joined two shells with a small stream made from the flexible liner mentioned above.) The shells we used are constructed of heavy-duty polyethylene, but you can also get ones made from fiberglass and other materials. Most shells have built-in ledges for plants and don't require as much planning and ground preparation as the flexible liners. Shells do limit your design to the shapes available, but linking several together increases your options. For a small water garden, shells offer a lot of convenience.

Preformed shells come in a wide variety of shapes and sizes. Our garden center stocked a dozen shells ranging in size from a 4-gallon mini pond to the 210-gallon butterfly-shaped shell we used. It could special-order dozens of other shells as well. You can buy shells with or without spillways, the molded lips that allow water to flow from one pond to another. You can even buy preformed streams and waterfalls for connecting a series of ponds. You can install a single pond, cascade a series of ponds down a hillside, plunk one in the middle of a patio or use one as a focus for a small retreat in a corner of your back yard.

Location, location, location

We elected to nestle our water garden into an existing flower bed about 20 ft. from the house. But remember, a water garden is a living thing—it makes noise, attracts wildlife and requires upkeep. Locate it where you can best appreciate it. And remember that you have neighbors, too.

Our experts gave us a few tips:

1. Select a location that receives four hours or more of direct sun a day if you plan on including aquatic plants.
2. Make certain the area has good drainage. Locate the pond away from the bottom of steep slopes so debris, fertilizers and pesticides don't run into your pond. If

you're connecting two ponds with a stream like we did, make sure you have an adequate slope. Position your pond so runoff flows downhill and away from any houses.

3. A lot of literature warns against positioning your pond under or near trees. But hey, this is the real world! If you wind up situating the pond in a treed area, expect to spend more time plucking out leaves, needles and branches before they decompose. And watch out for roots as you dig.
4. Think safety. Building codes in most areas are nebulous about water gardens. Most communities don't require barriers or fences, but ask before you dig in. Otherwise, let common sense rule. If there are toddlers in the house or neighborhood, consider building a barrier around your yard or pond.
5. Call your utility companies and have them mark out the path of all underground wires, cable and pipe. Their locations may very well require you to change your game plan. Digging into an underground wire or pipe can be expensive and dangerous—even deadly.

Remember, moving water isn't just for looks; it keeps the water filtered and aerated and helps prevent stagnation. If you install just a single pond, plan on including a pump, filter and some type of fountain to keep the water circulating, clean and fresh.

FIG. A: Construction details of ponds and stream
WATER IS DRAWN through the filter by the pump, then pushed through the circulating hose to the upper pond.

1 POSITION and adjust the preformed liners or shells until you find a design that fits the site and your tastes. Keep the shells away from steep downhill slopes where debris and lawn chemicals could run into them.

PREFORMED LINER WITH SPILLWAY

"BUTTERFLY" PREFORMED LINER

LEDGES

6" BEYOND EDGE OF POND

2 DIG a hole 6 in. wider and 2 in. deeper than the liner. Mimic the shape and depth of the shell, including the ledges. Test-fit the shell frequently to ensure a solid fit.

3 SPREAD a layer of coarse sand to protect the bottom of the liner and the ledges from sharp rocks. Sand also makes leveling the preformed shells easier.

COARSE SAND

4 LEVEL the liner in every direction. Make certain the bottom and ledges are resting solidly on sand. Use a level on a long, straight 2x4 to level lengthwise.

Install the pond shells

Before making any purchases, get copies of the literature showing the size and shape of the shells your supplier has available. Select a few models, then use a garden hose to create a rough footprint of where they'd go and how they'd connect. Play around with several configurations. We settled on the 210-gallon "Butterfly" pond (about $300) from Atlantic Water Gardens for the lower pond and the 165-gallon "St. Lawrence" pond with spillway (about $190) from MacCourt. See Buyer's Guide, p. 187, for more information.

Once you've obtained your shells, position them (**Photo 1**), then use a shovel to trench an outline 6 in. larger than the ponds. Remove the shells and dig (**Photo 2**) the hole for the lower pond. You need to create a hole that will support the bottom of the shell as well as the ledges. Lower the shell into the hole frequently to check the depth, shape and position of shell and ledges. Dig the hole about 2 in. deeper than the intended final elevation because the sand base you'll spread next will raise it back up (**Fig. A**). Make certain the lip of the shell will be at least 2 in. above the surrounding soil and mulch, or else dirt and muddy rainwater may flow in.

Next spread and level a 2-in. layer of coarse sand over the bottom of the hole (**Photo 3**). Set the shell in place and check everything out. Does the sand fully support the bottom? Is the shell level (**Photo 4**) in every direction? Is the lip at least 2 in. above the surrounding soil? Are the edges of any ledges supported? If the answer to all these questions is "yes," you can start backfilling the pond.

Fill the pond with 2 to 3 in. of water, then check the shell for level again. This is critical; the water in your pond will be level, so if

> **Tip** Use the level of the water in the shell as a guide for fine-tuning the height of the ledges; the ledges are flexible enough to lift or lower an inch or so to maintain a level perimeter.

LEDGE

RUN WATER IN POND WHILE BACKFILLING

COMPACT SAND AND SOIL AROUND LINER

5 BACKFILL around the liner with a 50/50 mix of sand and soil at the same rate water is filling it. Compact the soil and sand as you place it. Fully support the ledges when the backfill reaches that level.

TUCK CORRUGATED HOSE UNDER LIP ON LINER

6 TUCK the hose connecting the upper and lower ponds under the lip of the shell. Continue to extend and protect the hose from kinks and pinches as you do the stonework around both ponds.

7 POSITION the upper liner, again first digging an oversize hole, then placing it on a layer of sand to protect it. Make sure to provide a sufficient change in elevation so there's a strong, positive flow from upper to lower pond.

All the right stuff

If you want a long-lasting water garden, keep these buying tips in mind:

■ Some pond shells are flimsy and more likely to flex under the pressure of heavy backfill or freezing, expanding soil. Do some comparison shopping before you buy. Both manufacturers listed in our Buyer's Guide (p. 187) offer sturdy shells.

■ Buy the thickest EPDM rubber liner you can find. It commonly comes in 40-mil and heavier-duty 60-mil thicknesses.

■ Invest in heavy-duty hose for circulating the water. Once it's buried, it's hard to make repairs. The corrugated version we found was quite crush resistant.

■ Pump size is based on the desired flow rate, plus the height and distance it needs to push the water. Read the manufacturer's guidelines; when in doubt, opt for the larger pump.

■ Order excess flagstone. You'll be better off finding shapes that fit than doing a lot of cutting. You can use any leftover material to build a path, a small retaining wall or a garden border.

the shell is tilted, the water line will show it! Pack a mixture of half sand and half soil around the base of the pond as you fill it with more water (**Photo 5**). Be sure to pack sand under the ledges before the water reaches them; they're flimsy and need support.

Once we had the lower pond backfilled within about 8 in. of the top, we tucked the corrugated hose under the lip of the shell (**Photo 6**). This hose is used to recirculate water from

the pump in the lower pond to the "mouth" at the far end of the upper pond.

Dig the hole for the upper shell, then level it and line it with sand as you did the lower shell. Make sure you have an adequate height difference (**Photo 7**) for your falls and stream. If you're building on a slope, you may be able to bury the entire upper shell. Our site was flatter, so we used stone, sand and soil to partially build up around the shell.

CAPSTONES OVERHANG LIP ON LINER

SUPPORT STONES LEVEL WITH LIP OF LINER

BUILD UP EDGES OF SPILLWAY

PLANTER

SUPPORT OVER-HANGING PARTS OF LINER

CANAL WALL

ESTABLISH DOWNHILL SLOPE FROM SPILLWAY TO LOWER POND

8 INSTALL the flagstone. Set the first support layer of stone level with the lip of the liner. Overhang the second "cap" layer of stone to cover and disguise the lip of the liner.

9 CONTINUE to add stone to support the ledges of the upper pond. Create the walls and base of the canal leading to the lower pond at the same time. The planter area creates a stable surround as well as a more natural-looking transition between upper and lower ponds.

10 SPREAD a layer of sand in the stone canal, sloping it toward the lower pond. Continue packing and leveling the sand to create a solid "stream bed."

Build up the edges with stone

You can disguise the lip of your liner with overhanging plants, stone or a combination of both. We primarily used flagstone.

Spread a 1- to 2-in. layer of sand around the lower pond, then set a layer of flagstone so the upper surface is level with the lip of the shell (**Photo 8**). This allows you to cantilever the second layer of "capstones" over the lip of the pond without them weighing directly on the lip.

There's no exact science to the stonework part of this project. Use the ugliest, most irregular stones for the first support layer, since you won't see them anyway. Select and install capstones that conform to the shape of the pond edge. We built and rebuilt the stone layers around the bottom pond several times before we found a pattern we liked.

Once you have the lower pond surrounded with stone, build your way up and around the upper pond. Start with a wide stone base around the upper pond. This will allow you to lay a slightly sloped, stable wall as you build up to the lip. Solidly support the ledges of the pond with rock and soil when you reach them. We created a small rock planter (**Photo 9**) that stepped up to the upper pond and helped make a more natural-looking transition.

While you're doing the stone-work around the upper pond, snake the free end of the corrugated hose (**Photo 6**) to the far end of the upper pond. Bury it and cover it within the rocks, but don't pinch it. Extend the free end of the hose so it discharges into the far end of the upper pond, then secure and disguise the hose with cap rocks.

Build a lazy river

We created a small stream from the spillway of the upper pond to the lower pond. We began by building a small canal out of stone (**Photo 10**), then sloped a layer of sand across the bottom. We then laid the rubber liner into the canal (**Photo 11**), draped the excess liner up and over the walls of the canal, then added another layer of stone to disguise it. Make sure the canal is deep enough to prevent water from escaping.

Support the liner and curve it up and behind the spillway to contain the water. Make certain the other end drapes well into the lower pond. Use water from a garden hose to test the slope and flow of your little river as you build it. Again, don't expect to get everything right the first time. Building with irregular stone isn't the same as building with flat, square wood. Use small stone chips to shim and stabilize larger stones as you work.

Once you're satisfied with the design and watertightness of your stream, use pond foam (a black, weather-resistant expanding foam available through your pond dealer) to secure thin stone to the top and face of the spillway to disguise it (**Photo 12**). We added smooth stones to the bottom of the stream to help disguise the liner and create a more natural-looking flow.

Continue adding stone up and around the upper pond and upper pond lip. Use support stones and cap stones to support and disguise the lip of the upper shell just as you did when building up the edges of the lower shell.

POND FOAM

FILTER

PUMP

60-MIL EPDM LINER

11 LAY the rubber liner in place, draping it over the sides of the canal wall and into the lower pond. Tuck the liner up and behind the upper spillway. Use water from a garden hose to test flow and watertightness as you install the liner.

12 USING special pond foam, attach thin layers of stone to conceal the plastic spillway. Complete the stonework around the upper pond.

13 CONNECT the filter, pump and hose. Place the lower pond pump and the upper pond inlet hose as far from each other as possible. This will help ensure a more thorough water filtration and minimize stagnation. Keep an eye on the water level for several days to make sure there are no leaks.

Pumps, fountains and wildlife

If your ponds are full of sand, rock bits and other construction debris, siphon, pump or use a big wet-dry vacuum to remove the water and refill the ponds with fresh water.

Connect the filter and pump to your water circulating line so the water is drawn through the filter before it reaches the pump (**Photo 13**). We added a T-fitting to our pump so we could circulate water to the upper pond and to a small statue beside the lower pond.

Set the filter on a few small rocks so it doesn't rest directly on the bottom where it's more likely to become clogged with debris. Plug in your pump, then keep an eye on water levels and flow to make sure everything is functioning properly and there are no leaks. (See "How Do I Run Underground Cable?" on the next page for information on installing outdoor receptacles.) Pay attention to the pump and filter literature for maintenance information. Keep the upper end of the hose out of the upper pond to prevent a possible siphoning effect.

Maintaining clean water and establishing aquatic plants and fish are complex topics we won't even pretend to address here. Suffice it to say, understanding the dynamics of your pond and doing proper maintenance will make the difference between a pond you'll want to linger around for hours and one you'll want to fill in with dirt and plant with petunias in a few years. See "For More Information," at right, for more help. 🏠

Oops! While we were photographing the story, someone stood on a sharp rock in the spillway, creating a pinhole tear in the liner. We didn't discover this slow leak until several days later. The pump in the lower pond kept circulating the water, but hour by hour, water leaked through this small cut, and less water was making its way back to the lower pond. Eventually it nearly went dry. If we hadn't caught it, we would have burned out the pump and most likely killed the flowers and fish. Water loss from even dinky leaks or splashes adds up fast.

Buyer's Guide
Water garden supplies can be found at many large garden centers. Three manufacturers:
- ATLANTIC WATER GARDENS: (609) 927-8972. www.atlanticwatergardens.com. Lawn ponds, filters, skimmers and accessories.
- BECKETT CORP.: (888) 232-5388. www.beckettpumps.com.
- MacCOURT: (800) 552-5473. www.maccourt.com. Preformed lawn ponds.

For More Information
- "Pools, Ponds and Waterways," Dawn Grinstain, Grove Press, 1992. www.suttonbooks.com
- "The Complete Pond Builder," Helen Nash, Sterling, 1996. barnesandnoble.com

Ask™ Handyman

HOW DO I RUN UNDERGROUND CABLE?

I just installed a water garden and now need an outside outlet near the pond to run the pump. How deep should the line be and what type of wire should I use?

There are several different methods for safely running the underground wiring, but the 12-in. deep PVC conduit method we show is about the easiest and most practical for running a typical 15-amp line. A second method, 12-in. deep direct burial of type UF (underground feeder) cable, is another easy alternative. We recommend the PVC conduit because it offers more protection against physical damage. Both methods have to be GFCI (ground fault circuit interrupter) protected before the wires enter the ground to guard against electrocution in case the wire is accidentally cut while you're digging.

No matter which method you choose, you'll have to get an electrical permit first. Review your plan with the inspector and get instructions for inspections.

Tying into an existing garage outlet is usually the simplest way to power your outside outlet for two reasons. First, the electrical boxes are usually exposed for easy hookups, and second, any outlets in garages built after 1981 are supposed to be GFCI protected, which would automatically protect the new outside outlet as well. Unfortunately, there are plenty of unpro-

tected garage outlets out there, so you'll have to check the outlet before beginning your project. The safest way to check is to buy a GFCI receptacle tester (about $10) and test the garage outlets. If they're not protected, you'll need to install a GFCI as part of the job.

GFCI RECEPTACLE TESTER

You'll find all the electrical supplies you need for the new outlet project at a home center. Begin by installing a permanent post for mounting the pond outlet box and digging the 12-in. deep trench. You'll need these electrical supplies and parts for doing the electrical work:

- Two weatherproof electrical boxes: one for mounting the receptacle at the pond and a second for the garage to splice the transition between the cable and individual wires. Metal electrical boxes must be grounded to the bare or green insulated ground wire(s) contained in the box.
- A cable clamp for running cable through the back of the box from the garage outlet. Use duct seal putty to seal the wall penetration hole to keep moisture out of the box.

"GFCI PROTECTED" LABEL

TYPE NM-B CABLE

WEATHER-PROOF EXTERIOR BOX

EXISTING GFCI-PROTECTED OUTLET

CABLE CLAMP

PVC ADAPTER

DUCT SEAL PUTTY

CONDUIT STRAP

12"

PVC COUPLING

WHAT WILL KEEP MY CONCRETE POND FROM LEAKING?

In 1962, I built a small pond of poured concrete. I poured it in sections, but the joints where the sections meet have always leaked. I have tried many different types of cement to seal them, but nothing has worked. Any suggestions?

The joints in the concrete are opening and closing due to seasonal temperature changes. Because any rigid filler will crack, use a flexible urethane caulk. Many home centers and lumberyards carry products like this (one choice is Vulkem 116, for a local distributor call 800-321-7906, www.tremcosealants.com).

First make sure that the joint is at least 1/4-in. wide. If necessary, grind it out with an angle grinder or circular saw fitted with a masonry cutting carbide or diamond blade. Be sure to cut at least 1-in. deep. Wear eye protection, ear protection and a dust mask.

Next, wash out the top inch of the joint with a jet of water from a garden hose. Be sure the joint is debris free and then let it dry. For joints 3/8-in. wide or larger, push a polyethylene backer rod into the joint, leaving 1/2 in. for the caulk. Fill the joint flush to the surface with caulk and immediately tool the joint (try a small plastic spoon) to ensure a good bond to each side of the concrete. Let the caulk set up for 24 hours and then fill the pond.

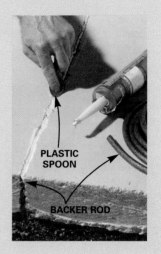

PLASTIC SPOON

BACKER ROD

■ "Schedule 80" PVC (1/2-in.) conduit, elbows and couplings for containing the wires and connecting the exterior boxes. Use PVC cement for joining the parts.

■ PVC adapters for connecting the conduit to the weatherproof boxes.

■ Type THWN moisture-resistant insulated wire to pull into the PVC conduit between the two weatherproof boxes. You'll need three different colors (green for the grounding wire, white for the neutral wire, and black or red for the hot wire). Match the wire gauge to the existing wire in the electrical box you're powering the new outlet from.

■ Conventional cable (Type NM-B) to connect the garage outlet to the individual THWN wires within the outside garage splice box. (Again, match the existing garage wiring when choosing the gauge.)

■ Rain-tight weatherproof covers to protect the plug and receptacle.

In addition, you'll need a receptacle, cable staples, conduit straps and wire connectors. Mark the garage outlet plate cover you're tying into with a "GFCI Protected" sticker (or handwritten notice). The inspector will want to examine the below-grade depth and connections, so don't backfill the trench until your work is examined. Otherwise you may be forced to redig the trench.

WEATHERPROOF EXTERIOR BOX

PVC ADAPTER

RAIN-TIGHT WEATHERPROOF COVER

1/2" SCHEDULE 80 PVC CONDUIT

PVC ELBOW

HOW CAN I IMPROVE MY GARDEN SOIL?

I can't get anything but weeds to grow in my garden. The soil is so hard and rocky. What can I do?

Sounds like you're between a rock and a hard place (sorry, we couldn't resist). Here are two ways out of your dilemma. The first is to dig out the top 12 in. of the old soil and replace it with a rich, fertile mix. But I think the better way is to build a raised planting bed. Creating one requires a lot more initial work and expense, but in the long run you'll reap these advantages:

■ The raised bed is filled with a quality garden soil.

■ The soil won't become excessively compacted because you don't walk on it. This allows for good drainage and air movement down in the root zone.

■ The garden is easier to plant and maintain because it's at a more convenient height. With the bed at 18 to 20 in., you can sit on the edge and work comfortably; 28 to 30 in. allows for wheelchair accessibility.

■ If you're working on a slope, the raised bed creates a level terrace.

■ The planter becomes a strong landscape design element.

Make the raised bed planter as long as you wish, but limit its width to 4 ft. so you can work the garden from both sides. Reaching in more than 2 ft. is hard on the back.

Consider the specific plants to determine the raised bed's depth. It should be a minimum of 8 in. This will accommodate the roots of lettuce and radishes, but root vegetables and many perennials require more depth, so consider building it 12 to 18 in. deep.

GARDEN SOIL

4'

12"

EXISTING SOIL

LAND-SCAPE FABRIC

SHALLOW TRENCH

12" WIDE, 4" TALL CONCRETE RETAINING WALL BLOCK

CAN TREATED WOOD CONTAMINATE VEGETABLE GARDENS?

I keep reading conflicting information regarding the safety of raised garden beds made of treated wood. Can you settle this once and for all? Is it dangerous to use treated wood around gardens, especially vegetable gardens? Will the chemicals in the wood find their way into our home-grown produce?

The predominant chemical used to treat wood to prevent decay is chromated copper arsenate. It's the arsenate (a form of arsenic) that gives people the jitters. But after numerous studies, there's little evidence that chemicals leach out of the wood and get into the food you're growing. A minuscule amount of the chemical will leach from the wood into surrounding soil, particularly when the wood is newly installed. Generally speaking, however, the molecules bind tightly to soil particles near the wood and don't migrate very far into your garden. One study done by Texas A&M University indicated that there was no difference between the amount of arsenic naturally present in soils and the amount in soils contained by CCA-treated wood.

If you're still concerned about using conventional treated wood, call around and see if there's a local supplier of treated wood that doesn't contain arsenic. The most common kind is Type ACQ-D (the preservative is called alkaline copper quat) manufactured by Chemical Specialties Inc. You can call the company at (800) 421-8661 to see if there's a supplier in your area. Or you can build your garden walls out of precast concrete landscaping blocks, cedar or redwood.

For more information on treated wood, contact:

■ American Wood Preservers Institute at (800) 356-AWPI. www.AWPI.org

■ U.S. Dept. of Agriculture Forest Products Laboratory at (608) 231-9200. www.fpl.fs.fed.us/

HOW DO I RUN WATER TO A DISTANT GARDEN?

My vegetable garden is almost 100 ft. from the house and the nearest hose spigot. What's the best way to get a spigot out by the garden?

It's no fun to drag 100 ft. of hose out to the garden. Fortunately, there are several ways to make remote watering more convenient. The easiest is to extend the water supply with buried CPVC pipe. Keep in mind that the job requires some trenching and simple plumbing work. The buried water line is not freeze-proof in Northern climates. You'll have to drain or blow it clear before freezing temperatures arrive.

To prevent contaminated water in the garden hose from being sucked back into the house's water supply, you'll need to install a backflow valve. We used a pressure-type backflow valve that's commonly used with irrigation systems. Check with your building inspector for specific local requirements. Mount this valve on the house's exterior wall at least 1 ft. higher than the new garden spigot regardless of its distance from the house.

To find a water source, tie into a 3/4-in. water line at a point before it runs through a water softener. Cutting a T-fitting into an existing outdoor spigot line is ideal. Include a shutoff and drain in the new line. Run this line through the wall and connect to the backflow valve.

From the backflow valve, run a 3/4-in. CPVC pipe into the ground and along the trench. Bury it at least 12 in. deep to protect it from shovels, tillers and other tools. At the other end, bury a post about 18 in. deep and run the pipe up the post to a hose spigot. We hollowed out a cedar post to hide the pipe, but you could just run it on the surface of the post. If you have freezing winters, be sure to shut off the water and blow all the water out of the line.

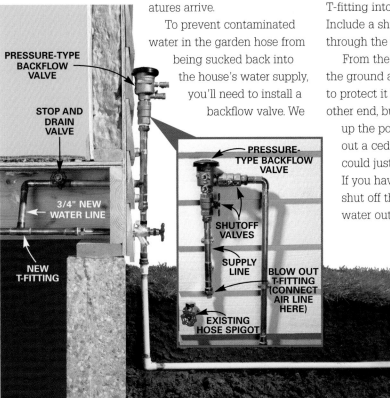

PRESSURE-TYPE BACKFLOW VALVE

STOP AND DRAIN VALVE

3/4" NEW WATER LINE

NEW T-FITTING

PRESSURE-TYPE BACKFLOW VALVE

SHUTOFF VALVES

SUPPLY LINE

BLOW OUT T-FITTING (CONNECT AIR LINE HERE)

EXISTING HOSE SPIGOT

REMOTE HOSE SPIGOT

3/4" CPVC PIPE

IS THERE A BETTER WAY TO START A LAWN?

Our new house is surrounded by bare soil. Sod is expensive and heavy; seed requires lots of tending. Are there other options?

If you're debating whether to seed or sod your lawn, consider a new technique called hydroseeding—especially if your soil is heavy clay or you have shady areas where sod won't thrive. (Sod is made up of bluegrass and other varieties that often require full sun.) Hydroseeding allows you to custom-mix the grass varieties that will grow best in your soil and sunlight conditions.

This process mixes grass seed, mulch, fertilizer and water in a solution that's sprayed onto a lightly tilled seedbed using a high-powered spray gun. The mulch

not only protects it from birds and wind but also decomposes to improve your soil. Although starting from seed doesn't offer instant results, your patience will be rewarded with a thicker, healthier lawn.

Hydroseeding is quick and convenient, but you can't do it yourself. It costs about 75¢ per square yard, about half as much as having your yard professionally sodded. Find a hydroseeding company through professional landscapers (look under "Landscapers" in your Yellow Pages).

Great Goofs™
True tales by real readers!

I pushed and I pushed . . .

The previous owners of my new home left the yard looking like a hay-field, so I was anxious to get mowing. Not yet a proud lawn mower owner, I asked the clerk at the local hardware store to show me their mower selection. I quickly picked out the model I liked best but only half listened to his brief explanation of how it worked. "How hard can it be to run a mower?" I thought.

I hauled the mower home and got right to task. After about an hour of pushing, I was soaking wet and panting like a dog after a foxhunt. I stopped for a break to refill the tank. While pouring the fuel into the tank, I noticed a handle with three icons: a rabbit, a turtle and a stop sign. Suspecting these symbols to be more than decoration, I started the mower and pushed the lever toward the rabbit sign. The mower lurched forward. As I ran to catch the now-self-propelled mower, I vaguely remembered the sales clerk saying something like "It practically mows by itself!"

Dig, dig, dig . . .

Recently married and new homeowners, my wife and I wanted to get started on build-ing a new deck. The first step was to dig the footings. My father (my chief con-sultant and laborer) and I went to the rental store to pick up a power auger. The auger made quick work of the first two holes, and we could see that we'd easily make it back and qualify for the half-day rental fee. The guy at the rental store had warned us that the auger could get stuck and that we shouldn't try to remove too much soil without periodically clearing the hole. His warning faded when we neared the bottom of the third hole (about 3 ft. down) and the auger got stuck. We tried and tried but no amount of tugging would free it. And because we were close to the bay window, we couldn't turn the machine to free it. We each grabbed a shovel and dug. Three hours later, with a hole diameter of about 5 ft. and a full day's rental fee, we finally got the auger free.

It's a gusher!

The exterior hose bib on my house had been leaking for years. The constant dripping finally got to me, so I went inside and turned the valve off that fed the pipe going to the bib. I went back outside and started wrenching the rusty old bib. I turned it several times until I felt it come loose, then noticed water coming through the brick. I sprinted inside and saw water gushing from the basement ceiling. I quickly shut off the main to the house and then surveyed the problem. I'd not only turned the hose bib but also completely loosened the interior shutoff valve!

How brown was my valley

Last spring, I'd had it with the weeds in my lawn, so I went to the local hardware store to get weed killer. I selected a product I thought might work really well because it was easy to apply and didn't require a mechanical spreader. As soon as I got home I sprayed the entire lawn. I didn't bother to read the directions until a few days later when everything was dead: the weeds, the grass and even some flowers. I'd sprayed the lawn with Round-Up—formulated to kill almost all plants. Several weeks later I had my entire lawn replaced with new sod for $2,500!

I told you so!

Several years ago, my wife and I decided to build a new fence along the property line. My wife insisted that I call the local utilities (gas, phone, water, etc.) hot line before I dug the holes, saying, "After all, it's just one number to call and the service is free." Well, I never got around to it and started digging the fence postholes. All was fine until I got to the last post. I jammed the digger down and hit something that felt like a rock, so I gave it another hard thrust. Oops! I could hear hissing out of the pipe and smell gas rising out of the hole. I told my wife and she notified the neighbors and the gas company. Needless to say, I felt about 2 ft. tall as they all gathered across the street looking at me standing by the hole as the gas truck came rushing up the street. I could see my wife staring at me and mouthing the words, "I told you so!"

A soaking surprise

Last summer I had to move the outdoor water spigot several feet to accommodate our new deck. I got all my plumbing parts ready, shut off the water supply inside and then opened the outdoor spigot to drain any remaining water. Just as I put the wrench on the spigot, water came gushing right in my face! My wife had turned on a faucet upstairs to wash her hands and released the vacuum pressure holding the remaining water in that pipe.

FALL GARDEN CHECKLIST

I'll admit that garden chores aren't my cup of tea. For the most part, a bit of chaos reigns in my yard and gardens. But if we have enough warm fall days and winter holds off, I'll get to most of my fall chore list. Even a serious procrastinator shouldn't put off some of these.

■ Rake leaves, but instead of bagging them and sending them to the dump, shred them with the power mower and compost them or use them to mulch the garden. They'll decompose over the winter and be ready for spreading and improving the soil come spring.

■ Prune away old and dead wood, crossing branches, etc. on trees and shrubs after the leaves fall and the trees and shrubs have gone dormant. Pruning for shape and maximum flowering varies with the plant and region. Check with a local nursery for the best times to do this.

■ Seed new lawn, fill in bare spots and overseed existing lawn to thicken it. Use a seed mix consistent with the shade conditions in your yard. Fertilize the lawn to get it through winter and off to an energetic start in the spring. Use a balanced fertilizer (look on the sack for 10-10-10 or something close to it).

■ Clean up garden tools. Scrape away dirt with a wire brush, then apply light cooking oil with a rag or spray to all metal surfaces. Brush boiled linseed oil onto rough wooden handles to preserve them.

■ Leave perennial grasses, plant stalks and seedheads standing to beautify the winter garden, feed and shelter wildlife, and insulate plants.

■ Pull up any prolific self-seeding annuals that may become a nuisance next summer.

BIRDBATH CLEANUP

Stubborn stains in a birdbath are usually caused by chemicals in rain, tap water or well water as well as organic debris. Fill the basin with a quart of water, add 1/2 cup of household bleach, then scrub the basin with a wire brush until any gunk or discoloration disappears. (Use a soft scrub brush rather than a wire brush on shiny ceramic surfaces.) Take care that you don't splash bleach on surrounding vegetation. Rinse well to ensure the birdbath remains chemical-free.

BLEACH

WIRE BRUSH

WATER

CONCRETE BIRD BATH

RAIN SAVER

Rain is better for plants than chlorinated municipal water or well water, and it's free. Catch and store the rain that falls on your roof by connecting a rain barrel to a downspout. However, you don't want water overflowing and draining against the foundation of your home. Also, standing water can breed mosquitoes and endanger small children. Look for a barrel that has a secure lid with an opening that attaches to the downspout and a faucet that lets you hook up a hose or fill a watering can. Expect to pay at least $60. One example is a covered rain barrel from Gardener's Supply ($100, www.gardeners.com, 888-833-1412). For more information and many more choices, use the Internet. Type "rain barrels" into a search engine.

6

Your home may well be the largest investment you'll ever make. Here are projects and tips for keeping it running safely and efficiently.

Energy Savings
& HOME SAFETY

TIPS FOR
ENERGY-SAVING

Here are three dozen low-cost ways for you and your family to save fuel, electricity and cold, hard cash; most take less than an hour.

by **The Editors of Family Handyman magazine**

Sure you can spend a small fortune on new windows, more insulation, a higher efficiency furnace and other energy-saving products. But before you do, take a look at these smaller projects and steps you can take. Some — like turning down your thermostat a few degrees at night — don't cost a thing. Others-like installing fluorescent bulbs-require spending a little up front to reap larger rewards further down the line. Pick and choose what's right for you.

ENERGY-SAVING
COMPACT
FLUORESCENT
BULB

INSTALL and use an automatic setback thermostat. You can reduce your heating and cooling costs by 5 to 15 percent.

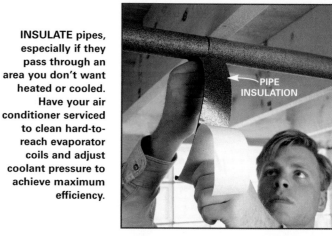

INSULATE pipes, especially if they pass through an area you don't want heated or cooled. Have your air conditioner serviced to clean hard-to-reach evaporator coils and adjust coolant pressure to achieve maximum efficiency.

PIPE INSULATION

CHANGE furnace filters every month, more often if needed.

HAVE a furnace tuneup to clean and adjust burners and improve fuel-burning efficiency.

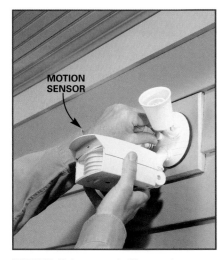

INSTALL light controls like motion sensors, photocell switches and timers to shut off lights automatically when they're not needed.

CLEAN the air conditioner condenser coils and fins when you see grass and airborne debris collected on them.

SHADE your windows with trees, awnings, overhangs, shutters or other devices to keep direct sunlight from entering your home. Add window tint film.

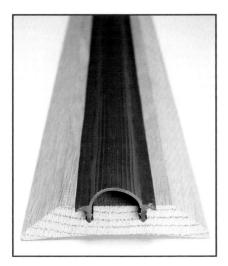

REPLACE worn-out thresholds and weather-stripping around windows and doors.

You can also:

■ FIX leaky faucets; dripping hot water can cost $35 per year.

■ BUY gas stoves with electronic ignition rather than pilot lights.

■ INSTALL a reflector (shiny aluminum foil over cardboard will do) behind radiators to reduce heat driven into and through the wall. Save 5 percent.

■ REDUCE hot water usage by replacing high-volume showerheads with low-flow heads (2 to 3 gallons per minute). Save up to $40 per year.

■ REPLACE recessed light fixtures with airtight models when you remodel.

Heat from wastewater

Every time you take a shower, the heat and money spent warming the water go down the drain. The GFX drainwater heat recovery system is a 30- to 60-in. long, large-diameter copper pipe you install in place of a vertical section of drainpipe. Wrapped around this is a continuous coil of copper pipe that incoming water spirals through on its way to the water heater. The heat from the wastewater raises the temperature of the incoming water by as much as 30 degrees F, resulting in less fuel use by your water heater. (When water flows down a pipe, it clings to the walls, making the transfer of heat very efficient.) This preheating can triple the shower capacity of an electric water heater and halve the cost of a shower.

The company has recently married the GFX to a tankless electric water heater to create an extremely efficient water heating system (Adtec Heaters, 888-253-5350). The GFX alone costs $200 and up.

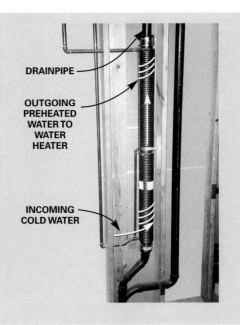

DRAINPIPE

OUTGOING PREHEATED WATER TO WATER HEATER

INCOMING COLD WATER

REPLACE light bulbs used more than two hours per day with compact fluorescent bulbs. Fluorescent bulbs last longer and use only one-third as much energy as standard bulbs.

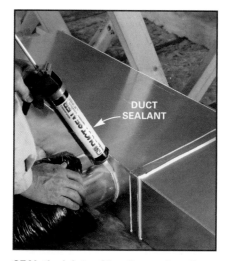

DUCT SEALANT

SEAL the joints of heating and cooling ducts that run through attics and basements with a high quality duct sealant.

WRAP the tank of your gas-burning water heater in a special fiberglass blanket to decrease heat loss. Check your owner's manual to make sure a blanket is recommended for your model.

21 money-saving and energy-saving ideas that don't cost a dime

1 Lower the indoor temperature a few degrees in winter (you'll save about 2 percent per degree). Set it even lower at night and a full 10 degrees lower when you're on vacation.

2 Close the fireplace damper when the fireplace isn't in use. If it's never used, seal the flue with a plastic bag stuffed with insulation.

3 Open shades and blinds to let in sunlight during the day and close them to reduce heat loss at night. For cooling, close them during the day.

4 Close off unused rooms and lower the temperatures by adjusting the registers and dampers. You'll save up to $50 per year.

5 Clean your furnace's blower fan with a soft brush and vacuum cleaner.

6 Turn off lights not in use. Reduce bulb wattage and use dimmers when you can.

7 Reduce humidity in bathrooms and kitchens with exhaust fans. When dehumidifying a basement, keep basement doors and windows closed.

8 Ventilate and cool your home with window or whole-house fans during the cooler hours of the day.

9 Fill clothes washers and dishwashers for more efficient energy use, rather than cleaning partial loads.

10 In warm weather, set the thermostat higher (75 to 78 degrees F) and rely more on ceiling and table fans for cooling, even when the air conditioner is running.

11 Skip the dishwasher's drying cycle (and cut the energy use by about half!).

12 Wash clothes in cool rather than hot water.

13 Flush your garbage disposer with cold water rather than hot. Grease solidifies in cold water and will wash away.

14 Clean refrigerator coils with a soft brush annually, or more often if you have pets that shed.

15 Clean clothes washer and dryer lint screens after every use.

16 Run major appliances late in the evening or early in the morning when electric loads are less (off peak).

17 Cook more efficiently using microwaves, Crock-Pots and pressure cookers.

18 Turn off room air conditioners when you leave for an hour or more. You can quickly cool the room later.

19 Recycle. Reuse. Take your bike instead of your car.

20 Consider higher-efficiency appliances when purchasing new refrigerators, freezers and dishwashers. The energy savings usually pays back the extra costs within a few years. The same goes for furnaces and water heaters.

21 Lower your water heater setting to 120 degrees F for both energy savings and safety. (Measure hot water temperature at a faucet with a cooking thermometer if the water heater setting isn't calibrated in degrees.)

Which
Should I buy?

WHAT'S THE BEST HEARING PROTECTION?

I'm getting into woodworking and spend about 10 hours a week using my router, planer and table saw. I'd like to hold on to my hearing. Should I buy earmuffs or earplugs?

Both offer adequate hearing protection; the key is selecting a protector that's comfortable and convenient so you'll actually use it.

Disposable foam earplugs that you twist, then let expand into your ear, are the very best because they block the ear canal completely. They're cheap (as little as 10¢ a pair purchased in quantity), unobtrusive and lightweight. But I personally can't get used to these; they feel like insulation stuffed into my ears. And they're so effective that they make me feel disconnected from my surroundings. I need to hear some of the whine of the router and whir of the circular saw to know that I'm not forcing or binding the tool. Jaw movement can dislodge them, they're tough to use when you have an earache and, of course, you need to remember to replenish your supply. But if your ears are very sensitive and the feel doesn't bug you, these might be right for you.

Earmuffs generally don't block quite as much noise, some people consider them hot and clunky, and if you have glasses or long hair they may not seal completely—but I'm partial to them. They offer adequate protection, and wearing them is second nature now. (When they're not in use, I automatically prop mine up and out of the way atop my head like Mickey Mouse ears.) They serve as ear warmers in chilly weather, and more than once they've absorbed the impact of a blow that would otherwise have been absorbed by my noggin.

Reusable molded earplugs, often on a cord or headband, offer the least protection of the group. But they're lightweight and cheap, so it's convenient to keep a couple of extra pairs around. And even if they're not the best performers, they're adequate for most situations.

Hearing protectors have a noise reduction rating (NRR) printed on the package. Noise is measured in decibels (dB); each 10 dB jump reflects a doubling of the noise level.

The idea is to get the noise reduced to a safe and comfortable level; for a two-hour stint in your workshop, that should be less than 90 dB. Foam plugs offer an NRR of about 30 dB; earmuffs about 25 dB; molded plugs slightly less than 25 dB. For extremely loud operations, wear both plugs and muffs to attain an NRR of 35 db or more.

NOISE REDUCTION OF 25 DB OR MORE

NOISE REDUCTION OF 30 DB

NOISE REDUCTION OF 25 DB OR LESS

Common sound levels

Normal conversation	60 dB
Shop vacuum, table saw	95 dB
Belt sander, jigsaw	100 dB
Router, circular saw	110 dB
Chain saw, nail gun	120 dB
Jet engine, pain threshold	140 dB

DIY trivia
The 30,000 tiny hair cells arranged in our inner ear's snail-shaped cochlea are responsible for transmitting sound. The hairs nearest the opening are responsible for transmitting high-frequency noises and are the first ones damaged by loud noise. That's why people with hearing damage can hear a low-pitched male voice with better clarity than a higher-pitched female voice.

INSTALL A DOORKNOB REINFORCER

Install a door reinforcer on your entry and garage service doors to help discourage break-ins. Reinforcers are three-sided metal plates that encase and strengthen the door around the latch, which is a door's most vulnerable area. The $18 reinforcer shown is meant to strengthen door latches (**Photo 3**), but you can also buy reinforcers that strengthen deadbolts (about $12). It's fairly simple to install them on fiberglass, wood or steel doors as shown in **Photos 1**

through 4. A reinforcer extends the door edge about 1/32 in., and so may rub the door frame of tight-fitting doors. If so, slightly deepen the hinge mortises with a chisel to widen the gap at the latch side. Or chisel a 1/32-in. recess into the door edge so the reinforcer fits flush.

Door reinforcers are found at home centers and well-stocked hardware stores. For more information, contact Mag Security, (714) 891-5100 or www.magsecurity.com.

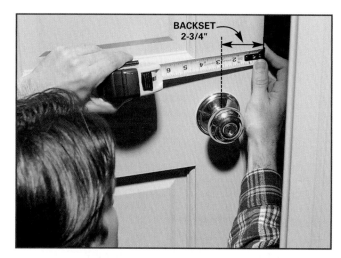

1 MEASURE the "backset," the distance between the door edge and the center of the door knob; the thickness of the door; and the knob hole diameter. Buy a reinforcer that fits all those measurements.

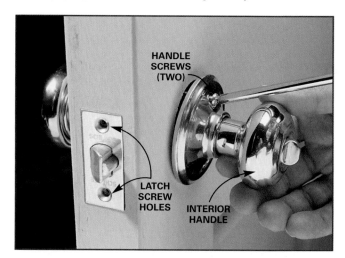

2 UNSCREW the two screws on the inside knob and remove both knobs. Also remove the two 3/4-in. latch screws, but leave the latch in place.

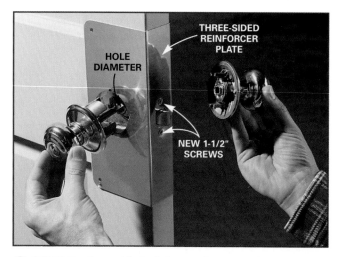

3 SLIDE the three-sided reinforcer plate onto the door. Secure it to the latch with the two 1-1/2 in. screws provided and remount the doorknobs.

4 DRILL four 3/32-in. pilot holes into the door and install the corner screws on the interior and exterior sides of the reinforcer plate.

Have you ever lost your house keys and been worried that a stranger could get in? Unless you're the first occupant of the property, you never can be sure how many copies of your keys exist. Lock-smiths typically charge up to $10 to rekey an individual lock. Since most homes have multiple doors with multiple locks, rekeying can get expensive.

You can rekey a lock like a pro and at a fraction of the cost. Rekeying kits are available for most lock brands, but they're not interchangeable. You have to buy a kit for each brand of lock used in your home. (If you're lucky, they'll all be the same brand!) Made by Change-A-Lock, they're available in home centers and hardware stores and on-line at www.change-a-lock.com.

Each $8 kit will rekey six locks, but you can order extra pins if you need more. The kit will work on entrance and deadbolt locks, and it comes with two keys and all the tools you'll need, except a screwdriver. But keep your current keys — you'll need them to remove the cylinder. We used a Schlage brand lock for this story, so if you have a different brand, be sure to check the instruction sheet for minor variations.

Insert the key in the lock and turn it until the door is unlocked. Remove the doorknob and lock cylinder housing as shown in **Photos 1 and 2**. Use the special retainer ring tool supplied with the kit to force off the thin retainer ring (**Photo 3**). Set the ring aside so you can replace it later.

The most critical part of this operation comes next. **Photo 4** shows the cylinder plug being removed from the cylinder. The top of the cylinder contains pins and springs, which keep pressure on the keyed pins. You must keep the plug follower tight to the cylinder plug until it's completely removed so that the pins and springs don't pop out of the cylinder. If they do fall out, it's not the end of the world—just make sure you pick them all up and refer to the enclosed instruction sheet for reinserting them. Check **Photo 5** to see how the new pins are inserted into the cylinder. Once the new pins are in, reverse the steps to reassemble the lock.

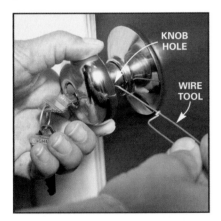

1 INSERT the wire tool (included in the kit) into the knob hole and depress the knob clip. Pull the knob off the door.

2 PUSH the cylinder out the back of the knob assembly to pop off the knob sleeve, and remove the cylinder.

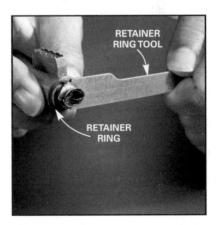

3 PUSH the special retainer ring tool against the retainer ring to pop it off the cylinder.

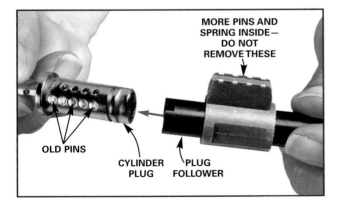

4 INSERT the old key and turn it either to the left or right. Remove the plug by pushing the plug follower (supplied in the kit; see photo on p. 200) through the cylinder. Make SURE to keep constant pressure between the plug and follower so the pins and springs don't pop out.

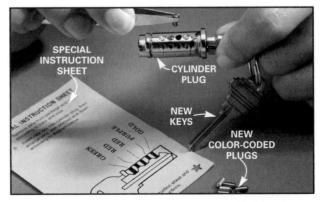

5 DUMP OUT the old pins, insert the new key, and use a tweezers or small needle-nose pliers to match the new colored pins to the color code on the special instruction sheet included in the kit.

7 UNEXPECTED
WAYS FIRES START

Most heartbreaking losses are surprisingly easy to prevent. Sit down with your family and go through this guide tonight. It could save a life.

by **Travis Larson**

Most fires are unexpected because they're caused by the most ordinary, everyday items that you normally consider safe: a stove burner, a candle, an electric space heater, the water heater, an extension cord, a cigarette. What typically makes them dangerous are mental lapses, poor judgment, hurried actions and simple carelessness.

While everyone makes mistakes, you can vastly cut down deadly fire risks by exercising good safety habits and simple prevention steps. In this article, we'll outline the "Big 7" most common causes of preventable fires, share some true but tragic stories and tell you the simple things you can and should do to keep them from starting.

#1 SOURCE: COOKING FIRES

The problem

The grease in an unattended frying pan catches on fire and ignites nearby combustibles, which in turn ignite curtains, cabinets or anything else in the vicinity.

The statistics:
23% of fires, 9% of deaths

A true fire story

WAUSAU, WI—A sleeping 4-year-old girl died of smoke inhalation in a house fire that started about 30 minutes after her mother left her alone to run errands. Apparently, a stove burner was left on under a frying pan containing grease used for frying chicken. The four-year-old was the only person home at the time of the fire.

On average, every year one out of every eight homes will have a kitchen cooking fire. Cooking fires mostly occur on the cooktop, usually in the first 15 minutes of cooking. A common scenario is an unattended frying pan on a hot burner. If a fire starts, don't carry the pan outside; slip a lid over the flames from the side to keep from burning your arm. Many grease fires become full-scale house fires when a flaming pan is carried through the house, dripping a flaming grease trail along the way.

The solution
- Never leave the kitchen while something is cooking on the stove.
- Keep combustibles at least 3 ft. away from the cooktop. This includes curtains and wall hangings.

TIP: Post a reminder note near the range for a week or two until everyone gets the message.

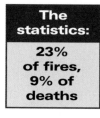

FLAMMABLES OVER STOVE TOP

GREASE FIRE

PAPER TOWELS TOO CLOSE TO STOVE

TOWEL TOO CLOSE TO STOVE

#2 SOURCE: HEATING EQUIPMENT

The problem

Wood stoves and space heaters igniting nearby combustibles are responsible for the lion's share of heating fires.

A true fire story

WINSTON-SALEM, NC—An electric space heater caused the death of a 3-month-old infant left at home with her brother and her

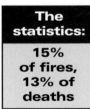

The statistics:

15% of fires, 13% of deaths

two sisters early one morning, fire officials said. Manuel, age 11, smelled smoke in an upstairs room and was able to get two of his sisters outside but was unable to rescue his 3-month-old sister, who was asleep in the master bedroom. An electric space heater in the bedroom appears to have ignited a nearby pile of clothes. The mother was driving her husband to work when the fire started. A smoke detector had been installed near the kitchen, but the family took it down because it would go off when they cooked.

Most deaths from heating equipment occur when wood stoves and space heaters are in use and ignite nearby combustibles while everyone's asleep. Here are other common ways that wood stoves cause fires:

■ If they're not disposed of properly, embers in discarded ashes smolder for up to two weeks and can ignite other trash.

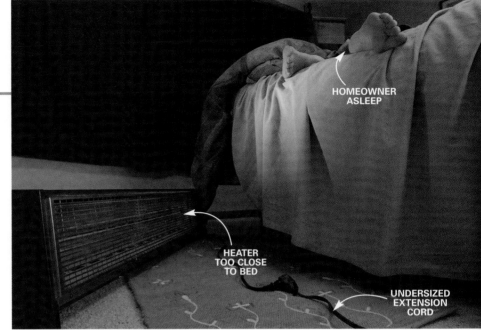

HOMEOWNER ASLEEP

HEATER TOO CLOSE TO BED

UNDERSIZED EXTENSION CORD

■ Chimney disrepair and creosote buildup can combine to create a chimney fire that can ignite adjoining wall framing.
■ Sparks or even just heat can ignite combustibles that are located too close to the wood stove.

The solution

■ **Keep space heaters at least 3 ft. away from drapes, bedding and other flammables.**
■ **Plug space heaters directly into outlets, not into extension cords.**
■ **Don't use space heaters while sleeping.**
■ **Empty wood-stove ashes in a metal container and store them outside away from combustibles for at least a week before dumping them into the trash.**
■ **Have your chimney inspected and cleaned every year.**
■ **Keep any and all combustible objects at least 5 ft. away from the stove or fireplace.**

TIP: Establish a designated space heater zone in rooms where space heaters are used. The zone should be clear of blowing drapes and at least 5 ft. away from other combustibles.

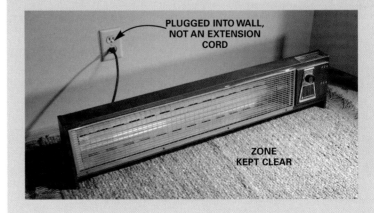

PLUGGED INTO WALL, NOT AN EXTENSION CORD

ZONE KEPT CLEAR

Smoke alarms

According to statistics, this year fire will claim the lives of 30 of Family Handyman readers and the homes of 500 others. Don't become part of this statistic. Well over 60 percent of house-fire fatalities occur in homes that are missing smoke alarms or have disabled alarms or alarms with dead batteries. Test your smoke alarms every month and replace units that are more than 10 years old.

#3 SOURCE:
ELECTRICAL FIRES

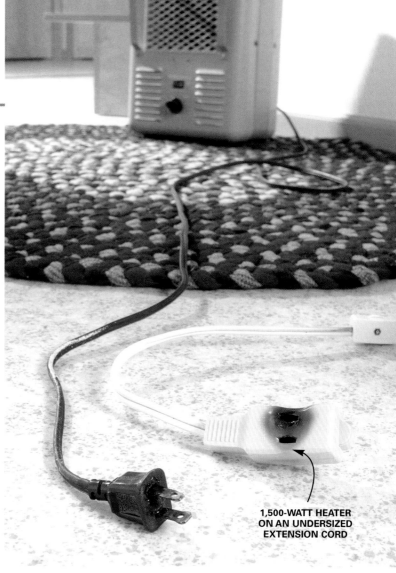

The problem

Overloaded extension cords, hidden electrical shorts, bad connections, and oversized bulbs and fixtures can ignite nearby combustibles and burn down your house.

A true fire story

FLORIDA—Fire and smoke spread through a single-story home, killing two in a late-night blaze. Investigators determined that an electrical short in a five-outlet power strip overloaded with seven appliances started the fire. Excessive heat melted plastic wires and ignited the carpet and a television stand. Crews

The statistics:

9% of fires, 10% of deaths

doused the flames and removed a 74-year-old man and a 59-year-old woman from the home. The man had already died of smoke inhalation and the woman later succumbed to second- and third-degree burns.

1,500-WATT HEATER ON AN UNDERSIZED EXTENSION CORD

Electricity and heat caused by shorts, overloading or bad connections go hand in hand. The heat generated is often enough to ignite combustibles such as wood framing, rugs or even the insulation around the cord or wire.

While a few of the electrical causes are tough to spot, there are telltale clues that can tip you off to dangerous concealed wiring hazards.

- Electrical cords that are warm to the touch can signal overloading.
- Charred or plastic burning odors may indicate oversized bulbs and light fixtures.
- Warm switch or receptacle plate covers may mean a poor electrical connection.
- Frequently tripping circuit breakers may be caused by a defective breaker or possibly a short in the cables buried in walls or ceilings.

The solution
- **Replace extension cords that are undersized or frayed.**
- **Never run extension cords under rugs.**
- **Replace undersized cords with larger-gauged ones or plug appliances directly into outlets.**
- **Call an electrician to track down hidden problems causing frequently tripping circuit breakers.**
- **Call an electrician to open up and troubleshoot electrical boxes that have warm covers.**
- **Check all the light bulbs in your home to make sure bulb wattages don't exceed the fixture's recommended maximum.**

#4 SOURCE: APPLIANCES

The problem

After problems with stoves and heaters, the biggest culprits in appliance fires are lint in dryers and combustibles near gas water heaters.

A true fire story

PORTSMOUTH, VA—Clothes piled against a water heater started a fire that took the life of a 7-year-old girl. A neighbor who noticed the fire was able to kick in the back door and rescue five of the children ages 2 to 10, but dense smoke made it impossible for him to save the 7-year-old. The mother had gone to the store and left the children in the care of her next-door neighbor, who wasn't with the children when the fire broke out. A fire department spokesperson said, "There should be plenty of space between a water heater and any other materials," and "there should never be anything within two feet of any heating appliance."

The statistics:

7% of fires, 4% of deaths

Since water heaters are often in the same room as the laundry, clothes tend to get piled up against the water heater near the flame. The problem is worse when that flimsy cover plate falls off the burner access.

Dryer vents catch on fire when built-up dust and lint ignite from either the burners or the heating elements and create a fire path to built-up lint within the vent hose. Especially dangerous are dryers that are vented with flexible vinyl hoses. The vinyl then catches on fire and lights anything near it.

MISSING COVER PLATE

CLOTHES PILED AGAINST WATER HEATER

The solution

- Make sure protective water heater combustion chamber covers are in place.
- Pull the back service panel from the dryer cabinet and clean all the lint from the interior and around the drum.
- Clean built-up lint from the vent line.
- Replace vinyl vent lines with smooth-walled metal ducts.

TIP: Mark a "combustible-free" zone 3 ft. away from your water heater with masking tape.

COVER PLATE

3'

#5 SOURCE: **SMOKING**

The problem

Smoking kills more people than any other cause of fire because the fires usually start when everyone's asleep.

A true fire story

MINNESOTA—A man died after he fell asleep while smoking in bed. He awoke to find his bed and clothing in flames. Disoriented, he opened a closet and ignited the clothes hanging inside before struggling through the bedroom door and collapsing on the hallway floor where his clothes lit the carpeting on fire. He was pronounced dead at the scene and the fires were extinguished.

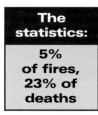

The statistics:

5% of fires, 23% of deaths

If a cigarette smolders in the bedclothes or drops on the carpet when the smoker falls asleep, the gases from smoldering fabrics will actually lull the smoker into a deeper and deeper sleep. Live butts that fall between cushions or are tossed into trash cans can take hours to ignite, and when they finally do, the household's in bed, asleep.

CIGARETTE IGNITES BEDDING

UNSTABLE ASHTRAY

The solution
- Don't smoke in bed.
- Use large ashtrays on tables.
- Soak ashtrays under the faucet before throwing cigarette butts in the trash.

TIP: When nagging isn't doing the trick, it might be time to buy a sign like the one shown.

#6 SOURCE: **CHILDREN PLAYING WITH FIRE**

The problem

Not only do children playing with fire start 5 percent of the residential fires; they're also the most likely ones to die from those fires.

LIGHTER AND MATCHES STORED WITHIN EASY REACH OF CHILDREN

The statistics:

5% of fires, 8% of deaths

A true fire story

TENNESSEE—A 2-year-old and his 23-year-old mother died when a fire spread through the house. The children's 28-year-old father, who rescued his three daughters before reentering the house to search for his wife and son, also died. There were no batteries in the kitchen's smoke alarm.

The fire apparently began in a front bedroom under a bed. They believe that one of the children was playing with a lighter or matches and ignited a foam mattress. Flames then spread to the hallway, living room and kitchen. A padlocked door prevented the victims from leaving the home.

Children will often start fires while hiding in places like closets or under beds, where they're surrounded by combustibles. Their first reaction is often to hide from you or the fire after it starts. There, they become overcome by smoke and/or make it difficult for firefighters to find them. It's obvious that you shouldn't leave matches and lighters lying around, but you also have to be vigilant around burning candles.

The solution
- Store matches and lighters up high, well out of the reach of children.

#7 SOURCE:
CANDLES

The problem

Like cooking fires, most candle fires occur when candles burn unattended near combustibles—usually in bedrooms.

A true fire story

INDIANA—A 23-year-old woman and her two daugh-

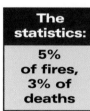

The statistics:

5% of fires, 3% of deaths

ters, ages 11 months and 2 years, died when wind from an open window blew curtains across an unattended candle, spreading flames to nearby combustibles. The house had two smoke alarms, one battery-operated, the other hard-wired. Both were inoperable. Firefighters found the 11-month-old girl in a crib in the living room, dead from smoke inhalation and burns. Her mother and sister were found next to a bed, dead of smoke inhalation. All three had been napping when the fire broke out.

The recent popularity of candles and the 50 percent surge in candle-initiated fires in the last 10 years is no coincidence. Couple that with burning candles near combustibles or on shaky holders and there's a huge potential for a catastrophic fire.

Using candles safely calls for the utmost in attention and care. They're simply a high-risk item because you can easily set them near combustibles without noticing, leave them unattended and forget about them entirely. They'll often get soft and fall out of a holder and ignite nearby combustibles or even ignite an underlying wooden holder or shelf. (It's wishful thinking, but if I had my way, we'd only burn candles at the dinner table and nowhere else.) 🏠

FLAME TOO CLOSE TO COMBUSTIBLES

TIPPY HOLDER ON UNSTABLE SURFACE

The solution
- Use only tip-proof containers.
- Burn candles only while you're awake and in the same room with them.
- Keep candles at least 3 ft. away from combustibles.
- Never burn candles that have combustibles (flowers, leaves and potpourri) cast into the wax.

TIP: Go through your candle and candleholder collection and throw away tippy holders and candles with combustibles cast into them.

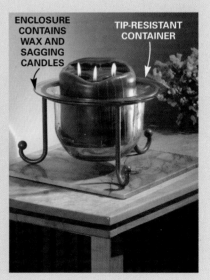

ENCLOSURE CONTAINS WAX AND SAGGING CANDLES

TIP-RESISTANT CONTAINER

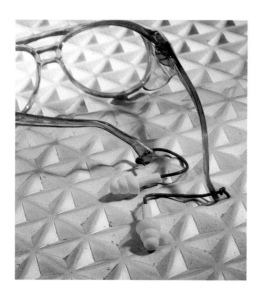

SAFETY GLASSES/ EARPLUGS COMBO

Here's a good way to keep your vision and hearing protection together. Drill a 3/32-in. hole near the end of each earpiece of your safety glasses. Pick up a pair of corded earplugs ($3) at a home center or hardware store. Cut the earplug cord in the middle, and thread each half through the holes. Knot the ends about 2 in. from the plugs and cut off the excess.

HANDY HEARING PROTECTION

Buy several sets of hearing protection ear muffs and keep them stored on the handle of your mitersaw, wet-dry vacuum and lawnmower. You're more likely to use them when they're handy.

FLAG CLAMP

If you have to pick up long lengths of wood from the lumberyard, throw a spring clamp in the back of your vehicle. Use the clamp to attach the warning flag to the end of the protruding lumber. The clamp's easy to slip on and off, and you won't have to fuss around with staples, nails or string.

BROKEN GLASS CLEANUP

Use a lint roller to clean up small shards of broken glass. After picking up the large pieces by hand, roll the tacky tape of the lint roller around to pick up the smaller ones. It just might save you from a painful glass splinter in the bottom of your foot.

PROPANE TANK CARRIER

Whenever I took my 20-lb. propane tank to be filled, it always rolled around in the trunk of my car. To solve the problem, I stuck it in an old milk crate. The crate's wide, flat base keeps the tank stable.

COUNTERTOP

RUBBER ERASER

RUBBER ERASER CHILD PROTECTOR

Small children always seem to bump their head on the underside of a countertop when they stand up. To protect them from future bumps, glue a rubber eraser to the underside of the counter corner. Use a C-clamp to hold the eraser until the glue dries.

MOUSE PAD JAR OPENER

Throw that extra mouse pad in a kitchen or workbench drawer and use it to loosen caps on jars and cans. The rubber on the back of the pad grips stubborn lids so you can break them loose.

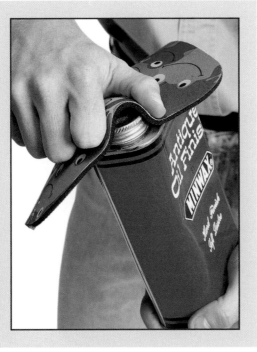

SAFETY FIRST

Making long cuts can be dangerous. Before you try it, read the following safety precautions.

■ Wear safety glasses and hearing protection and avoid loose-fitting clothes. Tie back long hair.

■ Set the saw blade to cut about 1/4 in. deeper than the wood's thickness.

■ Secure boards less than 6 in. wide with nails and wider boards with clamps.

■ Stand beside, never behind, the blade when you're cutting. Keep bystanders away from the area behind the saw.

■ Wedge the saw cut open with a shim if the board starts to pinch the blade and cause it to bind.

■ Make sure the blade guard is operating freely. Never block or wedge it in the raised position.

REDUCE THE THREAT OF
CARBON MONOXIDE

Keep your energy-efficient home safe. Follow these two steps to keep this silent killer at bay.

by **Duane Johnson**

1 INSTALL CARBON MONOXIDE (CO) ALARMS

Why? How dangerous is CO?

Accidental carbon monoxide (CO) poisoning accounts for several hundred deaths in the United States every year. The deaths are particularly tragic because most could have been easily prevented with a warning from a $20 to $40 CO alarm.

What is CO?

CO is an invisible, odorless gas that's produced by fireplaces, furnaces, stoves, water heaters and heaters that burn natural gas, propane, oil or wood. Usually chimneys and flues safely carry these combustion by-products up and out of your home. *But not always.* Flue blockage, poor natural drafting, leaks and other problems sometimes cause CO and other combustion gases to spill out into your living space and pollute the air you breathe (**Fig. A**). The CO is gradually absorbed into the bloodstream. Light doses of CO cause flu-like symptoms and larger doses can lead to unconsciousness and death.

Cars, lawn mowers and snow blowers also produce a lot of CO, especially at start-up. If you have an attached garage, natural drafts tend to pull that CO into your home, even if you have the garage door open! As a rule, never let a car engine idle in a garage.

Is the CO threat greater in energy-efficient homes?

Sometimes. Reducing air leaks in your home is one of the best ways to make your home more energy efficient. Air tightening includes such things as closing up attic bypasses, weatherstripping, caulking around doors and windows, and installing new windows. But as your home gets tighter, flues and chimneys can't vent CO and other combustion gases to the outside as easily, because they won't have as much makeup air. *CO alarms are simple, inexpensive insurance to warn you if CO spillage reaches a hazardous level . . . even if your home is new or you haven't taken steps to improve energy efficiency.*

Where do I put the alarms?

At a minimum, put an alarm near the sleeping rooms on each level in your home. CO accumulates in the bloodstream, and you're most vulnerable during long periods of sleep. Position alarms on ceilings or walls, away from drafts and solvents. (Read the directions for more details.)

What's the best CO alarm to buy?

Look for a CO alarm with a UL listing on the package. It can be either battery-powered or a plug-in type (often with a battery back-up; **photos on p. 211**). All alarms have a test/reset button that you should push weekly to make sure the alarm is operating.

We recommend the plug-in type alarm with a digital readout that tells you the peak CO concentration whenever you push the peak level button. The CO level might not be high enough to trigger the alarm. But detecting a low level can alert you to a potential problem, so you can trace the source before the CO reaches a higher, more dangerous level. This is particularly important if you have more vulnerable folks in your home such as young children, the elderly and those with certain illnesses.

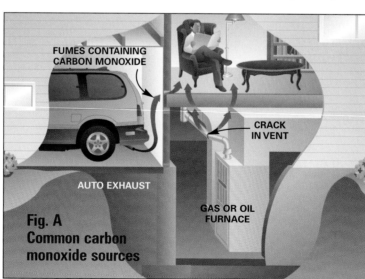

FUMES CONTAINING CARBON MONOXIDE

CRACK IN VENT

AUTO EXHAUST

GAS OR OIL FURNACE

Fig. A Common carbon monoxide sources

CARBON MONOXIDE is produced by gas-, oil- and wood-burning devices. Auto exhaust and poorly vented furnaces are the most common dangerous sources in a home.

What should I do if an alarm goes off?

Here are general guidelines taken from the more detailed instructions that come with your alarm.

1. Push the test/reset button. (This is easier with a wall-mounted CO alarm.)
2. Call an emergency number, 911 or your fire department in most areas.
3. Go outside or move to a well-ventilated area like next to an open window or door. Make sure all family members are accounted for. Wait for emergency services to arrive; they'll make sure your house is well aired out.
4. If the alarm goes off again within 24 hours, follow steps 1 – 3 above and call in a qualified technician to test your fuel-burning equipment and find the problem. Be aware that furnace start-ups can set off the alarm under some conditions, as can starting cars in an attached garage.

Warning: If an alarm sounds, you have a potentially lethal amount of CO in your home! Take the alarm seriously. Make every effort to find an explanation. You don't want any level of CO in your home, much less a lethal level. Unfortunately, CO sources can be difficult to pinpoint. Don't hesitate to call in a heating and ventilating technician experienced in CO issues to search out the probable causes and recommend corrections.

Also be aware of the symptoms of CO poisoning: slight headache, nausea, vomiting and fatigue (all flu-like symptoms) from mild exposures, and throbbing headache, drowsiness, confusion, fast heart rate or unconsciousness from heavier exposures.

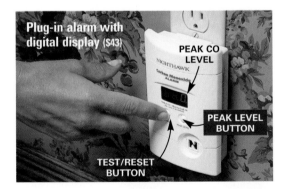

Plug-in alarm with digital display ($43)

PEAK CO LEVEL

PEAK LEVEL BUTTON

TEST/RESET BUTTON

BOTH TYPES OF CO ALARMS sound an alarm when hazardous levels of CO are present. The type with a digital display will also show the peak CO level in your home when you push the peak level button. It will not record very low levels.

Battery-powered alarm ($20)

TEST/RESET BUTTON

First Alert

2 ASK A HEATING SERVICE TECHNICIAN TO CONDUCT A COMPLETE BACKDRAFTING TEST AT YOUR ANNUAL HEATING EQUIPMENT CHECKUP.

Backdrafting occurs when the combustion gases can't go up and out flues and chimneys because outdoor air is already flowing down them (**Fig. B**). This often occurs when you run a clothes dryer, powerful range fan or any combination of venting fans. All suck air out of your home. If your house can't get enough makeup air leaking in around windows doors and through cracks and gaps in walls, the makeup air may come down the flues or chimney. Then your furnace, water heater or wood-burning fireplace may not vent properly, and combustion gases, including CO, will spill into your living space. (Studies have shown that backdrafting is common even in homes that are not energy efficient or airtight, so this test is worthwhile regardless of any energy-efficiency improvements you've made.)

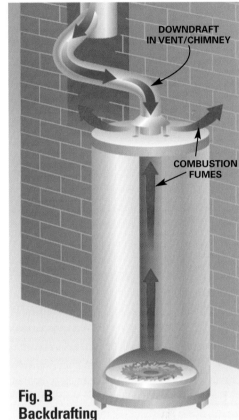

DOWNDRAFT IN VENT/CHIMNEY

COMBUSTION FUMES

Fig. B Backdrafting

BACKDRAFTING is a condition in which air flows down a flue or chimney rather than up, and combustion fumes can't flow out. The fumes spill into your living spaces.

A complete backdraft test only takes about 10 minutes. The service technician should close all doors and windows and turn on your ventilating fans, creating a worst-case situation. The technician will then turn on your water heater and test it for combustion gas spillage, and test the furnace as well.

If you have significant spillage, the technician should inspect your venting system and recommend solutions. ⌂

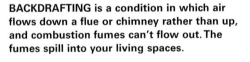

Buyer's Guide

CO alarms are available at hardware stores, home centers and discount stores. The brands shown at left are First Alert (800-323-9005) and Nighthawk (800-880-6788).

AN 8-STEP STRATEGY FOR
ENERGY SAVINGS

You can save energy and money lots of different ways — but there's a logical order in how you should proceed. Here's the lowdown.

by **Duane Johnson** and **Spike Carlsen**

If you wince every time a gas or electric bill arrives in your mailbox, take heart. You can easily reduce energy use in your home. And we don't mean by wearing three sweaters, taking cold showers and shuttering the windows. Energy efficiency and a pleasant indoor environment work hand-in-hand. You'll not only reduce the drain on your bank account but also find your home more comfortable.

In this article, we'll give you the BIG picture on how to evaluate your home's energy performance, determine where the biggest savings lie and maintain a healthy indoor environment. Other articles in this section deal with the specifics: simple steps you can take to save energy and money (p. 196), and "21 money-saving and energy-saving ideas that don't cost a dime" (p. 198).

We'll tell you right off that big energy savings aren't as easy to get today as they were 30 years ago. During the energy crunch of the 1970s, many homeowners added insulation and caulked around windows and doors to capture the biggest savings. And since then, new homes have been built to higher energy-efficiency standards. Still, if you follow these simple steps, you'll find plenty of savings still out there.

1. HIRE AN ENERGY AUDITOR

It's worth hiring a pro to evaluate your home and help you sort out the many possible energy-saving strategies. Call your local utility company to find energy auditors. It may supply this service for free or recommend an auditor. An energy audit typically costs $35 to $250, but sometimes community programs subsidize the bill. The energy auditor will inspect your home and rate its current performance in terms of insulation levels, air leakage, condition of heating or cooling equipment and other criteria. (You can also conduct a somewhat crude energy audit yourself using the calculator at www.homeenergysaver.lbl.gov.)

The auditor can then tell you which upgrades are cost effective and estimate your energy savings. Cost effectiveness is the key. You can spend thousands of dollars for upgrades that won't save you much, and a good auditor will steer you away from those. For an improvement to be worthwhile, the estimated savings should cover the cost of the improvement in about seven years. For example, adding $200 of insulation to your attic will be worth it if the estimated savings are about $30 per year ($210 after seven years). But installing a new efficient window for $200 won't be worth the cost if you save only $10

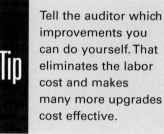

Tip Tell the auditor which improvements you can do yourself. That eliminates the labor cost and makes many more upgrades cost effective.

Tip Schedule a time when you can walk through your home with the auditor. Ask lots of questions. You can learn a ton about your home and how it works.

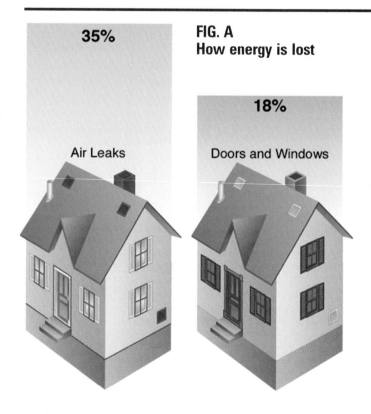

**FIG. A
How energy is lost**

35%
Air Leaks

18%
Doors and Windows

per year ($70 after seven years). The auditor's report should clearly specify the estimated savings.

Keep in mind that as energy costs go up, more retrofit ideas become cost effective.

2. REDUCE AIR LEAKAGE

Think of the warm air leaking out through gaps, cracks and holes in your home's walls and ceilings as your energy dollars floating away (Fig. A). Sealing these openings is one of the most cost-effective ways to save energy.

Stopping air leaks in the attic is usually enough. You don't have to work your way through every room caulking every crack, inside and out. Just get the largest and worst offenders, which are almost always in the attic.

You'll notice that your house feels more comfortable too, because you'll have fewer drafts. The less warm air that leaks out, the less cold air that leaks in to replace it.

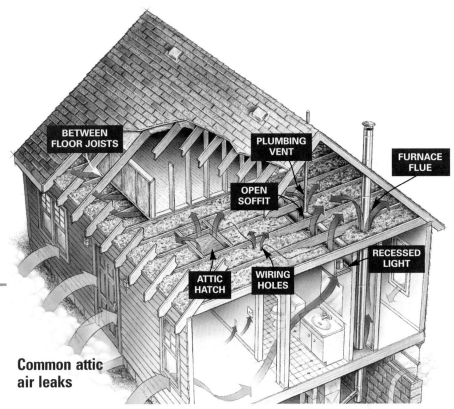

Common attic air leaks

BETWEEN FLOOR JOISTS · PLUMBING VENT · FURNACE FLUE · OPEN SOFFIT · RECESSED LIGHT · ATTIC HATCH · WIRING HOLES

To reduce air leakage, plug the largest holes first. Insulate open soffits and between floor joists first, then flash around chimneys and vent pipes. Finish up by caulking and sealing small holes. For complete information on sealing air leaks (and testing for backdrafting when you're done) see "Seal Attic Air Leaks," Oct. 2001, p. 46. To order reprints of this article, see page 220.

3. ADD INSULATION

Add 6 in. of insulation to an uninsulated attic and you'll reap substantial energy savings. Add 6 more inches and you'll get additional energy savings, but to a lesser degree. To find the point of diminishing return for adding insulation, consult Department of Energy charts at www.owenscorning.com or www.certainteed.com. The recommended values are based on climate, fuel costs and other factors. Adding more than the suggested amounts will result in a longer payback period for your investment.

The biggest culprits are air leaks (infiltration) and poor-performing windows. But every home is unique. An energy auditor will tell you where the biggest savings lie in your home.

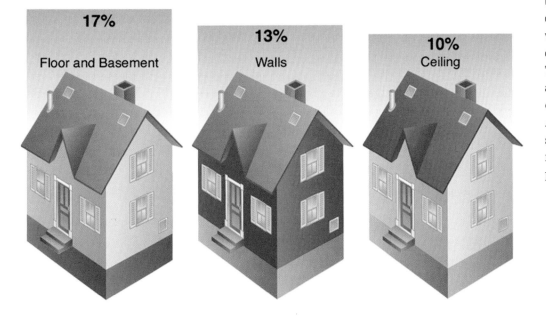

17% Floor and Basement

13% Walls

10% Ceiling

4. CONSERVE ENERGY

FIG. B: Where energy goes

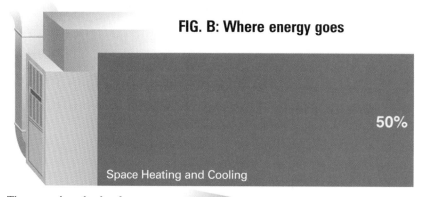

50%

Space Heating and Cooling

There are hundreds of energy-saving steps that cost little or nothing. Some ideas involve a small investment of time and money, for example, installing a programmable thermostat or caulking around windows. Others involve a small investment of energy—yours. These simple steps include lowering the temperature setting on your water heater and closing the curtains. See "Tips for Energy-Saving" on p. 196 for more ideas.

22%

Water Heating

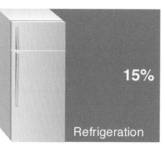

15%

Refrigeration

5. SHADE YOUR HOME

Shading is the best way you can save energy dollars in the summertime with your own sweat equity. Shading saves energy because it blocks out the direct sunlight that is responsible for about 50 percent of the heat gain in your home. Most of it strikes the roof and works its way through the attic, then down through the ceiling; the rest comes in mainly through windows. If you upgrade your attic insulation to at least 12 in. thick (about R-36) and make sure to buy light-colored roofing next time you reroof, you'll stop most of that roof heat. And steps like planting trees, attaching awnings and extending roof overhangs will shade the most vulnerable south-facing windows as well as those facing east and west. Most of these are low-cost, do-it-yourself strategies.

13%

Appliances and Lights

About half of the energy consumed in the average home goes to space heating and air conditioning. But all areas are targets for energy improvements, especially as energy costs rise.

6. PROTECT YOUR HEALTH AND THE HEALTH OF YOUR HOME

Energy-efficiency improvements can increase the risk of carbon monoxide (CO) poisoning. This can occur in homes with devices that burn gas, oil or wood and in homes with attached garages. At a minimum, install a CO alarm.

Watch your windows for excessive condensation. Most energy-saving measures reduce air leakage, allowing excessive moisture to build up inside. This moisture can cause mold and rot and an unhealthy indoor environment. Condensation on windows is common at the beginning of the heating season but should largely disappear except during cold snaps. Usually the best prevention strategy is to find the moisture sources (some of the worst culprits are improperly vented dryers, bath fans and the rooms they're in) and eliminate them or improve ventilation. For more details, see "Clearing up Condensation," Nov. '98, p. 94. To order a copy, see p. 220.

See "Prevent Carbon Monoxide Poisoning" on p. 210 for information on detectors and placement.

WARMTH WITHOUT ITCH

If you itch and sneeze just thinking about fiberglass insulation, check out UltraTouch cotton insulation. Made from scrap denim and cotton fibers, UltraTouch doesn't irritate skin and lungs, and can be installed without protective clothing or masks.

UltraTouch is treated with a boron-based product to meet fire-resistance standards and help it resist mildew, mold and pests. It's available in R-13 batts for 2x4 walls and R-19 batts for 2x6 walls, putting it on a par with fiberglass with respect to R-values. The 16.5- and 24.5-in. widths

7. STOP AIR CONDITIONER DUCT LEAKAGE

Studies have shown that an average duct system loses 10 to 40 percent of the cool air through gaps in the duct joints. This cooling is wasted when the ducts run outside the interior conditioned space, in an attic or a crawlspace. While sealing ducts is a common practice now, few air-conditioned homes have had this done. Sealing ducts is difficult. You'll have to rely on professional services (see "Air Conditioning" in your Yellow Pages) to test the ducts for leakage and to retest to show the effectiveness of their work.

8. BUY HIGH-EFFICIENCY WINDOWS
(when it's time to replace them)

Windows are the weakest link in your home's outer defenses against heat loss, accounting for about 18 percent of the heat loss in the typical home. But windows are also expensive, so it isn't cost effective to replace them just to save energy. If they're worn out, however, it's cost effective in all but the southernmost regions to upgrade to double-pane windows with low-E coatings. Your window specialist will help you choose the type of coating that works best, depending on whether you mostly need to slow heat loss or reduce solar gain. ⌂

(available for both thicknesses) ensure the batts completely fill standard stud and joist cavities. It's perfect for attics, crawlspaces and other places where insulation is typically left exposed. Another benefit is its high density, which provides superior sound insulation.

The downside? The R-13 UltraTouch costs about 60¢ per square foot and the R-19 about 80¢ (plus shipping), making it two to three times as expensive as fiberglass. Acoustical Surfaces, 123 Columbia Court N., Suite 201, Chaska, MN 55318; (800) 448-0121. www.acousticalsurfaces.com

How to buy weatherstripping

You can usually find the types of weatherstripping shown below at well-stocked hardware stores and home centers. Many other types are available, but you'll probably have to order them from a catalog. Ask to see a catalog at your local hardware store and order through the store if possible. (An on-line catalog is available at www.mdteam.com.)

We like the wrapped foam type (A and B below and shown in our story). It's durable, retains its shape, withstands abrasions and conforms to a wide range of gaps. The metal flange with slots for screws (B) is a bit more adjustable than the nail-on wood flange type (A).

The vinyl or silicone bulb type (C) won't cover wide gaps as well as wrapped foam, but it has a smaller profile with a cleaner look.

Finding new weatherstripping to match the exact profile of the old can be difficult. If you know the door manufacturer or where the door was purchased, try there first. (Check the door and frame for a label.) Otherwise, call a local door or window repair service. (Look under "Doors, Repair" or "Windows, Repair" in your Yellow Pages.) It may stock the materials or tell you where to call. Replacement kits for the wrapped foam and magnetic (for steel doors) types are sometimes available at hardware stores and home centers.

A good Internet source for weatherstripping is the Energy Federation Inc. at www.efi.org.

Common weatherstripping types

WRAPPED FOAM WOOD FLANGE

WRAPPED FOAM METAL FLANGE

VINYL BULB METAL FLANGE

Ask™ Handyman

NEW SAFETY RULE FOR PROPANE TANKS

Can you tell me the "what, when and why" behind the new-looking propane tank valves?

If your gas grill is powered with a propane tank, be advised that the tank may no longer be refillable.

On April 1, 2002, a code change took effect that states that all 4- to 40-lb. propane tank valves must be equipped with an overflow protection device (OPD). This device addresses the danger of tanks leaking because of overfilling. About half the states have adopted the new code, but most major propane suppliers will no longer fill noncompliant tanks.

The OPD valve handle has three lobes (see photo); the non-OPD valves don't. Your non-OPD tank can be fitted with a new code-compliant valve, but the cost may well exceed the cost of a new tank.

Tip: The easiest way to replace an obsolete tank with an OPD-equipped one is through a cylinder exchange program.

IS YOUR HOME UNDERINSURED?

Our agent is pestering us to review our house insurance policy with him. Is he really trying to help us or just make a fast buck?

If you're like most of our other readers, you've made significant improvements to your home since you moved in. Studies show that 73 percent of homeowners are underinsured by about 35 percent. If you've added a room, remodeled a bath or kitchen, collected jewelry or artwork, installed expensive appliances, or finally bought that nice furniture, you should check out your homeowner's policy. Call your insurance agent for an "insurance to value" assessment to make sure that you have the coverage you need. For a few extra dollars a month, that insurance phrase "replacement value" could actually mean you'll get the money you need to replace the things you've accumulated.

IS TREATED LUMBER HAZARDOUS?

I'm enclosing my yard with a fence and I'd like to use treated wood. Will the arsenic in the treated lumber be a hazard near my well?

You shouldn't have any trouble. When it's used appropriately (not for cutting boards, countertops or food containers), lumber treated with chromated copper arsenate (CCA) is not considered a health hazard by the Environmental Protection Agency. But because of continuing health concerns about the arsenic in the preservative, the treated wood industry is voluntarily switching over to non-arsenic wood preservatives for the residential market. The changeover will be completed by the end of year 2003.

You can currently buy non-arsenic treated lumber at many lumberyards and home centers, and most retailers can order it if they don't stock it. It's sold under the brand names of ACQ Preserve, NatureWood and Wolmanized Natural Select. Go to www.treatedwood.com, click on distributor locator, then enter your zip code, click on the retailer box, and check the Preserve and Preserve Plus product boxes to find a local supplier.

All treated lumber that contains arsenic carries a label with a red arsenic warning.

AM I LIKELY TO GET SHOCKED?

Each winter, I plug a set of Christmas lights into an exterior receptacle in my garden. The plug gets wet in the rain and snow. Could I be shocked when I go out to unplug it?

It's not likely if you have a GFCI-protected outlet. A GFCI (the outlet with test and reset buttons) is specifically designed to prevent lethal shocks and is required by code in exterior situations. What's more likely is that the wet cord and plug will cause the GFCI to shut off the power and your lights to go out. Also, the outlet will eventually corrode.

To prevent this, install an in-use cover like the one shown to keep the cord end and the outlet dry. The National Electrical Code now requires these covers to be installed on new exterior receptacle boxes. We recommend a sturdy all-metal cover. These covers are available at home centers, hardware stores and electrical wholesalers.

GFCI OUTLET

CORD RUNS THROUGH THIS NOTCH WHEN COVER IS CLOSED

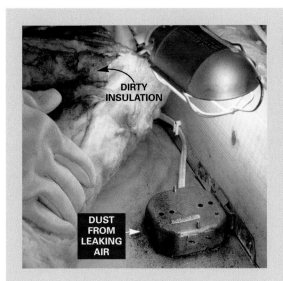

DIRTY INSULATION

DUST FROM LEAKING AIR

HOW DO I FIND ATTIC AIR LEAKS?

I know I'm losing a substantial amount of heat through my ceiling. Any tips on tracking down the cracks and gaps?

Even though most of the gaps spilling warm air into your attic are buried in insulation, you'll still see evidence of the escaping air. While in your attic, look for areas where the insulation is darkened (see photo), a result of filtering dusty air from the house. In cold weather, you may see frosty areas in the insulation caused by warm, moist air condensing and freezing as it hits the cold attic air. In warmer weather, you'll find water staining in these same areas. If you pressurize the house with a window fan (see "Pressurize Your House," p. 47), you may be able to feel the leaks with your hand as the air finds its way into the attic.

WHAT ARE ARC-FAULT INTERRUPTERS?

I'm remodeling my house and I've heard talk about needing to use these new arc-fault circuit breakers. What are they for and why do I need them?

To prevent fires, arc-fault interrupters (AFCIs) are designed to trip when they detect low-level arcing (also called an electrical short) that won't trip a standard breaker. The AFCIs fit into the same slots of your electrical service panel as the standard breakers they replace.

As of January 2002, the National Electric Code (NEC) requires AFCIs in all 15- and 20-amp bedroom branch circuits. Not all states have adopted the AFCI requirement, so check with your local building officials. Does this mean you'll have to replace old circuit breakers in your house? Only if you're building a new addition or undertaking major remodeling. Again, check with your local building officials for exact local requirements. New AFCIs cost about $40 per breaker at home centers or through electrical supply companies.

AFCI BREAKER (FITS IN SERVICE PANEL)

RESOURCES

10 SPECIALTY SUPPLIERS OF SPECIALTY PRODUCTS

Need something a little unusual or hard to find? These companies will deliver it right to your door.

PartsDirect

A service of Sears, this is a mail-order parts source for appliances, lawn equipment, power tools and home electronics of most major brands. Site boasts 90,000 diagrams to help you track down the exact part and number you need.
(800) 366-7278; www3.sears.com

McFeely's

These guys carry literally thousands of screws and fasteners with a real focus on square-drive screws. Whether you need an everyday 1-1/4 in. drywall screw or a 6 in. stainless steel lag bolt, you can order it here. They've expanded into finishing supplies, tools and hardware.
(800) 443-7937; www.mcfeelys.com

Blaine Window Hardware

The company stocks over 40,000 parts for windows, interior doors and exterior doors, both current and obsolete. You can even send them your old busted part and they'll find the exact replacement part for you!
(800) 678-1919; www.blainewindow.com

Klingspor

Carries sheets, belts, discs and rolls of sandpaper of every size, composition and grit. When you buy in bulk, a single sheet of sandpaper can cost as little as 20 cents. A good selection of other woodworking supplies, too.
(800) 228-0000;
www.orders.woodworkingshop.com

PRO TECT

Whether you need liquid masking tape, shoe booties or a plastic barrier complete with zipper door to keep remodeling dust out of your house, they carry it.
(800) 545-0826; www.pro-tect.com

Conney Safety Products

They stock everything even remotely connected to safety: safety goggles, fire extinguishers, fall protection equipment, warning signs and the latest in ergonomic work wear. Same day shipping in most cases. Good technical support help line, too (you get to talk to a real person that really knows their stuff).
(800) 356-9100;
www.conney.com

Outwater

Offers a wide array of moldings, columns, exterior millwork, tin ceilings, wrought iron and other architectural building products. These guys sleuth out the coolest, most useful (and sometimes weirdest) stuff and make it available to everyone. It's downright fun browsing through their catalog and Web site.
(888) 688-9283; www.outwater.com

Northern

Suppliers of pressure washers, generators, jacks, small engines, air tools, water pumps, hydraulic valves and other big noisy tools and equipment. Sold through a chain of 40 stores in midwest and southern states, by phone or Internet.
(800) 556-7885; www.northerntool.com

Constantines

Fantastic source for hardwood lumber, veneers, finishing supplies, and hardware. They've been around since 1812 and clearly know how to keep their customers happy.
(954) 561-1716; www.constantines.com

Real Goods

Their tagline "products for an ecologically sustainable future" pretty much explains their focus. Compact flourescent bulbs, water filters, solar lighting equipment and energy efficient water heaters are a few of the products offered.
(800) 762-7325; www.realgoods.com

10 GREAT PLACES TO GET GREAT DEALS ON GREAT TOOLS

If you're willing to dig a little, you can unearth some great tool deals.

Factory Authorized Service Centers

All major tool manufacturers have factory authorized service centers for repairs and warranty work. Often these centers will sell reconditioned tools, complete with warranty, for substantially less than new tools. Contact the companies below to find a service center near you.

- Bosch Tools, (877) 267-2499, www.boschtools.com
- Milwaukee, (262) 781-3600, www.milwaukeetools.com
- Skil Tools, (877) 754-5999, www.skil.com
- Makita Tools, (1,046 factory and authorized service centers); (800) 462-5482; www.makita.com.
- DeWalt, (1,085 factory and authorized service centers); (800) 433-9258; www.dewalt.com
- Ryobi, (800) 525-2579; www.ryobitools.com
- Black and Decker, (800) 544-6986; www.blackanddecker.com
- Porter Cable, (800) 487-8665; www.portercable.com
- Sears Craftsman, (Sears stores often carry reconditioned power tools); (800) 469-4663; www.sears.com

Grizzly

Grizzly manufactures tools overseas, using quality control engineers on-site, then sells them direct with no middlemen. This allows the company to sell solid tools at a solid price. Their specialty is stationary power tools like tablesaws and drill presses, but they carry tons of accessories and smaller tools, and tools from other manufacturers. They have a unique customer-referral service that puts you in touch with someone in your area that has purchased a tool you're eyeing so you can get a first-hand report. Contact them for a catalog at (800) 523-4777 or visit www.grizzlytools.com

Amazon.com

Amazon flung itself into the powertool business with the purchase of Tool Crib of the North a few years ago. They frequently have great sales and free shipping and offer a lowest price guarantee. You can even buy and sell used tools at the Amazon Marketplace by clicking on the "outlet, used and reconditioned" button. www.amazon.com

Tools on Sale

The main store located in St. Paul, MN has over 900 power tools on display. You can order all of these, plus zillions of accessories through a mail order catalog. No on-line ordering, but send for a copy of the 640 page catalog if you live in the upper Midwest. (651) 224-4859; www.7cornershdwe.com

uBid.com

An on-line auction house for new and refurbished items. Click on the "Home Improvement" button to see what's being offered. A recent glance showed over 5,000 products ranging from hammer drills to arc welders. Register and learn the rules of the game before you bid. www.ubid.com

Harbor Freight

Mail-order source for more than 7,000 name brand and off-brand tools. They offer "lowest price" and "100% satisfaction" guarantees as well as free shipping on orders of $50 or more. Their Web site also hosts auctions and clearance sale sections. (800) 423-2567; www.harborfreight.com

Colonial Black Book of Tools

They cater to professionals, and you need to set up an account before ordering, but they'll sell to anyone. Thousands of top-notch tools. Their motto? "Accuracy is a duty, not a virtue." (800) 345-8665; www.blackbookoftools.com

Your local want ads

Many newspapers have a "Tools and Machinery" or "Building Materials" section in the classified ad section. Paying cash is one of your strongest negotiating points. Check out tools carefully, once you've bought 'em, they're yours.

eBay

eBay is the world's largest Internet auction site and a fascinating place to buy new, used, reconditioned and antique tools. The seller pays eBay a listing fee and commission; buyer usually pays the shipping. You need to register first and become familiar with the bidding rules, but once you get the hang of it, it's fun. www.ebay.com

Used tool specialty stores

Most large cities support a store specializing in used tools. Some buy and sell tools outright, others work on a consignment basis. Look under "Tools—Used" in the Yellow Pages. Ask about guarantees and return policies before plunking down your cash.

50 GREAT DIY WEB SITES (IN 5 WORDS OR LESS)

www.aaawatertesting.com.
www.waterlab.com.
Water purity testing by mail

www.americanwoodworker.com
Woodworking projects, tips, techniques

www.backyardgardener.com
Plans, plant lists, reference

bookstore.gpo.gov
Inexpensive energy, safety, restoration information

www.buildingonline.com
Deck plans, manufacturer links

www.carpet-discounts.com
Carpet buying, installing, allergies, warranties

www.cedarbureau.com
Cedar shakes and shingles information

www.closetmaid.com
How-to and organizational advice

www.construction-cost.com
Prices, calculators, estimating, product information

www.customclosets.com
Design advice and project estimates

www.decoratingstudio.com
Ideas, books, classes

www.diygranite.com
Stone countertop products, information

www.doityourself.com
Repairs, projects, decorating, finance, referrals

www.energycheckup.com
Energy tips, funding, finding contractors

www.energycodes.gov
Software, calculators and energy tips

www.epa.gov/hhiptool
Saving energy and money

www.familyhandyman.com
DIY projects, tips, techniques

www.firesafehome.org
Fire safety products and info

www.gaf.com
Roof Selector eliminates guesswork

www.gardeninglaunchpad.com
Links to 4,700 gardening sites

www.gethomeideas.com
Inspiring decorating ideas galore

www.handymanusa.com
Helpful expert forum

www.hardwoodcouncil.com
Everything about hardwoods

www.homedepot.com and
www.lowes.com
Shop or just browse online

www.home-repair.com
An online home improvement community

www.hometips.com
Expert advice for your home

www.houseofantiquehardware.com.
Antique and reproduction hardware

www.howstuffworks.com
A treasure trove of information

www.improvenet.com
Network of 30,000 contractors, referrals

www.livinghome.com
Interior design, trends, products, calculators

www.mailordergardening.com
Order 100s of seed catalogs

www.masterhandyman.com
Radio personality Glenn Haege's site

www.nationalgardening.com
Gardening zones, identification, news, community

www.naturalhandyman.com
Home repair help, humor, encouragement

www.nesf.org
Home, school, work electrical safety

www.oldhouseweb.com.
Vintage products, information, discussion boards

www.owenscorning.com
Loads of asphalt roofing facts

www.pavementpro.org
Tips for avoiding pavement scams

www.paintinfo.org
FAQs, lead paint, how-to, safety

www.repair-home.com
Discussions, resources, contractor directories, projects

www.scottscompany.com
Indentify nasty weeds and bugs

www.southernpine.com
Everything here is about pine

www.the-home-improvement-web.com
Helpful regional information

www.turf.uiuc.edu
Tons of information about turfgrass

www.usawallpaper.com/wallpaper-calculator.html
Calculates your wallpaper needs

webpages.charter.net/crush11
Garden ponds, fish, plants, information

www.weekendhandyman.com
Repairs, home and woodworking plans

www.woodfloors.org
Wood floor care, design, repair

To order photocopies of complete plans for projects shown in the "Gallery of Ideas" and other sections, call 715-246-4344 or write to: Copies, The Family Handyman, 511 Wisconsin Dr., New Richmond, WI 54017. Many public libraries also carry back issues of The Family Handyman magazine.

INDEX

For a complete 5-year index of The Family Handyman magazine, visit us at www.familyhandyman.com

ACKNOWLEDGMENTS

FOR THE FAMILY HANDYMAN

Editor in Chief	Ken Collier
Editor	Duane Johnson
Executive Editor	Spike Carlsen
Senior Editor	Dave Radtke
Associate Editors	Jeff Gorton
	Carl Hines
	Travis Larson
Senior Copy Editor	Donna Bierbach
Senior Art Director	Bob Ungar
Art Directors	Hope Fay
	Becky Pfluger
	Marcia Wright Roepke
Office Administrative Manager	Alice Garrett
Technical Manager	Shannon Hooge
Reader Service Specialist	Roxie Filipkowski
Office Administrative Assistant	Shelly Jacobsen
Administrative Assistant	Lori Callister
Production Manager	Judy Rodriguez
Production Artist	Lisa Pahl Knecht

CONTRIBUTING EDITORS

Bonnie Blodgett	Jeff Timm
Jeff Larson	Bruce Wiebe
Susan Moore	

FREELANCE ART DIRECTORS

David Farr	Barb Pederson
Mark Jacobson	Gregg Weigand

PHOTOGRAPHERS

Mike Habermann, Mike Habermann Photography
Mike Krivit, Krivit Photography
Phil Liesenheimer, LA Studios
Bill Zuehlke

ILLUSTRATORS

Steve Bjorkman	Don Mannes
Roy Doty	Doug Oudekirk
John Keely	Eugene Thompson
Bruce Kieffer	

CONSULTANTS

Charles Avoles, plumbing
Al Hildenbrand, electrical
Kathryn Hillbrand, interior design
Dave MacDonald, structural engineer
Jon Jenson, carpentry
Bob Lacavita, automotive
Mary Jane Pappas, kitchen and bath design
Ron Pearson, environmental issues
Tom Schultz, drywall
Dean Sorem, tile
Costas Staurou, appliance repair
John Williamson, electrical
Ron Zeien, appliance repair
Les Zell, plumbing

For information about advertising in *The Family Handyman* magazine, call (212) 850-7226

To subscribe to *The Family Handyman* magazine:
By phone: (800) 285-4961

By Internet: www.familyhandyman.com.

By mail: The Family Handyman Subscriber Service Dept.
P.O. Box 8174
Red Oak, IA   51591-1174

We welcome your ideas and opinions. Write to:
The Editor, The Family Handyman,
2915 Commers Dr., Suite 700, Eagan, MN 55121.
Fax: (651) 994-2250.
E-mail: fheditor@readersdigest.com
Web site: www.familyhandyman.com